The Last Romantic

Books by MARTIN BIRNBAUM

ANGKOR AND THE MANDARIN ROAD. 1952.

JACOVLEFF AND OTHER ARTISTS. 1946.

VANISHING EDEN: WANDERINGS IN THE TROPICS. 1942.

JOHN SINGER SARGENT: A CONVERSATION PIECE. 1941.

BEARDSLEY ET WILDE: DEUX ESSAIS. PARIS. 1939.

ARTHUR RACKHAM: A LIST OF BOOKS COMPILED BY FREDERICK
    COYKENDALL WITH AN INTRODUCTION BY MARTIN
    BIRNBAUM. 1922.

OSCAR WILDE: FRAGMENTS AND MEMORIES. LONDON. 1920.

INTRODUCTIONS: PAINTERS, SCULPTORS AND GRAPHIC ARTISTS.
    1919.

PRINCE ULRIC'S MINSTREL: A SHORT STORY.
    PRIVATELY PRINTED. 1916.

MARTIN BIRNBAUM
Photographed at the age of 80 by Russell Kuhner

The Last Romantic

THE STORY OF MORE THAN A HALF-
CENTURY IN THE WORLD OF ART

Martin Birnbaum

INTRODUCTION BY UPTON SINCLAIR

TWAYNE PUBLISHERS :: New York
1960

To

EMILY WINTHROP MILES

whose interest and forbearance
helped make my undertaking
a pleasure

For their helpful suggestions, I acknowledge
with gratitude my indebtedness to:

      Mrs. Alice Lewisohn Crowley
      Mrs. Stevenson Scott
      Dean Jay, Esq.
      The late Carl Henschel, Esq.
      Carman Messmore Esq.
      Sir Alec Martin
         and
      Welles Bosworth, Esq.

                  M. B.

Contents

Illustrations

Introduction

Martin Birnbaum is my oldest living friend. He came into this world four months and ten days ahead of me, but when you have passed your eightieth year, that is not a great difference. We were together at the age of twelve, in the old Public School Number Forty, on the East Side of New York. At thirteen, we entered the City College of New York, and were in the same class for six hours a day, five days a week, forty weeks a year, for five years—that adds up to 6,000 hours, and you can learn to know each other very well in that time. When I came out from college I became a writer of "half-dime novels," and Martin became my violin teacher for a matter of three years. Since that time we have met when fate made it possible, and have corresponded frequently.

Martin became an art expert—one of the best known in that profession; and the stories he told me impressed me so that when I started the Lanny Budd series of novels, I decided to have Lanny follow in Martin's footsteps. From that time on, Martin was my unnamed collaborator, mostly by mail. He read in manuscript all the three million words in those eleven large volumes. He gave me not only the priceless art stories in those books, but he corrected everything about Europe; and is to be thanked for the fact that scores of Europeans from a dozen countries wrote me expressing amazement at my familiarity with their native lands.

Such a service is beyond thanks; and when Martin told me recently that he was writing his memoirs, as I had urged him to do, I gave him my best advice—which was to get to the art business quickly. "Remember you're writing for Americans, and it's the big money they are interested in. When you are dealing with million-dollar paintings, and have a couple of millionaires fighting over their possession, you have a real story." I tell you in advance that there are some of the richest names in America in Martin's book, and he had the making of one of the greatest of our museum collections. His views of art are sound, and his knowledge of artists and their works is infinite.

Martin was born near a part of Hungary known as the Puszta, and when he was a child he was saved from death by being put up on a high stove when the home was flooded and hundreds of other people were drowned.

Martin was brought to America as a child and raised on the Lower East Side of New York, which is very certainly not a fashionable neighborhood. When he was still young he earned a scholarship in the National Conservatory of Music. He had a great teacher, Leopold Lichtenberg, and might have become a violin virtuoso, but his father insisted on making him a lawyer.

So when he got through college he attended Columbia Law School and became a legal advisor to a title insurance company—about the dullest occupation that could be imagined for a lover of all the arts. He was saved by the fact that an elderly rich lady took him abroad to attend to some legal matters for her. He traveled all over Europe, visited art galleries, and met many artists—and that ended the law business. Coming back to New York, he continued his art studies and took charge of the New York office of the Berlin Photographic Company, which dealt in photographs of all the world's art works; and that is where his art romance really begins in this volume.

But first, I am going to finish my short story of him—and steal one of the good stories from his book. I was living in California, and on one of his last visits I took him to dinner at the home of Rob Wagner, editor of *Script* and Hollywood correspondent of the *Saturday Evening Post*. Present at the dinner was Charlie Chaplin, who at the moment had just finished his wonderful satire on Adolf Hitler called *The Dictator*. When Charlie had a work in progress, or just completed, he was always "full of it," and he told us all about it; and after dinner in the drawing room he enacted one or two of the scenes for us.

Martin, of course, was delighted, and told the story in his book. What I have never told Martin, and what will give him a jolly shock, is that both Rob and Charlie made up their minds that he was a German spy! I find it hard to imagine why; I suppose they just couldn't imagine that anybody could really be so suave and elegant, so wordly-wise and serene—it just wasn't natural. We were all spy-conscious in those tormented days, and of course we sometimes had reason. It turned out that Charlie's own chauffeur was a Japanese spy; my wife had suspected him when she had observed him peering into our bedroom windows while his master was a guest inside. Rob had received a visit from two police detectives when the neighbors reported his strange habit of hanging a large yellow card board in a tree in front of his hilltop cabin—it was his signal to a Chinese peddler that he wanted to buy some vegetables!

So now here is the book—the life story of one of the kindest, gentlest and wisest men I have met during my life's pilgrimage. You may not know many of the artists or the art works that he tells about; I certainly know very few of them. But you will learn what love of art means and what it can do to make inspiring pleasure and to preserve the past alive in the present and immortal for the future. To collect these priceless treasures and put them into museums where the people of the future can come and see them—that is surely an honorable labor, and if it pays a man enough so that he can retire and become a world traveler and inspect the art works of Japan and China and Indonesia and Africa, and tell us about these fascinating things—that, it seems to me, is altogether to the good. In this book you will see reproduced a portrait of Martin playing the violin, as I have seen him so many times in my home. You will also see portraits of some of the artists and collectors he tells about, and when you have finished the book you will have memories to take with you when you visit the great art galleries which Martin Birnbaum helped to build.

UPTON SINCLAIR

I

Prelude to an Art Career

The gifted American painter, Georgia O'Keefe, and other friends, called me the last romantic. If there is any truth in their epithet, my romanticism began over three-quarters of a century ago, on May 10th, 1878, to be exact, when I was born on the outskirts of the city of Miskolcz. This city is near the northern boundary of the great Hungarian plain known as the Puszta.

My father was a self-taught engraver. He might have become an accomplished artist had he enjoyed intelligent guidance. But, unfortunately, he became an orphan at an early age; before he was twenty-one years old, he was obliged to support an ever-increasing family by engraving the coats-of-arms of Hungarian noblemen on silver, glass and letter seals which were then fashionable. He knew Munkacsy, the celebrated painter of *Christ Before Pilate*, a huge canvas that was afterward exhibited in the United States.

My parents wandered about on foot to the castles of my father's aristocratic patrons, leaving their young ones in the care of my maternal grandmother. I recall that our home in Miskolcz always rang with laughter and song, and indeed my eldest brother, Joseph, and one of my sisters, Amalia, became professional singers.

An ardent admirer of Louis Kossuth, my father longed to see democratic America. After a first visit he did not rest until he persuaded my mother to emigrate. All her brothers, soldiers in the Austrian army, had died on battlefields, and she was eager to take her sons to the United States, where conscription was undreamed of, and standing armies were not a threat to young mothers. It was a country that we all grew to love as our very own. Indeed, I have always maintained that we loved it even more than the average native-born citizen who takes its blessings for granted.

13

The family, including a grandmother over eighty-five years old, crossed the Atlantic in two sections. After we were united, we settled down in a little red brick house on Willett Street, on the Lower East Side of New York City. I was sent to Sheriff Street School (No. 22), the principal of which was a Mr. Merritt, a handsome old-fashioned example of American manhood.

To Magnus Gross, one of my schoolteachers, I owe a special debt of gratitude, for he encouraged my youthful interest in natural history, a branch of learning that became one of the passions of my life. Even while a boy in knee pants, I was permitted to join as an active member the New York Entomological Society. Its meetings were held in the American Museum of Natural History. Most of the members were professional scientists. On one occasion I had the audacity to deliver an address on phosphorescent insects. I made no startling discoveries after dissecting many beetles, but my talk was noticed in the Society's bulletin, and a distant correspondent who had greenhouses, not suspecting that I was merely an enthusiastic child, asked me to send him some large living phosphorescent click beetles. I did this by imprisoning specimens in hollow stems of sugar cane, and posting them to Scotland. My father, not realizing the importance and remunerative possibilities of a scientific natural history career, did not encourage me in these pursuits. Some of my happiest hours were spent in the garden of the Gross home on East Eighty-Sixth Street, then considered far uptown, where my teacher raised tropical waterlilies in tubs and introduced me to the pleasures and excitements of collecting plants, minerals and beetles.

Among my father's achievements in this period was a decorative engraved inscription on a cup or vase presented to John L. Sullivan, the champion boxer.

Fate had already begun to weave mysterious threads into my personal web of circumstance. One day my elder sister announced that the Infanta Eulalie, a royal Spanish princess, the first ever to visit America, was arriving as the guest of the nation, to help celebrate the four hundredth anniversary of the discovery of the New World. The aunt of King Alfonso, she died in 1958, aged 94. I saw her driving in a magnificent victoria up Fifth Avenue, hailed by cheering thousands. Her newly born son was called the Columbus Baby. Who could have foretold that about a half-century later I would visit her in Paris, and that her son would become the owner and occupant of my private suite of rooms in the Casa del Leone, an enchanting house rebuilt for me on the Giudecca in Venice?

In 1892 we moved farther north in the city. Magnus Gross had me transferred to a school on East Twenty-third Street, to the class of Mr. Furey, another sympathetic public school teacher. Two other new pupils were enrolled in my class almost at the same time. One was Upton Sinclair, whose parents had just come to New York from Baltimore. The other was David Keppel, who shared my enthusiasm for collecting coleoptera. He was the younger son of Frederick Keppel, the well-known art-dealer and publisher of etchings. David entered Mr. Furey's class because Columbia Grammar School, which he had been attending, had burned down. Although all three of us were only about thirteen year of age, we were permitted to take the entrance examinations to the College of the City of New York, and we passed them.

In the meantime, although I was a mere beginner on the violin, I won a coveted free scholarship in the National Conservatory of Music, founded by Mrs. Jeanette Thurber. I was chosen from among hundreds of applicants, probably on the strength of the childish assurance with which I played an etude. The faculty of the Conservatory boasted of such celebrated artists as Joseffy, Victor Herbert, Camilla Urso, DeVere Sapio, Rubin Goldmark, and other virtuosos; I was accepted as a pupil by Leopold Lichtenberg, the head of the violin department.

Lichtenberg had been the favorite pupil of the great Wieniawski, and he was at one time the youthful concert master of the Boston Symphony Orchestra. He rarely appeared as a soloist in public, but Nahan Franko persuaded him to play concertos by Viotti and Rode at a series of concerts of old music at the Lyceum Theatre. At one of these, conducted by Nahan's brother, Sam Franko, I sat just behind Franz Kneisel, whose quartet was then making musical history. When Lichtenberg finished a difficult unpublished cadenza written especially for him by Wieniawski, I overheard Kneisel say to his neighbor, "You will never listen to better violin playing than that!" At the time, I did not know as

much about violin technique as I do now, but although I have
repeatedly attended great performances by Kreisler, Ysaye, Cesar
Thomson, Kubelik, Heifetz, Zimbalist, Elman and all the gifted
younger performers of the present generation, I still think that I
have never heard anything more perfect or more dazzling than
Lichtenberg's playing. His bowing in particular was superlative
and unique.

When Richard Strauss came to America and introduced us to
his *Don Quixote,* the *Sinfonia Domestica, Ein Heldenleben* and
other amazing compositions, he could find no violinist to play some
of the solo passages that had to be performed by the concertmaster.
They were declared unplayable, *"unviolinmässig,"* as the Germans
would say. Hermann Hans Wetzler, who was the orchestra's assistant conductor, came to the rescue by rediscovering Lichtenberg
and urged him to come out of his retirement if only to prove that
the difficult passages could be played.

My eminent teacher, however, was a highly nervous, irritable
perfectionist. Although he had a number of gifted pupils he did
not perpetuate his great style through a succession of young followers, as did Auer, Sevcik, and other famous teachers. Lichtenberg could be a cruel master, and he terrified me by pulling my
hair, pounding time on my back, and even breaking a priceless
Tourte bow on my fingers. I finally refused to go to the conservatory, and what promised to become a successful musical career
came to a sudden end. In any event, Mrs. MacDowell, the mother
of the famous American composer and an important official on
the conservatory board, would have insisted that I give up college
and devote all my time to music or lose my scholarship. My father
would never have consented to such a stipulation. His preju-
dice against music as a profession arose from the fact that even
the most talented gipsies were treated with scant respect, although
with patronizing affection, by Hungarians. He would not permit
my brother Joseph, who was already a leading juvenile in Francis
Wilson's company, or my sister Amalia, who might have developed
into a second Scalchi, to study music. In my case, I think he acted
wisely, for it is doubtful whether I would ever have become a
virtuoso of more than average ability under Lichtenberg's harsh
guidance.

Never having attended a school, my father expected me, a college student, to develop an encyclopaedic mind, and this resulted in a kind of failure. In spite of my passionate fondness for music, art and natural history, my forces were always too scattered to achieve eminence in any particular field of endeavor. However, I never ceased to love my violin, and have always agreed with Oswald Spengler, who described it as "the noblest of all instruments that the Faustian soul has imagined and trained for the expression of its last secrets."

One incident of my National Conservatory days deserves mention. Anton Dvorak, the Czech composer, had been appointed director of the Conservatory, and one day he saw me, then a little boy with an enormous head of curly hair, enter the building with my violin case under my arm. He took me into his study and asked me to read at sight a composition in manuscript, which later proved to be his *Sonatina, Opus 100,* the slow movement of which was eventually transcribed by Kreisler and became known as the *Indian Lament.*

A few years later, Lichtenberg told my friend Mrs. Theodore Havemeyer, at whose residence he was playing trios with Leo Schulz and Herr von Inten, that I might really have been destined for a spectacular career as a musician had I remained his pupil. At any rate, as the result of his teaching, I did have the audacity to perform in public and to play privately from time to time before such artists as Kreisler, Remenyi, Schnabel and Mancinelli (a gifted composer who was a leading conductor at the Metropolitan Opera House for many years). I can even boast of having shared a program with the celebrated contralto Schumann-Heink, although the performance was only the usual benefit for the Seamen's Fund given on board an ocean liner. I also enjoyed many years of quartet playing with Dr. Leo Buerger, the celebrated surgeon, husband of the pianist Germaine Schnitzer, Dr. Herman Fischer of the German Hospital, and Robert Haven Schauffler, a writer of biographies of celebrated composers. Schauffler, who married a fine pianist, afterward became a professional cellist, and he and his wife were members of the trio formed by the remarkable blind violinist Edwin Grasse.

At the College of the City of New York, which I entered in the class of 1897, my outstanding teacher was Professor Herberman, head of the Latin Department. He was a profound old-fashioned German scholar, and was further recognized as the leading Catholic layman in the country. After he was stricken by total blindness, I would often escort him from the college on Twenty-third Street to his home, and on these walks he taught me the beauties of the classics in a way that would never have been possible in a crowded classroom.

Professor Hardy, who lectured to us on English Literature, was also a prominent Catholic. His favorite book was Cardinal Newman's *Apologia pro Vita Sua*, which he never tired of holding up as the perfect model of English prose. Before his untimely death, while I was still a student in his class, he was gratified to learn that Upton Sinclair and I had already begun to publish our efforts, but I have always thought that Upton treated him shabbily in *The Goose Step*.

One of the memorable incidents of my career at C.C.N.Y. was a meeting with Theodore Roosevelt, then New York's police commissioner. I had been chosen by my fellow students to find judges for a public debate between student members of two literary societies and I called on "Teddy" to ask him to be one of the judges. He at once put me at my ease, and I was fascinated by his smile which revealed a fine set of teeth. He would have accepted the invitation had the debate not occurred on a Friday. That night each week, he reserved for his family, and he would allow nothing to interfere with his Fridays at Oyster Bay. In his place I secured the services of Joseph Choate, the brilliant ambassador to Great Britain.

I had been encouraged by my parents to see great plays and actors, although I could afford only the cheapest balcony seats or standing room. I became an inveterate opera-goer as well, and managed to hear all the stars of the great galaxies gathered together by Conried, Gatti-Gasazza and Hammerstein.

My introduction to the world of visual art dates back to this period. David Keppel's father was an enthusiastic amateur musician, and I often spent hours at his home playing the violin while he accompanied me on a small organ. The Keppel residence on the north side of Stuyvesant Square was filled with fine etchings and mezzotints; it was not long before I became familiar with the works of Whistler, Sir Seymour Haden, and the famous English mezzotint engravers. A fine impression of Haden's *Shere Mill Pond* particularly stirred my imagination. Frederick, the elder son of Mr. Keppel, kept me at a distance for some time, but after I graduated from Columbia Law School, and he became the head of the Carnegie Foundation, we became good friends. Later he not only furnished me with valuable letters of introduction to the scholars working among the pre-Columbian ruins of Guatemala and Honduras, but we spent some pleasant days there together. I regarded his death, shortly after his visit to Central America, as a national loss.

Leo Buerger, another classmate, became a brilliant surgeon who successfully amputated the leg of Sarah Bernhardt. As I have mentioned, he was an excellent violinist too, and was a member of a string quartet I belonged to. In the class of 1897, other luminaries were Angelo Patri and Waldemar Kaempffert. Nor should we forget Aaron Salant, our brilliant valedictorian whose understanding and sympathy always warmed my heart. It is peculiarly fitting that a group of his admirers established a Fellowship at Harvard University in his honor.

The most celebrated of all my classmates is Upton Sinclair. I was his violin teacher after we became fellow students at Columbia University in 1897. He made such remarkable strides that he finally decided to consult the great French violinist Henri Marteau, who was then touring America. Although Marteau was temporarily laid up by a serious attack of measles, Sinclair braved the dangers of infection and went to his hotel to play for him. The virtuoso was surprised when he learned that Upton had been playing for only a few months, and advised him not to change his teacher. Our acquaintance, begun at school in 1891, ripened into a friendship that has never been interrupted. I helped to launch his first major literary effort, *Springtime and Harvest,* and was even suspected of having written *The Journal of Arthur Stirling,* which was published anonymously. When he began his famous Lanny Budd series, Sinclair asked me to help him with facts relating to art, travel and music, and to correct any blunders that I might discover while reading the manuscript. Zoltan

Kertezsi, Lanny's art teacher, one of the more important characters, is a fairly faithful portrait of me, and had I not been afraid of libel suits, my real name would have been used by the author.

Among other pleasant encounters which I owe to Upton was a memorable evening spent with Charlie Chaplin at the Beverly Hills home of Florence and Robert Wagner, editors of the weekly magazine *Script*. Chaplin's picture, *The Dictator,* had not yet been released, and the inimitable actor, after seeing some of my photographs taken on a trip across North and Central Africa, very graciously offered to favor me with a private view. I was, however, obliged to forego the pleasure because I was leaving for Hawaii on the following morning. To satisfy my ardent curiosity, Chaplin then gave us a detailed account of the plot, acting out many of the scenes with amazing liveliness and ending his entertainment with a moving delivery of the profound speech with which the picture comes to an end.

After receiving our degrees at the College of the City of New York, Upton took some post-graduate courses at Columbia University, while I, to please my father, entered the Law School where William Keener, who used the Socratic method, was the brilliant new dean. He taught me how to think, and my training under John Bassett Moore, the outstanding specialist in international law, fitted me for some useful, if not heroic, military service. During the war periods through which I lived I was found to be either too young or too old for military service, or suffering from some temporary physical ailment, and after repeated vain attempts to find a niche in the war efforts, the only position offered me was an insignificant, almost humiliating post on the Legal Advisory Board of the district in which I resided.

My legal studies did not really interest me, and I would cut lectures to attend a matinee of Otis Skinner's fine production of Browning's *In A Balcony.* My romantic streak would also manifest itself in essays like one on "Threnodies" which appeared in the *Columbia Literary Monthly* (February, 1900). Between lectures I was obliged to earn a living and support my parents by teaching and playing chamber music with Ambassador Henry Morgenthau's wife, with Rabbi Gustave Gottheil, and with other amateurs. I passed my State examinations, however, without difficulty, and in 1901 I was admitted to the New York Bar. For a time I struggled along giving violin lessons after my work at the law office was done; occasionally a vacation of a week or two would result in meetings with celebrities who seemed romantic and exciting. Violin playing almost always served as my letter of introduction.

I spent several weeks each summer at the quaint little town of Siasconset on Nantucket Island, where William Verplanck Birney painted groups of red-coated hunters sitting around tables, conversing and drinking. He was a kind, sweet-natured man, an American Dendy Sadler, living in one of the island's century-old miniature houses, which were so low that one could barely stand upright under their roofs. My bedroom was so small that I had no space for a chair, and my clothes hung from the nails on the walls surrounding my bed. Through the Birneys I met the artists and the group of actors who spent their summers at Siasconset. I even took part in performances given by the famous old actress Mrs. Gilbert, adored by thousands of Americans who attended the theatre of Augustin Daly. Clyde Fitch wrote *Granny* for her last starring play. I always sat at the same dinner table with Douglas Fairbanks, who was to become one of the great figures in the cinema world. The golden-haired matinee idol, Harry Woodruff, belonged to our group, and Robyn of Detroit, who had composed the music for the successful musical comedy *The Yankee Consul*, was my boon companion. The man who was to become the most famous of all the vacationists was *Signor* Marconi, then an unknown young scientist making revolutionary experiments with wireless telegraphy. I was to meet him later in Venice when he was world famous, and again in England at Melchett Court, in the New Forest. By that time he had become owner of a magnificent yacht.

When the Birneys left, I too forsook Nantucket and went to a hotel on Montauk Point, where Ada Rehan, Daly's leading star, was a regular visitor after her retirement. When she found that the young violinist had seen her, in her entire repertoire, from Wycherley's *The Country Wife* to Portia in Shakespeare's *The Merchant of Venice* from a cheap balcony seat, we became good friends and often went for a row together in the fresh-water lakes that studded the end of Long Island. After such romantic meetings I would return to the title company that I worked for with reluctance. Almost the only bright moments of my legal career were the free luncheon periods browsing in the bookshop of Mr. Luyster, where I spent my last pennies buying my favorite authors' first editions. I soon realized that I was too ardent by nature to reconcile myself to the law's delays, and when an opportunity arose to start a new career in the field of the Fine Arts, I abandoned the practice of law without hesitation. But I anticipate my story. . . .

While still an unhappy, frustrated lawyer, I had become acquainted with Mrs. Robinson Smith, whose charming daughter, Gertrude, is still a stimulating force in our musical world. Their "at homes" in New York and at Northeast Harbor on Mount Desert Island were like miniature salons. In those days such affairs had not degenerated into cocktail parties, and a young man could always count on meeting guests of more than average interest. Another home that I visited even more frequently was the modest apartment of Minnie and Virginia Gerson and their aged father, a picturesque nonagenarian lovingly known as "Popsy." I soon regarded them all with deepest affection. They introduced me to their brother-in-law, William M. Chase, whose collection of paintings by Alfred Stevens later became the *clou* of my first attempt at an art exhibition. I regarded Chase with awe, not simply because he was a prominent painter and teacher, but also because his portrait by John Sargent hung in the Metropolitan Museum, and he had been a bosom friend of the waspish butterfly, Whistler. Other habitués of the Gerson salon were artists like John W. Alexander, the brothers Reynolds and Gifford Beal, Duncan Philips and his wife, the art dealer Edward G. Kennedy who published the standard work on Whistler's etchings and whose portrait by Whistler is in the Metropolitan Museum, the interesting photographer Gertrude Kasebeer, John Corbin, the *New York Times* drama critic, and well-known actors like Otis Skinner, Ferdinand Gottschalk, Annie Russell and Leo Dietrichstein.

Clyde Fitch, the most prolific playwright of his time, was the closest friend of the Gersons, and very soon I was invited with some of the celebrities named above to Fitch's exotic home on East Fortieth Street and to Quiet Corner, his country place at Greenwich, Connecticut; I was included probably because I could help to entertain the house guests with my violin. There I would meet the gifted Eleanor Robson (now Mrs. August Belmont), the beautiful Maxine Elliot and her husband Nat Goodwin, all of them stars in Fitch's plays; there were literary figures like Kate Douglas Wiggin, and one met there the financier James Hazen Hyde before the scandals of the insurance world forced him to reside abroad. One celebrity whom I regrettably missed meeting at Fitch's home was Edith Wharton, whose *The House of Mirth* was a literary sensation, but Clyde consoled me by presenting me with the manuscript of the dramatization of that fine novel in the handwritings of the playwright and the brilliant novelist, whom Fitch described as "a devilishly clever woman." The play was one of Fitch's failures.

Virginia Gerson had written and illustrated a charming children's book, *The Happy Heart Family,* published by Pitts Duffield, whose lovely wife often graced Fitch's circle. Virginia also helped Mrs. John W. Alexander design the costume of forest leaves worn by Maude Adams when she won the theatre-going public with Barrie's *Peter Pan.* Eventually Virginia became one of the co-authors of Clyde Fitch's biography. I owe Virginia Gerson a special debt of gratitude, for she was directly responsible for my meeting Grace Wood who, in turn, introduced me to Mrs. Annie Bertram Webb—as will be narrated in due time.

Among other visitors to the Gersons was an ambitious young novelist whose first book, like one of mine, was dedicated to Virginia. This was Weymar J. Mills, who tried to pose as an eighteenth-century dandy, and hoped to take New York by storm like another Lord Byron. He expected to accomplish this by arranging a costume ball at the old Astor House, then on Lower Broadway, but since demolished. Up to the outbreak of the Civil War it had been the scene of the smart Assembly Balls, and Mills, with the aid of the Gersons, the Misses Grosvenor, and other society women, sought to revive those historic festivities. All the

invited participants were asked to dress, if possible, in the original
gala costumes of their American ancestors, but an exception was
made in deference to a few foreign-born like myself. We prepared
for the occasion by studying the old square dances of *ante-bellum*
days, and on the snowy night when the ball took place we drove
downtown, the ladies, dressed in hoopskirts, arranging themselves,
with some difficulty, in the hired Fifth Avenue bus. Our group,
which included the Gersons, the Beals, and Miss Nora Godwin,
William Cullen Bryant's granddaughter, stopped on our way
downtown at a few famous old houses to pay our respects to distinguished hostesses, like the descendants of Peter Cooper, who
were unable to attend the delightful revival.

It was one of the three memorable balls I attended. If I may
digress for a moment, the others were the Ball of the Gods and the
Venetian Ball, arranged in New York by Albert Herter and his
former fellow students at the Beaux Arts, in Paris. For the first of
these glamorous occasions, Leon Bakst designed a remarkable
costume of green and gold for me, and my body was painted blue.
When the coloring matter dried on all exposed portions of my
body, I seemed to be made of silken velvet. For the Venetian Ball,
a scene of great splendor, I wore a long crimson silk damask cloak,
and Belle Greene lent me one of Mr. Pierpont Morgan's priceless
jeweled necklaces, so that I really looked like a Giorgionesque
figure. Baron de Meyer took some fine photographs of me, and I,
or the Morgan jewel, created a mild sensation.

The weekend parties given by Fitch to which I was invited
with the Gersons were always brilliant. Once when we gathered
at Quiet Corner on the eve of our host's annual departure for
Europe, I bemoaned the mundane nature of my existence, adding
that I seemed doomed to spend the rest of my days in a law office.
On hearing this, Grace Wood, a well-known interior decorator,
said that had she known of my discontent a few days earlier she
would have introduced me to Mrs. Annie Bertram Webb, a lady
known as the patroness of the opera star, Geraldine Farrar. At the
moment, Mrs. Webb was trying to find a lawyer who could protect her interests in Capri, where she thought she had been
victimized by an unscrupulous hotel proprietor. Grace Wood—
forever be her name blessed—feared that it might already be too

late for me to reach Mrs. Webb, but she promised to make an effort. She sat down at once and sent a letter to Mrs. Webb's last-known American address.

On my return to New York I chanced to meet Mrs. John Ames Mitchell, wife of the owner of *Life*. Mollie Mitchell, as her friends called her, cordially invited me for afternoon tea on the following day, and I accepted. A little white-haired lady, gaily dressed in a light turquoise-blue gown, was the only other guest, but I did not pay close heed to her name when I was introduced. She showed an interest in my musical anecdotes, and both ladies encouraged me to chatter on and on. When I finally arose to leave, the little woman offered to give me a lift in her car which was parked outside.

We had hardly closed the door of the Mitchell residence behind us when she mystified me by saying that she rarely discussed her private affairs even before intimate friends. My mystification cleared when she went on to say she had received a letter from Grace Wood. This letter suggested that I might be the right person to act as her attorney in proceedings she was planning to start against a man in Capri who had cheated her, and now owed her a considerable sum. So this gay little lady was none other than Mrs. Annie Bertram Webb! Even now, by a coincidence, she was on her way to see Mrs. Wood and her sister Miss Florence Mosher, who was another of Mrs. Webb's protegées; she had studied in Vienna, she informed me, under Leschetizky, the great piano pedagogue. Strangely enough, not only had Mrs. Mitchell spoken well of me, but unbelievable as it might sound, a Dr. Davenport, who had met me at Northeast Harbor, had also mentioned my name as that of the very man Mrs. Webb needed to protect her interests. Unfortunately, Dr. Davenport had not known my address. This curious chain of coincidences convinced Mrs. Webb, who was a strong believer in Spiritualism, that I had been brought to her attention by some mysterious, perhaps even by a divine, agency! Without even raising the question of my right or ability to conduct a lawsuit in an Italian court of law, she made me a very generous offer on the spot. I immediately accepted, on condition that I could get a leave of absence from the title company where I was working as a specialist in real estate law; I would need time to terminate any legal action I might commence for Mrs. Webb in Capri. Subsequent events, I must say, really gave Mrs. Webb some reason for believing in supernatural intervention, and for supposing that I was a kind of medium, under the guidance of some benevolent occult power. For myself, all I can say is that this Salem-born lady—Mrs. Webb was the daughter of Captain Bertram, owner of a fleet of sailing vessels engaged in the Far East trade—produced a most beneficent revolution in my life.

The defendant in the Capri lawsuit was a Hungarian hotel proprietor. He was quite innocent of any dishonesty, but had been the victim of Mrs. Webb's jealous scandalmongering entourage. He met the boat from Naples on the wharf at Capri, singled me out of the crowd of tourists as I came ashore, and explained his position clearly. On finding that I was a native of Hungary, he threw himself on my mercy, and to avoid a lawsuit agreed to follow any reasonable suggestion I might make. Within twenty-four hours after my arrival, the entire situation was straightened out in the office of Mr. Jerome, the American Consul, to the satisfaction of both parties, and eventually every cent of the loan was paid back to Mrs. Webb, with interest.

Mrs. Webb, delighted at this quick result, now insisted that I should remain as her guest for the remainder of the term of my leave of absence, for she had paid me for the entire time in advance. I was lodged in a little glass house in the garden of the Villa Certosella, where De Locle had written the libretto for Verdi's *Aida*, when he had stayed at Capri.

The fear of a law suit being now only an unpleasant memory, we took drives along the coast over the famous road from Sorrento to Amalfi and Paestum. It was in the old Convent of the Capu-chins—now a hotel—that I first met Ernest Longfellow, the handsome son of the poet, and he in turn introduced me to his nephew, Richard Henry Dana, Jr., a never-to-be-forgotten friend about whom I shall have more to say as this story develops. Ernest Longfellow had been a pupil of Couture, and it was at his home in Manchester, Massachusetts, that I first met John Singer Sargent and the inspired Negro orator and head of Tuskegee, Booker T. Washington. Colonel House, President Wilson's advisor and agent, was Ernest Longfellow's summer neighbor, and we all met the

President. However, Harry Dana, Richard's brother, was justly suspected of being a too-ardent pacifist and I have no doubt that I, his
friend, was closely watched by private detectives while President
Wilson paid his visit.

When the beauties of the enchanting region around Capri were
partially exhausted, I was given carte blanche to plan a trip north
in Mrs. Webb's car, through Italy and France, to her residence in
Paris, at 40 Avenue Henri Martin.

First, however, she wanted to pay a short visit to Sicily, where
her friends, General and Signora di Majo, were expecting her.
Signora di Majo had been born in America, the daughter of Luigi
Monti who had been Longfellow's friend at Cambridge; Luigi
Monti, in fact, figured as the Sicilian in one of Longfellow's narra-
tive poems.

Signora di Majo's maternal grandfather was T. W. Parsons, the
famous American translator of Dante; her father lies buried in the
Protestant Cemetery near the wall of Rome, where lovers of Keats
and Shelley, who are also buried there, come to dream and mourn.
As a young girl, during a visit to Italy, Luigi Monti's daughter had
fallen madly in love with the handsome di Majo, then a colonel,
and considerably older than she, but under the Italian military
law they were not permitted to marry because neither of them
had any money. Mrs. Webb served as a fairy godmother, and
provided a suitable *dot,* which smoothed out all the difficulties
of the lovers. Small wonder then that Mrs. Webb, affectionately
called Donnina, and all her friends were cordially received when
we arrived at General di Majo's *palazzo* in Catania, at the foot of
Aetna, where the General, a former governor of Sicily, lived. I
spoke only a few words of Italian and General di Majo could not
speak English, but my taste for raw *finocchi* instantly established
a bond.

The di Majos accompanied Mrs. Webb to Taormina, which
was then in its glory. The almond blossoms were at their best, and
I reveled in the magnificent views of snow-clad Aetna seen from
the flowery-decked arena of the ruined Greek theatre and framed
by its columns.

Robert Hichens, to whom I had a letter from Clyde Fitch, was the most celebrated person in Taormina. He had already written the *Garden of Allah* and *The Call of the Blood,* and I recall a dinner he gave at the Hotel Timeo, where we ate at a table completely covered with petals of many-colored pansies. I gave a concert for the benefit of the local charities, playing on one of the most perfect violins ever made by Stradivarius. It belonged to Colonel Shaw-Hellier, an Englishman who could not play but collected great instruments. Soon I was known to the whole foreign colony. Baron von Gloeden, the German photographer who posed his models in pseudo-Hellenistic settings, was one of the colony's outstanding figures and Mrs. Webb enjoyed the exotic parties he gave in her honor. The Baron urged me to climb one of the high neighboring hills on the summit of which Ludwig Wullner—probably the greatest of all *lieder* singers—lived like a hermit near the clouds. Although his voice was almost gone, he later made an unforgettable sensation when he gave his first American recital. His incomparable accompanist was the Dutch pianist Conraad van Bos, who died in New York in 1955. When the First World War broke out, von Gloeden and all other Germans were either interned or obliged to leave Italy, but the photographer returned in triumph when hostilities came to an end. I often wonder what became of his "Golden Book," in which a long list of famous visitors had written appreciations of the ancient Greek colony and of the gentle Baron's hospitality.

Another outstanding resident of Taormina was Alec Hood, the Duke of Bronte, to whom I was introduced by Robert Hichens. His title was inherited from Admiral Nelson on whom it had been bestowed by a grateful Italy. The Duke's Villa was famous for its matchless gardens overlooking Mount Aetna and the coast of Sicily. It was an ideal spot in which to sit and dream, while gentle winds scattered the almond blossoms into snowlike drifts. The house itself was Victorian in atmosphere; many inscribed photographs of the English Royal Family in neat silver frames were a feature of the drawing room. An extraordinary incident took place in the course of a luncheon party to which the Duke of Bronte had invited the well-known aesthete, Baron de Meyer, photographer, dress designer and interior decorator. A startling but cruel caricature of de Meyer by Max Beerbohm, dating from this period, is still in my possession. At the time of his visit to Taormina he was mourning the loss of his beautiful wife who had often posed for their friend, Charles Conder. De Meyer prided himself on his original taste, which was obviously offended when we sat down at the luncheon table dominated by a large, branching, silver *epergne* filled with flowers and bonbons. De Meyer exclaimed that the ugly ornament interfered with his view, and with a swing of his arm he swept the whole decoration to the floor! The silence of the amazed guests was broken by the dignified unruffled host who rang for his Italian butler and ordered him to sweep the floor and rearrange the table. De Meyer never afterward crossed the thresh-hold of Bronte's villa.

After we left Sicily, traveling north from Naples in Mrs. Webb's luxurious Renault, we stopped for days at a time not only at great centers like Rome, Perugia, Sienna, Venice and Milan, but also at smaller towns like Monte Cassino and Assisi. We would leave the beaten track to see the so-called Bronze Victory of Brescia, an incorrectly restored bronze. I was allowed to pay homage to the memory of the great violinmakers at Cremona. I devoured Baedekers all along the route, so that no outstanding art treasure should escape me. I hardly slept, for each night I had to study and prepare myself for the next day's wonders and aesthetic adven-tures. We read the sonnets of Petrarch beside the waters of the fountain at Vaucluse or re-read the adventures of Tartarin in Daudet's beloved Tarascon. We defied the dangerous blasts of the treacherous Mistral to see the strange little town of Polignac where Mrs. Webb, like a ministering angel, purchased quantities of lace from poor, almost blind old women who plied their bob-bins in the streets, while I went off to test the echoes of the ancient Roman oracle of Apollo, of which the huge neglected stone mask was still preserved. We even braved the rapids of the Gorge du Tarn. The stalwart, powerful men who guided us were amused when the little silver haired old lady, youthfully dressed, followed their instructions, and lay face down flat on the raft to which we were obliged to cling. Mrs. Webb's incredibly small feet were also a source of wonder and our guides never stopped laughing while we enjoyed the thrill of being swept for miles swiftly downstream through the Gorge, the steep walls of which were covered with shrubbery filled with countless nightingales warbling an enchanting accompaniment to our wild ride. The motor car was waiting for us at the lower end of the Gorge and we continued our drive, visiting every important shrine on the way north to Paris.

Paris, *la ville lumière*, was even more exciting. Not only did I visit all the museums repeatedly, but I had the opportunity to hear operas and symphonies new to me. I saw the performances of Isadora Duncan and Loie Fuller, and a galaxy of other stars. Sensation followed sensation, and I met many celebrities at the home of Mrs. Webb, who enjoyed entertaining them. One memorable afternoon performance that I arranged with Loie Fuller's assistance was a Japanese play in which the chief performer was the diminutive Madame Hanako, whose expressive features inspired Rodin to create a marvelously sensitive bronze mask. Long afterward I secured a cast of this for Grenville Lindall Winthrop's collection, now in the Fogg Art Museum at Harvard. In the short one-act play for which I arranged the Japanese musical accompaniment, Madame Hanako took the leading role of a poor beggar maiden who finds a parcel while wandering in a forest. It contains the resplendent dress and jewels of a royal princess. She yields to the temptation to try on the priceless costume, and while thus attired a prince walks by and immediately falls in love with her. However, when he discovers that she is only a beggar, he spurns and abandons her, and the short play ends on a tragic note.

The finely proportioned drawing room of Mrs. Webb's apartment at 40 Avenue Henri Martin, in which Farrar and Caruso once sang, lent itself admirably to such entertainments, and I had the pleasure of meeting many well-known people at these gatherings.

The day of my departure for New York to resume my work with the title company arrived far too soon. I returned with great reluctance to my old desk, but fortunately I did not remain chained to it for long. A few months later, David Kimball, brother-in-law of Mrs. Webb, appealed to me to return to Europe without delay and extricate Mrs. Webb from another legal predicament. Her secretary, Albert Helner had forgotten that her motor car insurance had lapsed. On his way to renew the policy Mrs. Webb's automobile struck a young Italian lad, coasting wildly down a hill directly in front of it, and the resulting injury was fatal. There were witnesses to prove that Mrs. Webb's chauffeur was in no way to blame, for he was driving very slowly. I had little trouble convincing the parents that they had better accept a sum that Mrs. Webb generously offered them than enter upon a lawsuit that she would undoubtedly win. The bereaved parents saw the wisdom and fairness of my offer, and once more I found myself the guest of Mrs. Webb for months to come.

We were soon in Capri again, just at the time when the world was horrified by the disastrous eruption of Mount Aetna and the total destruction of Messina. The island of the sirens continued to fascinate me. As soon as Mrs. Webb's arrival was known, all the local worthies came to call on her. I recall the handsome, picturesque American, Charles Coleman, known to everyone as "Cinque Cento" Charlie. His modest claim to fame rests on his pastel studies of the great eruption of Vesuvius, which he saw from Capri. Dr. Axel Munthe occupied the Villa Quattro Venti, a former home of Mrs. Webb.

Another frequent visitor was Appolonyi, the distinguished-looking sculptor, one of whose classical marble figures decorated the gardens of Baron Adelsward Fersen, scion of a great family. Fersen was a notorious homosexual poet, who wrote many volumes of verse dealing almost exclusively with homosexuality. He kept the international colony busy with gossip about his scandalous amours. Mr. Jerome, the American Consul, was the only neutral between the hostile camps of Fersen's friends and foes. Mrs. Webb was one of the Count's bitterest detractors, and I was warned not to meet him. Then there were the Wordsworths who, although they had little to offer, maintained a social position because they were related to the great English poet.

Lastly, there was the brilliant English writer, Norman Douglas, whose *South Wind* is the classical satire of life on the enchanting island. Maxim Gorki and Compton Mackenzie were later arrivals. Mrs. Webb's generosity to many of her friends is wittily, if not sympathetically, described by Douglas in *Looking Backward*. Douglas always regretted that he had not taken greater advantage of her charitable instincts. At the time of my first visit to Capri, which Douglas described as the Cuspidor of Europe, he was involved in an unsavory divorce suit. Mrs. Webb and her circle helped him to win the case. Furthermore, to help him financially, Mrs. Webb bought his remarkable collection of rare books dealing with the island. She told me that she had presented them to Harvard University. However, Philip Hofer, a member of the library staff, recently told me that after a prolonged search, he could find no such books, or any record of the gift. No one knows what happened to this unique collection.

To know Douglas in those days was a rare privilege. He had not yet written *South Wind,* which was to stamp him as one of the most original authors of our epoch, but for me, his essays on the jeweled lizards of Capri and other studies in natural history immediately made him an outstanding person in Mrs. Webb's group of friends. He was a fine linguist and his fund of information was remarkable. If I wanted an antique gem with a head of Antinous engraved on it, he knew where it could be found, and he would lead me to the shops of obscure art dealers hidden in the narrow streets of Naples until we discovered such an item. We rowed into every grotto, blue, red or green; we explored the great caves and climbed at low tide through the pitch-dark chimney-like passage to the top of the Monacone, one of the *fariglioni,* where traces of the rifled tomb of the architect of Tiberius could still be examined. He knew all the scandalous details of the life of Fersen and the love affairs of Coleman with handsome Capri peasant women. He was a tireless walker, and we would climb the heights above Ana Capri or descend to the ancient temple of Mithras (near the Arco Naturale) where the old Roman religious ceremony was once revived by Douglas with the aid of Consul Jerome. He once told me about the German, Hanns Heinz Ewers, who wrote an account of Wilde after the poet's release from prison, and there was never a dull moment in Douglas' company.

After Douglas and I had both left Capri, our friendship was still cultivated during occasional meetings, and when Douglas settled down in Florence in an apartment on the bank of the Arno I again saw a good deal of him—and his publisher, G. Orioli. We dined together quite frequently, and Douglas would invariably offer me a pinch of perfumed snuff from a beautiful silver box. At the first offering, I sneezed violently, and Norman exclaimed, "Why Martin, how delightful! You actually have a virgin nose!"

Orioli's influence was not altogether wholesome. They traveled about Italy together, and these wanderings were impudently described by the publisher in his amusing book, *Moving Along*. Douglas was always in need of funds. Orioli urged him to write the notorious *Some Limericks* adorned with the inimitable pseudo-scientific critical footnotes, and the less interesting book on aphrodisiacs entitled *Paneros*. Bibliophiles paid high prices for the small editions of these books. My copy of the *Limericks* is inscribed by Douglas: "To Martin Birnbaum, hoping it will do him some good, from his friend Norman Douglas, 22 September 1930."

I hope that someone will eventually collect the best letters of Douglas. The ones he wrote to me are among my prized possessions, second only to those that Santayana wrote me from his ivory tower in the Convent of St. Stephano in Rome.

It was Douglas, by the way, who first urged me to write. I am happy to reflect that our friendship was never broken, although his escapades in London and in Italy made him a questionable companion for a young man. He was a severe critic of his own work. I remember his telling me that an article on *South Wind* written by my friend Schofield Thayer, then editor of the *Dial*, was one of the best pieces written about him. Thayer was an ardent admirer of Beardsley, whose work I helped him to collect. When I last saw him in Martha's Vineyard, his promising career had come to an abrupt end, for he was suffering from a strange mental disease.

Robin, Douglas' elder son, whom I came to know in London, was a patient of my late nephew, Dr. Jerome Martin Ziegler. He had a certain talent as a writer, and his adventures as a rum-runner in New York during prohibition days are entertaining. Robin wrote an epicure's guide to London restaurants, and an autobiographical volume, *16 to 21*. When he came to see me in New York he was married. Soon afterwards he disappeared from the field of letters.

To return to my sojourn in Capri: At the time of the Messina disaster I was always on the lookout for acquaintances among the refugees from Sicily, and one of these was a distinguished German lady, Madame de Angelis, who had married a minor Italian official. When her house was utterly destroyed by the eruption of Aetna, she came to Capri with her two fine young sons to await the arrival of her sister, Frau von Unrúh, from their estate near Breslau. When the sister reached Capri from Germany, Mrs. Webb, with characteristic generosity, immediately came to the financial aid of both women.

Later we learned that their father, Count Roon, the celebrated Prussian War Minister, had been a great statesman during the reign of Wilhelm der Grosse, and his statue stood between those of Bismarck and Von Moltke in front of the Reichstag before it was burned by the Nazis. The sisters were the German Emperor's childhood playmates and enjoyed the highest position in the social circles of Berlin, although their landed estate was in the remote little town of Warkotsch, not far from Breslau.

One day, while watching the tourists disembark from the Naples steamer, I espied Richard Strauss, the famous German composer, and his wife, and offered them my services. Naturally, Herr Strauss did not recognize me when I introduced myself as a friend of Wetzler and a former pupil of Lichtenberg, the concertmaster of his American orchestra. I took the liberty of inviting Herr Strauss and his wife to the Villa Certosella, knowing that Mrs. Webb would be glad to meet the famous composer, who in turn, would be pleased to know the former patroness of Geraldine Farrar. It was only when Madame Strauss crossed the threshold of Mrs. Webb's villa that we became aware of the high social standing of the daughters of Count Roon. Madame Strauss seemed overwhelmed. She was a professional singer, the daughter of General de Ahna, and she afterward told me that she had descended the social ladder when she consented to become the wife of a mere musician!

Strauss loved to go walking and I guided the whole party over the hills, which were clothed with asphodels and studded with a tangle of other lovely spring wild flowers. Strauss begged the ladies not to pick the blossoms. He and I went ahead, leaving his wife with Signora de Angelis and Frau von Unrúh, whom she tried to cultivate. Strauss advised his wife not to talk too much, lest she say something foolish. *"Bitte, keine phrasen,"* he warned her. The composer seemed to enjoy my silent companionship, and the wonderful landscape with its inspiring Mediterranean panorama encouraged his meditations. We lingered on the winding road till the shadows slanted beneath the setting sun, and I refrained from disturbing him with small talk, while waiting for him to break the silence. The fact that Geraldine Farrar was no longer a guest under Mrs. Webb's roof was a great disappointment, for he had hoped that the lovely diva who had enjoyed a sensational success in Berlin, could be persuaded to appear as Salome in his opera of that name at the Metropolitan Opera House in New York. The honor eventually fell to Olive Fremsted.

After the departure of her distinguished guests, Mrs. Webb decided to accept Frau von Unrúh's invitation to her *Gut* in Warkotsch near Breslau, and the hospitality we enjoyed there in 1909 is still vividly remembered. Not only were we treated like old family friends, but Frau von Unrúh's august neighbors received us cordially on their fine estates. Von Moltke's nephew showed us the simple little cell-like bedroom of the noted statesman, which had been left undisturbed since he had died. We were invited to visit Prince Fürstenstein, who had, I think, married the authoress of *Elizabeth and her German Garden,* and we were shown his stables, unmatched in Germany.

A family more ancient than the ruling Hohenzollerns were the Richthofens, cousins of the famous German ace in the war that threatened to overwhelm us. The Richthofens at Stanowitz were followers of the Scotsman, Irwin, who believed that after the last of Christ's disciples were dead, He would rise again and put an end to all our fears and problems. Subscribing to this belief, the Richthofens, who were childless, were living like philanthropic lords of a great manor. They were giving away all their wealth, feeding the poor, housing all the aged in comfortable cottages, and teaching all the village children in free schools. They entertained, however, in regal style. At the luncheon in Mrs. Webb's honor, the portraits of their ancestors looked down on us from the walls while we sipped the best champagne, served in long, engraved crystal glasses into which hothouse peaches were dropped to give the wine a still more subtle flavor. On our return we were accompanied to Berlin by our hosts at Warkotsch, and my first undertaking was to climb the pedestal on which stood the marble statue of their father, Count Roon, and lay a huge wreath of flowers, Mrs. Webb's tribute, at its feet.

In the meanwhile, during the summer of 1909, we had agreed to meet Muriel Sanders and her future husband, Paul Draper, in Vienna, for he was anxious to study with the great Leschetizky, who had invited Mrs. Webb and her party to dine with him at his home. Leschetizky was an entertaining host, and gave us an imitation of a sentimental English governess playing the opening bars of the *Moonlight Sonata*. He told us that there were works of Beethoven that he did not like, but he described Schubert as "a miracle." Then he regaled us with fascinating stories of his most famous pupils, Gabrilowitsch and Paderewski. In his opinion Paderewski was not endowed with exceptional natural talent, but his application and indomitable determination to master his chosen instrument amounted to a kind of demonic genius. While telling us his stories, which I translated for Mrs. Webb with the help of Leschetizky's youthful third wife, the gifted raconteur was oblivious of the fact that the raspberry sauce on the dessert was trickling all over his shirt front.

Before we departed, Mrs. Webb asked the Leschetizkys to another dinner, and he accepted on condition that it be an absolutely informal al fresco repast in the Türkenschutz Park where Beethoven used to compose while promenading, and Mozart, not far away, created *Don Giovanni*.

I was entrusted by Mrs. Webb with the task of ordering the feast in advance. As we entered the enclosure on the appointed night, the orchestra leader recognized Leschetizky immediately, and from that moment only selections chosen by the guest of honor were played. Above all, he asked for a string of waltzes by his deceased friend, Johann Strauss, whom he loved more than any other human being, and the waltzes moved him to tears. "Yes, my dear," he added, addressing his young wife, "I loved him even more than I love you." He was distressed that funds for a monument to the great composer could not be raised in Vienna. When news of Strauss' death reached Leschetizky, he dressed at once and sat with the body of his beloved friend all night.

Knowing that Mrs. Webb's favorite dessert was a good soufflé, I had asked the maître d'hotel to prepare one, and when he proudly walked down the aisle carrying the dish, accompanied by his chef, in white uniform and the customary white cap, the dish the chef carried certainly looked like a masterpiece. We were all annoyed, however, because Leschetizky would not accept even the smallest portion, insisting adamantly that he had eaten enough and would join us only for a cup of black coffee. When Mrs. Webb saw that persuasion was useless, all her other guests were served and tasted the dish almost simultaneously. To Leschetizky's amazement, instead of swallowing the first spoonful, all heads were quickly turned from the table and, accompanied by choking, coughing and spitting, the poisonous concoction was disgorged on the grass as politely as possible. Leschetizky was puzzled and curious. He now agreed to try the strange mess, and took a tiny sample from Mrs. Webb's plate. He made strange grimaces but of course he could not swallow it. The maître d'hotel had left us before all this happened, and Leschetizky sent for him and ordered him to return with the chef and the remains of the soufflé. They arrived with the dish, beaming with pleasure, thinking we all wanted a second portion. But Leschetizky insisted that they too should taste their *chef d'oeuvre*. When they tasted it, they were horrified, and ran off the scene amid the shrieks of the orchestra and of the diners in the park. It developed that bitter rock salt, mistaken for sugar, had been beaten up with the eggs and the flavoring to concoct the horrible dish that was offered us.

Leschetizky, after an audition, refused to take Paul Draper as a pupil, believing that he was too old to develop into a virtuoso. However, the intelligent young American went to London to study singing with Raimund von Zur Muhlen and became a concert singer. I afterward heard him as a soloist with the Boston Symphony Orchestra. After a few years of married life, admirably described by Muriel in her fascinating book, *Music at Midnight*, she and Paul separated. Muriel Draper then proceeded to entertain her former husband and his second wife at a wedding breakfast, the table being entirely covered with fresh forget-me-nots!

Muriel was one of the most brilliant women I ever knew. She could master the essential rudiments of a language and speak it fluently in an amazingly short time, and she was the life of any party she attended. Her talented son, Paul Draper, and her gifted sister-in-law, Ruth Draper, the famous monologist, need no introduction. It is pleasant to record that Sargent's fine portrait drawings of Ruth Draper and many of her personal belongings were left to the Museum of the City of New York.

Leaving Vienna, we enjoyed Mozart operas at Salzburg, the art museums of Munich, and productions of Reinhardt, including the sensational *Lysistrata* of Aristophanes. Through Dr. Franz Blei, a talented writer, I met Meier Graefe, the author of a famous work on modern art, and together we visited Carl Sternheim. He was a rich collector who wore pumps over red silk hose, and one of his plays was staged in London. It was at his beautiful home, Belle Maison, boasting of a fine collection of first editions of Goethe, Heine, and Schiller, that I first learned to appreciate van Gogh and Gauguin, and there I met the strange genius Max Mayrshofer, at one time a muscular baker, whose nudes, some of which I still treasure, were afterward shown at the Armory Show in New York. Sternheim told me of his poetical drama based on the story of Don Juan. The chief character, he said, embodied all the strength and weakness as well as the charm of a "modern man," the best type being his own ideal, the German gentleman.

We motored to Nuremberg and thence to Bayreuth, to enjoy Wagner's operas, and on to Prague, and eventually to Breslau and and Warkotsch, where our stay with Frau von Unrúh has already been mentioned.

When we reached Paris on my second visit, in the spring of 1910, I again enlarged my circle of European acquaintances and spent considerable time introducing Mrs. Webb's musical protegés to leaders of French society who could help them to successful careers. Rita Fornia, a competent singer with an unusual repertoire, was engaged by the Metropolitan, but her contract was strangely drawn. She was rarely given an opportunity to sing, and although her salary was regularly paid her appearances were so rare that we called her salary "hush money." She was really engaged to hold herself in readiness to sing at a moment's notice should a more celebrated songstress became indisposed. Another admirable lyric soprano and actress, Marcella Kraft, who created the role of Elektra for Richard Strauss, was given an audition at the home of the Countess Grefühle, but failed to impress that great power in the French musical world. Her voice was too light for the vast spaces of the Metropolitan, but she made a single appearance with a minor company at a New York theatre in *Traviata*, and it was the most moving performance of the opera I have ever heard. The New York critics, however, had never heard of her, and damned Miss Kraft with faint praise.

I had, of course, ample time on these European trips to visit and study in the museums and I became a familiar figure not only in the Louvre, the Petit Palais, the Guimet, the Luxembourg, the Cluny, and the Carnavalet, but in smaller institutions like the Cernuschi, the Musée Gustave Moreau under the direction of the late Rouault, the Musée Rodin, the Maison Victor Hugo, the Orangerie, the rooms once occupied by Delacroix, the Jeu de Paume, and the enchanting Musée Jacquemart-André on the Boulevard Haussmann, which was founded by an admirable painter of flowers, after she married a wealthy Parisian.

In Paris the cheap galleries and the pit are the consolation and refuge of students, and for a small fee I bought a ticket to the Opera House, when Ida Rubinstein presented a new spectacle at which she attempted the speaking role of the heroine Semiramis. She ordered her settings from my friend Jacovleff, whose brilliant but too brief career I have described elsewhere. It is impossible adequately to measure how great a loss the world of art sustained when he died, and I often wonder what the ultimate verdict will be in a world encumbered by strange fallacies of art criticism.

On another night, I had Fenella, the gipsy girl who had posed for Rippl-Ronai in Hungary, as one of my dinner guests at the famous restaurant Lapérouse on the Left Bank of the Seine. She claimed kinship with Lovell, a king of the gypsies. Mrs. Webb came to her aid whenever she was in financial difficulties. Henry McBride and the celebrated Guillaume Apollinaire, an authority on avant-garde literature, were among those at the table. Apollinaire was rashly entrusted by me with the task of making up the menu. To impress me with his taste as a gourmet, Apollinaire ordered lavishly and the repast cost me a month's salary, but it really was a good dinner. After Apollinaire's death, I was asked to subscribe for his three posthumous volumes. I did not suspect the nature of his subject matter, and years later an accidental glance through uncut pages revealed the fact that the books of Apollinaire were inspired by the most shameless examples of erotic literature, reprints of which were edited by him and published on the Rue Fuerstenberg.

At that time, "Nico" Mazaraki, a gay young Greek, was one of my Parisian chums. He was a *marchand amateur,* and an intimate friend of Raoul Dufy, who painted an excellent portrait of him. Nico, who knew all the French contemporary artists, introduced me to Prince Nicholas of Greece, who had a certain talent as a painter, and gave exhibitions in Paris and London. His best work bore a faint resemblance to the work of Lepine, but he was more famous as the father of the beautiful Duchess of Kent.

Another of my friends in the foreign colony was Janet Scudder, who insisted on my accompanying her to visit Gertrude Stein and Miss Alice Toklas. Janet was certain that they would become my friends, but my visit on that stormy night was a dismal failure. Not knowing that every picture on the crowded walls, without a single exception, was by Picasso, I committed unforgivable blunders by praising a still life that, in the dim light, looked to me like a Cézanne, and by saying that another work showed the marked influence of Toulouse-Lautrec. This was followed by the worst possible gesture, when I commented favorably on a portrait of Leo Stein, Gertrude's brother, whose wife was regarded by his sister as a bitter enemy. To discover influences in the work of Miss Stein's unapproachable master was almost a crime, and was in itself sufficient reason for being regarded as an unwelcome visitor.

Mrs. Webb was a very restless person. The attractions of Paris did not hold her long. This 1910 European sojourn finally came to an end, and I was obliged unwillingly to return to New York and take my old place in the title company, although disturbed by an ever-growing consciousness of my dislike for the law.

Luckily Fate, or Dame Fortune, was still hovering over me. Another vacation at Northeast Harbor brought me into touch with Dr. and Mrs. Leonard Weber, and again through my violin this acquaintance ripened into a fine friendship. The doctor was one of the most prominent physicians in the German colony of New York, and I can only describe his wife, Meta Weber, as a Swedenborgian angel on earth, although she believed in no established religion. Mentally and spiritually she was one of the simplest and noblest human beings I ever had the good fortune to meet. Emil Werckmeister, a close European friend of hers, was the owner of the Photographische Gesellschaft (the Berlin Photographic Company). He had recently written her a letter saying that he was obliged to permit the manager of the American branch to resign, although he might find it impossible to find a suitable successor.

Tante Meta, as I fondly called Mrs. Weber, immediately thought of me, knowing that I was discontented in my profession, and she recommended me to Mr. Werckmeister. I had had no experience in this or any other commercial field, and the business of publishing photographs and reproductions of paintings was a complicated one. However, she believed in my ability, and in spite of my father's objections I accepted the position, and suddenly found myself free from the bonds of the law. This took place in 1910, and for six years I managed the American branch of the Berlin Photographic Company.

II

Debut in the World of Art

The familiarity with the masterpieces of art which I had acquired on my visits to Europe was, of course, excellent preparation for a career as an art dealer. It did not take me long, in fact, to master the details of my new venture, and I may say truthfully that I revolutionized the American branch of the Berlin Photographic Company. I at once noticed the high cost of maintaining the old premises on East Twenty-third Street and saw that I must reduce overhead expenses, which were wrecking the enterprise. I soon found an attractive building at 305 Madison Avenue that lent itself admirably to being gallery, showroom and offices. To avoid costly advertising, I hit upon the idea of giving a series of exhibitions that would attract the public and make our premises a well-known art center. However, I sometimes wondered whether I had jumped from the frying pan into the fire.

A fairly satisfactory answer was soon offered by Richard Henry Dana, one of my closest friends at that time. Architecture was his chosen profession, and I have never known a man who had higher ideals. The unique dwellings that Dick designed, built, and completely furnished for Mrs. Thomas J. Emery's housing project near Cincinnati were studied with a perfectionist's care, for when he was entrusted with a commission Dick would study every facet of a patron's needs and desires in a way that aroused my highest admiration.

When I discussed my future plans with my friend, he encouraged me with his assurance that to discover new talent among the artists of America was a high endeavor worthy of any man's efforts, for I might not only help to shape the lives of artists who might otherwise remain unrecognized, but I could also introduce new figures and great masterpieces into this country and help

43

furnish America with fresh inspiration. Dick was a pillar of strength in this *Sturm und Drang* period when I was searching for some justification of my activities, and I became, as it were, a nurse to artistic talent.

Quite recently evidence of the truth of my friend's remarks on the possible cultural importance of my humble efforts was unexpectedly furnished by the opening of certain period rooms in the Metropolitan Museum. Colonel Jacob Ruppert, who for years directed the business fortunes of the New York Yankees, was a fairly regular visitor to our galleries. On finding that I was an admirer of Saint Bernard dogs, he invited me to visit him at his residence on upper Fifth Avenue and later to go to see his baseball team. This took place long before I had become the slave of my magnificent boxer, whom I named Prince Ruppert after the colonel. My dog, after long association with me, developed a strong interest in art! When a picture was delivered at my home, he insisted on examining the opened parcel and looked at the painting with the air of a connoisseur. If the box contained a piece of sculpture, he expressed his approval by giving it a lick.

Colonel Ruppert and I had other interests in common, chief of which was the care of fresh-water aquaria. Our acquaintance resulted in his entrusting me with the decoration of his large drawing room, for which I procured a fine group of Restoration portraits by Lely, Kneller, and other artists, many of them in their original Sunderland frames. After his death they were bequeathed to the Metropolitan Museum, and were features of the admirable eighteenth-century rooms in the wing devoted to decorative arts, only recently opened by the late Francis Taylor, at that time the museum's able director.

I began my experiments at the Berlin Photographic Gallery with the first American Exhibition of the work of the great nineteenth-century Belgian painter, Alfred Stevens. Following the example of my old friend, Frederick Keppel, I wrote a not-too-lengthy introduction to the catalogue and had it printed at the renowned De Vinne Press. To my delight and surprise, on the day after the opening, my first effort in this field, I awoke to find myself locally famous. The art critics printed laudatory reviews of the exhibition, and treated my first essay on art with generosity. All the borrowed paintings that were for sale found ready customers, and many of the visitors who thronged the new gallery became purchasers of our publications. Madame Sarah Bernhardt, who had been a pupil of "Le Beau Sabreur," as Stevens was called, came in person to see her beautiful portrait, and other distinguished persons soon made a habit of regularly visiting all our exhibitions. The art dealers whom I did not know even by sight came to study the methods of the newcomer.

When our first success was followed by notable exhibitions of Aubrey Beardsley, Conder, Shannon and Ricketts, and the Americans Albert Sterner, Ernest Haskell and Robert Blum, we were recognized not only as publishers but as art dealers as well, and I found myself in a favorable position to encourage artists like Marin, Eugene Higgins and John Sloan who were then not too successful. Dr. Wilhelm Bode was at work for us in Berlin on a monograph on Franz Hals, and it was my assignment to obtain permission from all American owners of original paintings by the artist to photograph their possessions. Our most experienced photographers in Berlin were sent over with elaborate apparatus for that purpose. This brought me into personal contact with noted collectors like Collis P. Huntington, Charles M. Schwab, Senator Clark, Dr. Jacobs of Baltimore, Mr. John Grover Johnson of Philadelphia, Joseph Widener, and others. I did not hesitate to turn down Senator Clark's example by Hals and my opinion was accepted by Dr. Bode after he saw our photograph, but the senator was furious when he noted that his painting was not reproduced, and cancelled his subscription for a costly de luxe vellum copy of the work.

When I called on a similar errand at the great house of Mr. Collis Huntington, then standing on the southeast corner of Fifth Avenue and Fifty-seventh Street, I was ushered into the presence of Mrs. Huntington, the famous "Rosalie." She was in a wheel chair, and her face was an enigma, for she wore glasses so dark that no one could even attempt to read her thoughts. A secretary stood at the door of the room where we conversed. Obviously, no detail of the conditions that Mrs. Huntington imposed on the permission she granted escaped him. When I saw her again, some years later, she had become the wife of Henry Huntington, her deceased husband's nephew, who had divorced his wife to marry his invalid aunt. Subsequently, their great collection of pictures and incomparable library were bequeathed to the nation. It is strange that some biographer has not yet undertaken the task of delving into the amazing history of all the branches of the Huntington family. Henry Huntington was a charming, kindly man, and I was impressed by his gentle manners when he showed me his famous cactus gardens and the large flying cages in which his feathered pets were kept. As soon as they saw him approach, they flew toward him and kissed or rather pecked at his lips, through the bars of the great cage. When I asked him why he had chosen George D. Smith, who was not famous for his scholarship, to be his purchasing agent, he told me that Mr. Smith knew the price of almost all rare books. I did not venture to remind him that in almost every instance the necessary information was available in the published volumes of Book Prices Current.

Interesting as my visits to the Huntingtons were, they did not compare with another errand for Dr. Bode which took me to the simple unpretentious house of John Grover Johnson, on South Broad Street in Philadelphia. While the photographers from Berlin were busy I was free to roam about the house, which was filled to overflowing with paintings. The clothes closets were packed solid with them. Some of his pictures stood on the floor against bedposts, and a few were even hung on the chandeliers. In any nook, you might discover a Whistler, an important French Impressionist, or an early Flemish Master. Johnson, who was a distinguished attorney, numbered Morgan, Widener, and other great collectors among his clients, but he did not copy their methods. He was an independent man who rarely relied on experts, even though he weighed their opinions and their provenances with a careful legally-trained mind. He once cynically remarked that he bought works of art and not names, and after my visit to his house, I always thought of him as one of America's most brilliant collectors.

The Berlin Photographic Company published many other bulky volumes besides Bode's *Franz Hals*. The monograph on Velasquez by Beruete and the magnificent catalogue of J. Pierpont Morgan's possessions were notable examples.

My enthusiasm, however, was reserved for the series of exhibitions of Americans who had not had adequate recognition or of Europeans who were not sufficiently well known in the United States. All my vacations were devoted to study in museums, or to a search for salient figures in the art world who had not yet made an American debut. Naturally these travels brought me into touch with well-known figures in all the seven arts. One of the pleasantest of these encounters was a trip with Fritz Kreisler from London to Berlin. The celebrated violinist had just left the concert hall in London where he had appeared on a program with the delightful soprano Alma Gluck, who was making her successful English debut. By a happy coincidence I not only shared a stateroom on the channel steamer with Kreisler, but also a compartment on the train. We both carried our violin cases and soon became acquainted. I was surprised to find that he suffered from a nervous facial twitch, but fortunately this never seemed to trouble him when he was playing. When we both returned to New York, he often came to see my exhibitions, or we met in Mario Korbel's studio, where he posed for a bust, and I found that he was an exceptionally well-informed man on many subjects besides music. Small wonder that Sargent told me that he regretted never having had an opportunity to paint the great violin virtuoso.

Art exhibits were then not as common as they are now, and no artist could persuade me to accept payment for the privilege of holding an exhibition of his works at 305 Madison Avenue. My exhibitions followed one another in rapid succession, and became features of the art season, and my experiences thus gained were almost always pleasant. Occasionally, an interesting personality like Hamilton Easter Field or Pamela Colman Smith—an artist with a curious talent—would tempt me to give exhibitions of their works although they were not dominating figures in the field of creative art. I would often sit beside Pamela at a symphony concert while she with her sable brush in hand and a bottle of India ink on her lap, would follow the tempo of the conductor and improvise interesting drawings on the pad which she held. At her preview she sat on the floor in a corner of the crowded gallery and told Jamaican Negro stories which I am sure her guests will never forget.

My first meeting with Hamilton Easter Field also gave me a lasting impression. I had just returned from Europe, where men like Ricketts, Dulac, Rothenstein and Liebermann had introduced me to new names and movements, and Field was one of the few men in America who was thoroughly familiar with them. We discussed an exhibition of his own paintings which he wanted me to arrange, and I found in him an elusive personality, a quaint product of our complex civilization, whose dominant passion was for artistic and musical sensations. His strange, faltering, childish voice, his Quaker simplicity and peculiar unconventionality, repelled superficial observers, but his exceptional fund of information and rich store of anecdote soon won them over, and they became respectful listeners. He dressed badly, never giving the subject a thought. He was at his best while showing the beautiful possessions that he had collected in his fascinating home on Columbia Heights, Brooklyn, where he loved to draw aside the curtains of the rear windows and reveal to the astonished visitor the remarkable panorama of the East River waterfront, with its bridges and the innumerable gleaming lights of Manhattan beyond.

No one knew better than Field the happiest way to arouse your interest in an unfamiliar work of art. You never found him too tired to talk about his treasures; if he mentioned his favorite master, Fantin-Latour, or described his discovery at an auction of an unsigned Guys, which other connoisseurs had overlooked, his enthusiasm became irresistible. He could convincingly analyze the fine draftsmanship of Maurice Sterne, the dramatic quality of Sharaku, the special talent of Desvalliers or the vigorous power of a Madagascar woodcarving, and the most casual visitor would always be impressed by his remarkable eclecticism. He hung his Winslow Homer, Lafarge, Arthur B. Davies, Max Weber, or Legros, beside Chinese silks or above Greek marbles and Javanese bronzes, but a false note was rarely struck. This extraordinary sympathy with divers schools of painting, and his expert knowledge of all types of technique, weakened his own art. He was just developing a more definite personal style when he began a busy career as a professional art critic and editor. Devoting more and more time to teaching and organizing, he was always on the lookout for signs of talent, and younger men like the sculptor Robert Laurent and the talented wood engraver, Arthur Lewis, owed him a special debt. He not only encouraged the artists by purchasing their works, but his sympathy expended itself in many private friendships. He might with justice be described as an instructive art patron. It is difficult to weigh the loss art sustained when death cut short his career, just when he began to show his most engaging and valuable talents. Field was the executor of Fenellosa, and the estate of that distinguished Oriental scholar furnished me with material for a unique exhibition of the prints and original drawings of Hokusai, which Field chose and helped to arrange.

The commencement of my friendship with Ricketts and Shannon took place in the golden age before World War I, when they lived in a famous studio at the top of Lansdowne House. They spent their summers in the Keep at Chilham, said to be the oldest inhabited building in England. Sir Edmund and charming Lady Davis, who owned it, transformed the castle and the gardens into one of the showplaces of England, and Ricketts and Shannon helped to restore the keep and make it a unique artistic habitation. One felt grateful to the screaming peacocks that awakened a house guest at dawn, for one grudged every moment wasted in sleep. England, a land of enchanting gardens, may never again boast of such a delectable dream as Sir Edmund, the lord of the manor, created around the Jacobean castle that Grinley Gibbons had decorated. Many traces of early Roman occupation existed. King John is said to have slept there, and skeletons of former prisoners had been found in the dungeon. From the windows of stained glass made after designs by Burne-Jones, one caught glimpses of the lovely valley of the Stour and the road travelled by Chaucer's storytelling pilgrims on the way to Canterbury.

Such a setting was bound to create romantic artists, but Shannon and Ricketts were something more. Meier Graefe agreed with me that these artists had creative taste second to none. They had lived together so long that they were described as Siamese twins, and their friend Edmund Dulac made a beautiful caricature of them in that guise. After their American exhibition we became life-long friends.

Among the many celebrities to whom they introduced me was the distinguished Serbian sculptor, Mestrovic, who was then making a sensation in London. I had already seen his amazing one-man exhibition in Rome, besides many monuments in various cities in his native land. Later, Sargent, whose advice Mestrovic sought, asked me to arrange the sculptor's first American exhibition, but my premises were too small for such an undertaking, and he entrusted his works to the Metropolitan Museum, where I had pleasant conversations with him.

Another friend of Ricketts was Lucien Pissaro, son of Camille, the French impressionist who, by the way, was born in the Virgin Islands, now American territory. Although he is better known as the director of the handsome Eragny Press, Lucien was also a talented landscape painter. My visits to his studio were exciting, but I was always obliged to protect myself from the sharp claws of his many Siamese cats who flattered me with their dangerous attention.

Ernest Cole, a gifted young sculptor who was honored by a commission to make the Kitchener Memorial, was another friend and discovery of Ricketts. He worked, like Michelangelo, directly in the marble, without "pointing." Unfortunately the effigy was never completed, but I visited the artist in a room under the main floor of St. Paul's Cathedral, where Cole's father reclined, as though dead, dressed in Kitchener's uniform, posing for the figure of the deceased English hero.

Frequently I dined with Shannon and Ricketts at their long malachite table, on one end of which stood a life-sized ancient Greek marble torso, surrounded by blossoming lilies, gardenias and gorgeous amaryllis, set off by leaves of growing emerald-colored acanthus. We sipped old Benedictine while eating green gages served on lovely glass plates from Venice; the conversation at the feasts was worthy of such a setting.

Later, when they moved into a house near Regent's Park, tragedy followed them. Shannon fell down the stairs and suffered injuries that resulted in paralysis and malfunction of the brain. The gentle artist who had been inspired by the Venetians could recognize no one. To meet costly medical expenses, Ricketts was obliged to sell his wonderful unfinished Bihzad miniature, the celebrated drawing of a camel, and other Persian treasures, to Philip Hofer, now connected with Harvard University. Mr. Grenville Winthrop acquired from the same source some of the best William Blake designs for Dante from the Linnell Collection, but the strain of looking after his sick friend eventually ended in the sudden death of Ricketts himself.

On my summer vacations in Europe I would go off my beaten track to discover works I wanted to introduce to America. With Christian Brinton, I went to Scandinavia, primarily to see the first Italian futurist show. Although only a minor exhibition of the charming illustrations of Kay Nielsen resulted from this trip, I still had many interesting experiences. I met the widow and sons of Gauguin, the distinguished artist Edouard Munch, the collector Thorsten Laurin, the exceptionally talented painter, Prince Eugene, Jens Thies the director of the National Gallery in Christiania, Willemsen who wrote about the youth of El Greco, Hendrich Lund the lithographer, and a host of other prominent figures in the Scandinavian art world.

In Germany and Austria I was even more successful, and two of my exhibitions, one of German graphic art and one devoted to the artists of Austria, Bohemia and Hungary, were particularly interesting.

I traveled across the whole Austrian Empire into the very heart of Hungary to meet Rippl-Ronai, then recognized as the greatest living Magyar artist, and he let me have an important series of graphic works. Terey, director of the Budapest Gallery, furnished me with almost all the other examples I needed by artists of my native land. Svabinsky and Emil Orlik were the leaders among the Czechs, and their prominent publisher Artaria sent me the best available graphic works for the Austrian section.

My German exhibition was shown in several American museums and was described as sensational. The great sculptors Lehmbruch, Barlach, Kolbe and the talented Gaul, were among many artists presented for the first time in America by impressive groups of their etchings, drawing and lithographs. I borrowed some of the deeply moving prints by Käthe Kollwitz, a ministering angel among the poor of Berlin, whom I visited in her modest apartment in the German capital. I also secured drawings and etchings from Professor Lieberman, president of the German Academy until the Nazis forced him to retire. He lived in a luxurious home on the edge of the Wannsee, where I was overwhelmed in the entrance hallways which were lined with masterly drawings by Degas and Menzel. In my German Exhibition the works of a talented American, Lionel Feininger, then residing in Germany, hung near those of Kandinsky and Oscar Kokoschka, the brilliant colorist. The novel works by the *Blaue Reiter* group were shown with a large number of other revolutionaries who were still under suspicion. Occasionally a strange talent like Behmer's was singled out for a one-man exhibition.

The Armory Show, a turning point in the development of American art, had not yet familiarized us with the work of these men, who are now enthusiastically accepted but were then treated like anarchists. Childe Hassam, who visited one of these exhibits in a gay and loquacious mood after too many cocktails, condemned me unmercifully for introducing foreigners. Later we became friends, and I still have a charming water color that he dedicated to me some years later. I used many of his fine paintings, bequeathed to the American Academy, to decorate the auditorium of that institution.

In fact, after giving these controversial exhibits, I was even then proclaiming my surprise at the audacity and conceit of some of my exhibitors. They called themselves "expressionists," but they had so little of importance to express. I included some of their productions in my exhibition as a warning, or sometimes because I did not want to run the risk of neglecting a contemporary in our perplexed epoch merely because I did not understand him. Every generation, including our own, claims to have infallible critics who curtly dismiss predecessors and judge all the arts with absolute assurance, apparently ignorant of the fact that for a time even men like Shakespeare or Van der Meer have been neglected or forgotten, and had to be rediscovered. It is a simple matter to be fashionable, but few can anticipate or forestall the verdict of posterity, and I did not wish to assume the dangerous role of an artistic prophet. Santayana was unquestionably right when he wrote to me that we must "let the storm pass and the wreckage sink out of sight before we could survey the result and distinguish our veritable surviving treasure."

My suspicions were aroused by a deluge of exhibitions that began after the Armory Show. Amateurs without talent would pay the rent of certain galleries for the privilege of showing their preposterous irredeemably vulgar wares, and go to the additional expense of advertising them in the newspapers. The entertaining E. B. White has pointed out that in some cases ghost artists were employed, and to prove it he quoted a *Washington Post* advertisement that read: "Too busy to paint? Call on the Ghost Artists. We paint it . . . you sign it. Why not give an exhibition?"!! Does this account for the number of art shows opening daily during the season?

My exhibit of German graphic art was followed by the first chronological show of Persian and Indian miniatures dating from the twelfth-century illustrations in the manuscript known as the *Book of Automata,* down to works of the late eighteenth century, when the art of the Persians and their great Indian followers who excelled in portraiture, began to decline. This notable departure, arranged with the help of the scholarly Meyer Riefstahl, brought an entirely new group of visitors to the Berlin Gallery, and one morning I was surprised and gratified to be greeted by my friend, Belle Greene, of the Morgan Library. She introduced me to her escort, Bernard Berenson, already acknowledged to be the outstanding expert on Italian art of the Renaissance. I thought his special reason for paying this visit was to acquire the few pages of the famous *Book of Automata,* which were included in the exhibition. The greater portion of the manuscript is one of the treasures of the Morgan Library, and it was long considered the earliest illustrated Persian manuscript. B. B., as he was known to his intimate friends, told me that all these pages belonged at one time to the eminent authority F. R. Martin, and had been torn from the manuscript found in the Near East. He was pleased that our pages had not yet been sold, and immediately acquired them, as I then mistakenly thought, for the famous collection of his friend and patroness Mrs. Jack Gardner. Not long afterward, through my friends Ernest Longfellow, John Sargent, and Cecilia Beaux, I came to know the famous mistress of Fenway Court, and I had the temerity of questioning the authenticity of one of her acquisitions, a portrait of the Tudor Queen Mary, the original of which was in a European museum.

Naturally, B.B. examined all the outstanding items in my Persian exhibition, and we were soon involved in a warm dispute over an illustrated manuscript belonging to the painter Henry Golden Dearth, who claimed that it was more than a century older than F. R. Martin's *Book of Automata*. I had had it examined by Professor Jackson of Columbia and Professor Richard Gottheil, both experts in the linguistic field, who read and spoke Persian, and they told me that it was written in a dialect that had ceased to be spoken about the end of the tenth century. The small illustrations of soldiers on ramparts or engaged in battle showed marked Chinese influence and were drawn in the center of the pages, surrounded by the ancient script. This would be a sound basis for Dearth's claim. Berenson, however, asserted that the two professors were not art experts and knew little if anything of art history; the drawings, he declared, were probably drawn after the manuscript was written, in the blank spaces left for that purpose in the middle of many pages. Although such a practice was occasionally resorted to in later periods, I thought that this argument was far-fetched, to say the least. I did not press our claim, however, although Berenson had often modestly admitted that he was not infallible. I regret that after Dearth's death I was unable to trace the whereabouts of this interesting manuscript.

I did not see Berenson again until I had the pleasure of visiting his enchanting home "I Tatti," at Settignano, I went with Ned and Peggy Bruce, who had left Anticoli Corrado and were then living on the outskirts of Florence. The Berenson home was filled with visitors, but I had the good fortune of getting to know Mrs. Berenson, whose brother Logan Pearsall Smith and his literary master Santayana had been two of my idols.

The visit calls to mind a story that is attributed incorrectly to Belle Greene in S. N. Behrman's book about Lord Duveen. It appears that one of the wittiest members of the English colony in Florence was Reginald Turner, a man of charm and excellent taste, who lived in Italy under a transparent cloud after the Oscar Wilde trial. Berenson, generally recognized as Lord Duveen's exclusive expert, respected Turner's intelligence and finally the Englishman paid him a visit. Berenson showed him the literary and artistic treasures stored in Tatti, but as they wondered through the halls lined with books and paintings, not a word escaped Turner's lips. This piqued B.B., and finally he insisted on knowing what Turner really thought of his pictures. After a good deal of prodding, the Englishman whispered hesitatingly, "Oh—I think they are simply Duveen!"

Berenson himself was not only very witty, but caustic as well. More gracefully than anyone else, he could treat the enthusiasts for the contemporary with intellectual disdain, and I wish I had been present when he went to see the ultra modern collection of Peggy Guggenheim in Venice. The lady was overwhelmed when B.B. deigned to visit the exhibition, and gushingly told him that she had been his ardent admirer and had read and absorbed practically everything he had ever published. Berenson accepted her compliment, but did not seem flattered. For a moment he silently surveyed the surrounding walls, almost completely covered by sensational examples of modern extremists, and then said dryly, "And this is the result!"

I was not equal to the occasion when I called on the courteous collector in the famous unfinished palace on the Grand Canal, where Countess Casati once held sway with her python and other exotic pets. Mrs. Guggenheim was proud of having discovered Jackson Pollack who dropped blobs of paint on a piece of canvas until a desired effect was achieved. She had not yet acquired any examples of another artist who went a step further and from a distance hurled with abandon big splashes of wet paint on an innocent canvas, thus winning the approval of a "profound" critic who called one's attention to these color harmonies "confected with all the stylishness that is associated with the Paris-made object!"

It is a pity that Peggy Guggenheim did not direct her enthusiasm to the American Indian sand painters, whose miraculous manipulation of colored sand filtered through sensitive fingers, created magical designs of real beauty with which to heal their sick patients.

The Berensons were gracious hosts who could not have been more charming. When questioned, Berenson told me that he did not want to write an introduction to my exhibition of Rothenstein's works, because he did not know enough about contemporary trends. I dare say he was often obliged to give the same diplomatic excuse to other artists. The persistent Rothenstein, however, who had so often persuaded celebrities to pose for his lithographs, succeeded in getting no less a person than H. G. Wells to write a short preface, and it is to that exhibition the reader's attention will shortly be drawn. First, however, I want to interrupt my account of the sequence of exhibitions to comment on a more recent visit to B.B. in 1955, when the distinguished critic was celebrating his ninetieth birthday.

B.B. had just returned to I Tatti in Settignano from Tripoli, where he had been the guest of the Countess Cicogna, Count Volpi's attractive younger daughter whose wedding in the Church of San Marco I had attended years before. B.B. kindly sent his car to fetch me from Florence in time for lunch. I was amazed to find him as alert and as gay as ever. He attributed his good health to the care taken of him by his charming companion, Miss Nickey Mariano, and at once reminded me of our first meeting, warning me in advance that he would ask many questions. He became the interviewer instead of allowing me to take the initiative. He told me how surprised Billy Rose had been when he found that B.B. had never heard of him. When I mentioned that Rose had thought of asking Dali to paint a portrait of Barney Baruch, B.B. laughed and said I should encourage the commission, for "Baruch *is* a Dali," and the result would surely be entertaining. B.B. described Dali as a "timid" painter. "He hides his timidity under a cloak of meticulousness." When I contended that many of Dali's drawings were quite free, B.B. said they were not profound, and were merely examples of "calligraphy." He then went on to ask about Maurice Sterne's fatal illness (to which the artist succumbed in 1957) and over and over again B.B. proved that his memory was still amazingly good, reminding me of matters of slight importance that had happened forty years before.

Physically, B.B. looked fragile, and invariably after meals he wisely excused himself to take a rest, even if he had royal house guests. Nevertheless, he kept sending his contributions regularly to the *Corriere della Sera*, and only a week after I left him I read an admirable new article of his on the ruins of Leptis Magna which appeared in the issue of July 17, 1955.

I Tatti and its treasures were shown to me during my visit by Mostyn Owen, one of the intelligent young people whose society B.B. enjoyed. In the course of our wanderings through the great library, a plate by Picasso was the only modern work I saw on the walls, hung with many other treasures. I told B.B. of my recent visit to the Picasso exhibition in the Musée des Arts Decoratifs in Paris, which impressed, surprised and irritated me by its feats of virtuosity and many sudden changes of style, reminding me of the accomplishments of a sleight-of-hand magician who enjoys thrusting his cleverness upon his puzzled audience. Picasso is capable of painting searching portraits and characterizations like the head of Gertrude Stein, but he rarely tries to create works of simple, obvious and moving beauty. B.B. did not encourage any discussion of Picasso's accomplishments, nor, strangely enough, did he ever mention the name of Duveen. There were constant flashes of erudition in his remarks, and his brief excursions into aesthetics and philosophy were fascinating, for he was indeed a well of wisdom and impressed one by the enormous range of his learning. No one could improve on Leo Stein's estimate when he wrote to Mabel Weeks that "There was something robust about B.B.'s delicate sensitive organization that gives his thought and conversation a vitality that is rare." When I left him, I felt that his spirit had refreshed and aroused my own. What a welcome corrective his comments were to the verbiage of most of our critics! He was the prodigious man of the art world, as an Italian journalist happily described him.

And now to return to the Rothenstein exhibition alluded to earlier.

In those days there was an import duty of twenty-five per cent on foreign works of art, but an artist was permitted to bring over his own paintings or the work of another artist for exhibition purposes, in bond. If any of these items were sold, the duty could be paid just before the unsold portion of an exhibition was checked and shipped back to Europe.

I had had pleasant relations with William Rothenstein in London. We got on well together, especially after I agreed to arrange his first American exhibition of paintings, drawings and lithograph portraits of celebrities. His show was to be preceded by two exhibitions: an important group of original drawings by Beardsley; fans and paintings on silk by Rothenstein's deceased friend, Charles Conder. These two collections and his own were to be brought over by Rothenstein; I was to pay all expenses as well as the cost of Rothenstein's steamship ticket both ways.

Everything went well until I reminded him that he had offered to write the introduction to the catalogue of Charles Conder's works which were to be shown immediately after the close of the successful Beardsley show. Now that his explosion is only a memory, I can look back on it with amusement, but at the time it was infuriating. "I did not cross the Atlantic to write essays for you," he began, "and you are evidently trying to hurt or even ruin my reputation here by arranging to show my work after you exhibit Conder's delicately colored silk fans and panels. By contrast, my works will suffer, and you know it!"

I was amazed. I tried to convince him that no such thought had entered my mind. Indeed, the reason for the sequence of my exhibits was to help Rothenstein's financial success. I counted on disposing of many of his lithograph portraits as suitable gifts before the Christmas holidays, but there was still time to change the order of exhibitions. If he insisted, I said, I would arrange to show his works before Conder's. This seemed to placate him, but only for a moment. His manner was still one of distrust.

"Very well," he said, "please let me have all my lithographs and drawings so that I may have mats and frames made for all those which you are going to hang on the walls. You know," he continued, thrusting his index finger threateningly before my face, "you agreed to pay for the expense involved."

"Yes," I replied, "but I did not agree to let you do the framing and add to the mounting expense of your show. I think I can do your works justice, and at this moment there are a number of items hanging on the walls of this gallery that I think would meet with any reasonable person's approval."

He did not even give a casual glance at the frames and mats I wanted to point out to him.

"They may please you, but I am an artist," he said, with a withering sneer, "and you must not try to impose your business-man's taste, such as it is, on mine."

"Indeed," I answered, my anger rising, "you received me with open arms in London, and when I played my violin in your home you said I was the only artist whose playing had ever moved you. Well, Rothenstein," (he was not yet knighted) "your paintings are certainly not what one could describe as deeply moving. But we had better not continue this argument. It will lead us nowhere. Rightly or wrongly, I have been complimented on my taste in framing, and I would like to know what hidden genius you have discovered during your short stay here in America, who can improve on the mounting and framing shown on my walls."

"Well," he answered aggressively, "there is a Frenchman by the name of Dubernet whose work I like, and I must insist that he and not you shall handle my works."

I was now very sure of my position. However, my inward fury kept mounting although I tried hard not to betray my irritation and exasperation. Rothenstein had been staying for weeks as the guest of friends who are never even mentioned in his autobi-ography. Most of their drawings and pictures, which Rothenstein, of course, saw daily, I had been mounting and framing for several years.

"And so you think your man can improve on the mats I am trying to show you?"

"Certainly," he insolently replied.

Then I called down a shaft into the basement where my work-men were stationed.

"Dubernet! Come up here at once! You should meet an artist

who admires your work extravagantly! Tell him whose instructions you have followed for years whenever you made a mat, and that you have nothing whatever to do with the framing."

This really shook Rothenstein's equanimity. When I faced him again he was pale and trembling. I shouted at him: "And now you had better clear out of these premises. You can, however, sleep in peace. The mounting of your wonderful work will be entrusted to the very man you have selected."

I would not listen to his attempted apologies, and slammed the door of my office in his face.

The exhibit was fairly successful, but we never received any commission on his oil portrait of Samuel Untermeyer, the lithograph of my classmate Arthur Spingarn, and portraits of other visitors who first saw Rothenstein's work at my exhibition. The artist claimed that he had met all these clients socially outside of the gallery. Never having had a written contract with him—or for that matter with any artist—I dropped the whole matter. Needless to add, my name was not mentioned in the three interesting volumes of reminiscences that Rothenstein afterward wrote.

We patched up our differences after a fashion some years later, and he insisted on my spending a week end at his charming house at Far Oakridge, in Gloucestershire. I accepted, partly to convince him that I bore him no grudge, and furthermore I was promised the pleasure of meeting his other house guests, the late Max Beerbohm and his first wife, a talented American whom I first saw when she appeared successfully as the "chorus" in Richard Mansfield's magnificent production of Shakespeare's *Henry the Fifth.* I bought some of Rothenstein's portrait drawings of the great Hindu poet and philosopher, Rabindranath Tagore, who afterwards graciously signed them for me in Bengalese, and my host and Sir Max presented me with an early lithograph portrait of Beerbohm made when he was a young dandy at Oxford. This souvenir bears the following inscriptions:

For Mr. Birnbaum with best regards from Max Beerbohm, Oakridge, 1916, October 31.

This is mere swagger—the drawing has never belonged to me.

* * *

I beg to differ. My art, being a national asset, Mr. Beerbohm may fairly claim to have some small share in it.

W. Rothenstein, Far Oakridge.

A small exhibition of caricatures by Max, the first in America, was another item to my credit. Most of them belonged to Mr. and Mrs. Edgar J. Hesslein, Rothenstein's brother-in-law and sister, whose beautiful home in New York was filled with admirable works by Augustus John, Ambrose McEvoy, Charles Conder, Frank Brangwyn, Wilson Steer and other contemporary Englishmen. The Beerbohm show filled only half the gallery, the remaining rooms being given over to an exhibition of the Bulgarian painter Jules Pascin, with whose work I had become familiar in Berlin and about whom I shall have more to say presently.

Eric Gill, another Englishman to whose name and work my attention was first called by Rothenstein, would certainly have been introduced to America by me if a favorable opportunity had arisen. Rothenstein, always ready to exploit one's ignorance by talking impressively about artists of whom one had not heard, showed me an excellent carving in stone of a mother and child by Gill. Marchant, the progressive dealer on Lower Regent Street, was Gill's agent, and through him I acquired the artist's alphabets carved in stone, and many small sculptures that Gill reproduced in cheap material so that they would be available for admirers who had little to spend on works of art. Most of these items afterward found a place in the Winthrop Collection.

Long before meeting Gill I knew that he was no ordinary man. He was English to the core. At one time a group of his admirers, including the generous Count Henry Kessler, thinking that he might be inspired by Aristide Maillol, arranged a meeting between the two sculptors, and sent Gill across the Channel. When, however, Gill reached the crowded railroad station in Paris and the Grand Hotel, he felt lost and confused, and proceeded to take the first train back to the Channel port. Perhaps it was just as well!

Some time after Marchant's death, his widow, who continued to guide the fortunes of his gallery, sold me an important example of Gill's work entitled *Chloe*. It was the nude figure of a little girl carved in stone. Her hair, however, was painted a bright yellow, and this disturbed me. Mrs. Marchant suggested that Gill might be willing to remove the paint if I appealed to him in person. This I decided to do, and took an early train to High Wycombe, where Gill's studio and cottage on the top of a hill commanded a view of the surrounding country.

On reaching his grounds, I found lovely nude blonde children playing in the sunshine. Gill, wearing a monk's cowl, received me cordially. However, when I mentioned the special purpose of my visit he was rather annoyed and refused to touch Chloe's hair. He offered to buy it back, saying it ought never to leave England. I explained that it already belonged to the Winthrop Collection and I no longer had the right to return it. Then Gill commented bitterly on the fact that United States Custom House officials had attempted to confiscate books containing reproductions of his drawings (*Twenty-five Nudes* by Eric Gill, London, 1918), and he feared they might refuse an entry permit to *Chloe*, although he remonstrated that his drawings of the nude human body were as pure as the creations of God whom Gill worshipped. He had strong religious convictions which were reflected in his sacred works and in the noble bas-relief of *The Hand of God*, intended for Geneva, and shown at a Royal Academy Exhibition.

We discussed our affairs while standing in the open air in front of a particularly fine Crucifixion. He told me that he came of a family of missionaries. He complained of the cruel, senseless war. He had chosen this quiet spot in England for his studio, he said, only to find that an aviation field was being constructed in the immediate neighborhood, and now his life work would probably be blown to bits by enemy bombs. I told him that I would be happy to arrange an exhibition of his work in America, and that my friend, the late Everett Meeks had authorized me to engage him for a series of lectures to be delivered at Yale University and elsewhere. But Gill discouraged me, saying that he would prepare only one lecture, and he did not think the materialist swarms in America would care to listen to his views. Furthermore, he did not then have sufficient material for an exhibition. When he wanted to know to what I attributed my success as an exhibitor and dealer,

I told him that I introduced only items which for one reason or another I honestly admired. Gill preposterously twisted my statements in his autobiography, without mentioning my name, by saying that I was a prominent dealer who boasted of selling only the things I loved! However, I still feel grateful for the lovely inscribed drawings he gave me.

At about this time I came to know Kahlil Gibran, the celebrated Lebanese philosopher, poet and artist, but he did not have enough delicate portraits for an exhibition.

Another unique figure whose works I failed to show was the Frenchman Gaudier Brzeska, some of whose sculptures were already owned in America by John Quinn. Dulac told me that Ezra Pound had a considerable collection of Brzeska's work, and advised me to get in touch with Pound. I sent the poet a polite note, mentioning Dulac as the source of my information, and asked him to luncheon to discuss the matter. To my surprise I received a postcard in reply, addressed: "Martin Birnbaum, Claridge's Hotel, Brook Street." It read: "Afraid I am too busy to attend social functions at mid-day just at present. Yrs., E. Pound. 4-10-16." My answer to his rudeness was equally short, and was also on a postcard. It was addressed: "Ezra Pound, 5 Holland Place Chambers, Kensington, W.," and read: "You misunderstood my *letter*. I had no desire to meet you socially. Martin Birnbaum." Years afterward, when he was visiting Venice as the guest of Mary Baker, Pound arrayed in bizarre clothes, accosted me on the Via San Moise. "Haven't we met somewhere?" he asked. "Never socially," I replied, and went on my way.

To return now to the sequence of my New York exhibitions. I followed Rothenstein's show with the delicate silk panels, fans, lithographs and oils by Conder. Conder's panels for a boudoir brought me into relations with a famous lawyer and collector, the brilliant, erratic American-born Irishman, John Quinn. Quinn's fiery temper often exploded on slight provocation, and I shall always regret missing his heated encounter with Dr. Albert C.

Barnes. From conventional beginnings, he became known as a daring collector who acquired large groups of works by Gwen John, Epstein, Pascin and many of the controversial French innovators. Quinn was the outstanding patron of the historical Armory Show.

Madame Thaulow, the handsome widow of the Scandinavian landscape painter, Fritz Thaulow, who had befriended Wilde after his release from prison, asked me to sell the lovely panels by Conder which were originally made for Bing, the French dealer, who intended them for a lady's boudoir. When they were exhibited at the Berlin Photographic Company, Quinn brought Thomas Fortune Ryan (his client) to see them, and asked that the "riffraff" be ordered to leave the gallery while the great man paid his visit. This I refused to do, and I afterwards had the temerity to point out to the wild Irish-American that nothing unpleasant had happened to Ryan simply because he had been obliged to rub shoulders with art students from the East Side.

The Conder panels were eventually acquired by Quinn, for at that time he was thinking of marrying and installing the panels in his future wife's suite. However, he died a bachelor, and finally we sold the Conder panels to another Irish-American lawyer, Francis Garvan, who had married one of the Misses Brady. I tried in vain to persuade Mr. Garvan to have them mounted by Baron de Meyer, the famous photographer, but this unfortunately was never done, and the beautiful works still repose, I assume, in packing cases.

The Conder show calls to mind a strange sad incident. The painter's beautiful widow who owned almost the entire collection of Conders I had shown was found burned to death in bed. She had taken sleeping pills and lost consciousness while holding a lighted cigarette. She reaped no benefit from the sale of the items, one of which, a charming fan, was acquired by Mrs. George Blumenthal and presented to the Metropolitan Museum. When the unsold Conders were returned to England, some very fine items were stolen after they were delivered to the estate of the painter's widow. These have never been recovered.

Among my greatest successes at the Berlin Photographic Company's galleries was the first important showing of the sculptures of Paul Manship, after his return from the American Academy in Rome. Even when we entered into our verbal agreement he hesitated to entrust his work to me. However, after I published my introduction to his first exhibition, it did not take long to convince him that his fears were unfounded. Rarely if ever has a sculptor met with such a warm reception. Alden Weir started a wild scramble to acquire his works and entire editions of his small bronzes were sold out. The exhibition was a *succès fou*.

The enchanting bas-relief of his daughter Pauline, modeled when she was only three weeks old and inspired by the sculptors of the Renaissance, was acquired for the Metropolitan Museum of Art, where it remains one of the favorites of the visiting public. Today, Manship is more distinctively American, especially in his terra-cotta profile portraits, which are as far removed from the Renaissance as are the sentimental American groups by Rogers.

The entire art-loving public of New York came to see what was going on at 305 Madison Avenue, and dealers even bought items from me to study my methods more closely. Manship was immediately recognized as an important decorative artist. The beautiful gates of the zoological gardens in the Bronx, the children's playground in Central Park, the World's Fair fountains, the window flower boxes made for John D. Rockefeller, his candelabra and his armillary sphere are examples of his natural bent for decoration. He was given important commissions, among them the large sculptured marble plaque honoring Pierpont Morgan, the princely collector, and former president of the museum.

When Sargent was painting the portrait of John D. Rockefeller, Senior, as his contribution to the Red Cross Fund, he suggested that the aged financier sit for Manship as well, and Paul's sculptured bust of him is, in my humble opinion, one of the greatest portraits executed in our time, worthy of the Renaissance masters who inspired it. Sargent shared my enthusiasm, and after the completion of Manship's work I gave an exhibition of this remarkable portrait, resting it on an Italian Cassone between two noble paintings, one by Rembrandt and the other by Hals, with a priceless *mille fleur* tapestry lent by Joseph Duveen as a background. The impression it created was fantastic. I recall that one of the visitors who came to see it was William Rockefeller, the brother of the subject. He did not see me in the dimly lit gallery, and thinking he was alone, kept murmuring to himself, "Wonderful! It's wonderful!" On discovering that someone else was in the room, he introduced himself to me and added, "It shows my brother with his wig, in his gentle second childhood, exactly as he is!" I have never been able to understand why the family has never again arranged to have it publicly shown.

At Manship's exhibition in the halls of the Tate Gallery, in London, only the dead opaque plaster cast was exhibited, and subsequently Jo Davidson was given the order for a second sculptured portrait of Rockefeller. Although a competent piece of work, this was certainly influenced by, but not comparable to, Manship's masterpiece.

A close friend of Manship's, the late Mahonri Young, descendant of the Mormon leader, Brigham Young, was another American sculptor who made his debut at the Berlin Photographic Gallery. His success was hindered for a time by the disastrous sinking of the Titanic, but Young soon became well known for his admirable bronzes of laborers which remind one of the noble figures of the Belgian Meunier. His groups of boxers became popular sporting trophies. Visitors to Salt Lake City are familiar with his more ambitious public monuments. When I posed for a small bronze portrait as a violinist, I was agreeably impressed by his speed, and his virtuosity is also reflected in remarkable sketch books which deserve a place beside those of Jacovleff.

While busy with Mahonri Young's exhibition, Mrs. Mary Mowbray Clarke, the founder of the fascinating bookshop called The Sunwise Turn, introduced me to Herbert Edmund Crowley, a young Englishman who had studied singing with Sbriglia who taught the De Reszkes and Nordica; those who heard Crowley sing declare that he might have developed into a distinguished singer of ballads. Finally, however, Crowley gave up a tenor's career and the visual arts won his undivided allegiance. For a short time he went to the Academy in Paris, but soon found that they had little to teach him there. His family was not sympathetic and refused to finance his art training, so he went to work in the mines and banana plantations of Costa Rica. He had bitter economic struggles, until he began his professional artistic life, virtually an *auto-didakt*, by creating quaint comic strips for the *New York Herald*. These were called, if I remember rightly, the "Wigglemuch Series." This newspaper work, some of which is preserved in the archives of the Metropolitan Museum, reveals a rich vein of Celtic humor and imagination. When he made his debut in our gallery, with more serious drawings, his equipment as a draftsman was already so remarkable that I could think of no one who boasted of a technique that could create a drawing like his gossamer Palace of Dreams, an example of indefatigable power of concentration produced in fourteen months, often working sixteen hours a day. It might be called a collage because the topmost tower of his architectural phantasy is surmounted by a sparkling diamond, symbol of indissoluble life radiating light, inserted in the thick Whatman paper on which the palace is drawn. Has any artist but Daniel Vierge ever drawn more delicately with pen and ink? Everybody agreed that Crowley's works, many of which were produced in a remote corner of the Ramapo Hills, at Pomona, bore the imprint of an unusual personality and often the earmarks of genius. They were dream images, mysterious, refined and flawless. Discussing the importance of dreams, he said to me: "Hoping that dreams will happen has nothing to do with dreams. A dream cannot happen. A dream is. It seems to me that we are made up of three parts: the circumference, the centre and the space in between. The circumference combats evil; the centre is the conclusion we come to from that combat; the space in between consists of conclusions purified. From this space in between arises a cone-shaped figure of vibrating truth which rises higher and higher as experience comes to us. From this combat of good and evil, dreams are born. Life cannot exist without the dream. The dream cannot exist without life. Developed life develops the dream. The finer the conclusions, the purer the life and the dreams. The purer the dreams the purer the life to come."

Besides his drawings, Crowley created some small imaginary animals in coloured plaster, ceramic and bronze, and these were moulded with a professional knowledge of anatomy, but their correctness was subsidiary to the meaning of the image. Had he lived in a medieval period he would undoubtedly have found scope for his talents by decorating churches and monasteries with gargoyles like those on Notre Dame in Paris. Unfortunately, we cannot trace many of these fragile works. One of them, entitled *The Rent is Paid*, is set into the plaster over the kitchen door of Mrs. Mary Mowbray Clarke's home in Pomona, where many of Crowley's works saw the light. Only a few were cast in bronze and these display a curious undercurrent of human passions, reminding one of the strange insects of Behmer and Theodore Heine, and the wonderful caricatures and satires of Rowlandson and Hieronymus Bosch. Crowley had difficulty in coping with the life of our time. The meticulous order, precision and exactness of his work was a kind of apotropaic measure to protect himself from overpowering forces of evil. What he produced came through as if he were a medium, and while at work his hand at times seemed under a peculiar psychic control.

Rarest among his works were oil paintings and experiments in light and color. One picture in particular of a lonely Dantesque figure, wandering and meditating in a dark wood suffused with a beautiful deep twilight blue, is worthy of the best moments of the distinguished American painter, Albert Ryder. Fortunately Crowley's picture is well painted and shows none of the signs of ultimate disintegration from which many of Ryder's works suffer. His exhibition won high praise from men of taste. His Celtic wit which cropped out of most of his creations made one think that careful research into his ancestry would reveal an Irish gnome or pixie clinging like a Rackham or Segantini creature to the branches of his family tree. His letters were very amusing, and I regret not reprinting them.

After his exhibition and just when I began to pride myself on having introduced a salient figure into our art world, Herbert Crowley suddenly disappeared. Only after I retired did I discover that he had enlisted in the camouflage division of the British Army. In 1926 he married Miss Alice Lewisohn who, with her sister Irene, had founded the remarkable Neighborhood Playhouse on Grand

Street, New York, an admirable account of which was written by Mrs. Crowley. It was always an artistic adventure to go downtown with such friends as Maurice Sterne, Henry McBride, and Loeser of Florence, to see performances there. The Crowleys left for Europe, where Herbert died in 1939, at the age of sixty-six.

Herbert Edmund Crowley should not, of course, be confused with Aleister Crowley, a drug addict who was often referred to as The Beast and the wickedest man in the world, but he also claimed to be an artist. No dealer, I feel certain, would have had the audacity to exhibit his phallic, erotic output. In the ordinary course of events I would have met Aleister Crowley in Chelsea, in the sympathetic apartment overlooking the Thames occupied by my friend Gwendoline Otter, one of the most entertaining hostesses in London, and the last of Chelsea's bohemians, if we except the painter Augustus John. But, curiously enough, I met Crowley, the self-styled "Laird of Boleskine," through my staid and sober schoolmate David Keppel, the younger son of the print dealer and publisher of etchings, Frederick Keppel. By that time the name of Miss Otter, fortunately for her, had been scratched from the list of Crowley's strange women friends, whom he almost invariably tried to seduce.

When David Keppel introduced us, this singular man wore huge finger rings which made it dangerous to shake hands with him. He reminded me of Ezra Pound, not only sartorially, but also because he was a voluminous poet and student of oriental cults. Crowley was taken seriously by writers like Alice Meynell. At one time he and William Butler Yeats were active members of an occult society called the Hermetic Order of the Golden Dawn. Quite recently an early novel by Somerset Maugham, *The Magician*, was reprinted with a new preface; it aroused fresh interest in Crowley, who was the model for the hero. A few recollections of him may therefore be in order.

He was certainly not a mere poseur or charlatan. He was, in fact, a man of considerable erudition, and his exploits as a mountain climber in Central America and India were admirably spoken of at the Explorers Club. Especially famous was an almost completely successful attempt to climb, without proper equipment, Kantchenjunga, one of the most formidable Himalayan peaks. Augustus John made magnificent portrait drawings of him which are now in the Grenville Lindall Winthrop collection at the Fogg Art Museum, and John also devoted a few paragraphs to Crowley in his autobiography, *Chiaroscuro*. The list of his printed works is impressive. Many are devoted to "Magick" and the Cabala, but their meaning is beyond me. I found his bulky confessions full of tiresome efforts to appear perverse and diabolical, and the poems and stories rather dull, but they are now being collected by many bibliophiles. One handsome volume of privately printed poems, *Rodin in Rime,* flattered the great French sculptor, who presented Crowley with some good water color drawings and unique small *cire perdue* sculptures. Crowley first came to see me in connection with these, and I persuaded Sir William Van Horne, the Canadian collector, to buy them. When Crowley made an appointment to thank me for my efforts, he wrote in his usual extravagant style:

> Dec. 21, 1914
> The Wolcott
> 4 West 31st Street
> New York

My Dear Birnbaum:

  Magnificent surprise, the lithographs.* Really a success that beggars talk. The moment I am free—and I am moving to 40 West 36th Street tomorrow—I shall come around and weep upon your exquisitely chiselled neck, in the presence of 216 reporters, all sobbing in sympathy.

> Toujours,
> Aleister Crowley

  This effusion was followed by others, and I shall quote one other because it is typical of many.

---

* These were made from the drawings by Augustus John, mentioned above, now in the Fogg Art Museum.

55 Avenue de Suffren
Paris VII
February 28th, 1929

My dear Birnbaum,

Do what thou wilt shall be the whole of the Law.

I refrain from quoting the immortal words of Longfellow, subsequently mutilated by Beatrice Harrowden: But I should have so much have liked to had a "crack" with you.

I have been considerably under the weather since I left America, chiefly owing to asthma, which was maltreated by all the famous specialists, and ultimately cured by a perfectly simple operation. The upshot has been that I have never published anything for ten years. The enclosed prospectus indicates my resurrection.

If you count the stones of the Great Pyramid, the whole thing becomes perfectly simple. Not that I recommend your doing it, for it might be more illuminating to follow the meteoric career of Konody.

My personal opinion is that Matisse never painted anything. All he has done was to find a crypt, preferably in Styria, where were a large number of pictures of Fra Angelico, which he has passed off as his own work.

Although I have been a conservative during the whole of my present incarnation, my present approaching resurrection is largely attributable to the grand nephew of Lord Roseberry. His name is Yorke, which is excessively irritating, as we were honest Lancastrians in the Wars of the Roses. At the same time, I am compelled to admit that he does take a fairly reasonable view of my actual situation. Since the War, the gutter press has run the universe, and I have had a pretty bad time consequently. Nowadays, it is hard to think of anybody at all who has the courage to go on doing decent work. On the other hand, I think everybody is about sick of the present situation. We are approaching what Zoroaster called "the psychological moment."

Do let me hear more of you. You were a very bright spot during my exile in America—and the night is yet young.

Love is the law, love under will.

Yours sincerely,

Aleister Crowley

On every occasion when we met, he tried in vain to induce me to take hasheesh, cocaine and other drugs which he assured me would bring on unbelievably pleasant hallucinations. Such attempts and more questionable activities often landed him in law courts before he died in England, at Hastings, in 1947, at the age of seventy-two. Once I had a rather serious talk with him, and I could not decide whether he really wanted to detach himself from the world and exalt his spirit like an Indian mystic, or was he just "an enormously entertaining fake," as Maugham described him, a man who sedulously fostered a sinister reputation as a satanist, a black magician and symbol of evil. Perhaps, like the Roman Emperor Heliogobalus, he was slightly mad, and thought himself a divinity who was free to indulge in any vice or crime.

Instead of showing Crowley's sensational wall decorations which might have landed me in jail, I went off to Europe and brought back one of my most successful exhibitions, one which broke all records for attendance at the Berlin Photographic Galleries. This was the first American exhibit of the maquettes, drawings and water colors of Leon Bakst, the most famous of the decorators who worked for Diaghileff, the director and organizer of the Russian Ballet. Having seen Diaghileff's famous historic productions in Paris while I was Mrs. Webb's attorney and house guest, I did not rest until the leading Russian stage decorator agreed to let me have the honor of introducing his art to America. Our preparatory meetings took place in Paris and in Pavlova's dressing room behind the scenes of a London music hall. When Pavlova heard of my project, it won her enthusiastic approval. She not only promised to open the exhibition in New York where, with her partner Mordkin, she was already a favorite at the opera house, but she sealed the agreement with two artist's kisses, a passionate one for Bakst and a superficial one for me, his humble exhibitor.

I went to considerable trouble to see that Bakst's debut at my gallery should not pass unnoticed, and I counted on Pavlova's presence to add luster to the occasion. Beautiful special invitations, attractively designed by Bakst and printed on vellum, were eagerly sought for. On the opening night policemen were called to protect the gallery from art lovers who wanted to "crash" the show without cards of admission. Long before the hour set for the doors to open, the rather cramped galleries were already jammed.

Pavlova, I knew, had arrived from Buffalo that morning, and I sent a large corsage of orchids to greet her. However, when the hour agreed upon struck we waited for her in vain. It was difficult to keep the impatient women in order. I had naively assumed that they had come primarily to see Bakst's novel originals and not a celebrated dancer in her street costume. I tried to reach Pavlova again and again on the telephone, but the only response was that Madame's costumes had not arrived from Buffalo and she was therefore obliged to break her promise to her great friend Bakst. I did not wish to embarrass Madame by reminding her of those two carelessly bestowed kisses, but I did wickedly suggest that she would create an even greater furore if she appeared without any costume. Lady Constance Richardson would not have hesitated to come under those conditions. But my poor wit fell on deaf ears and did not have the desired effect. I was finally obliged to break the news to the disappointed women and interviewers and at a late hour the crowd dispersed. The publicity and my propaganda efforts had served Pavlova's purpose. Neither Bakst, as far as I know, nor I ever received an apology from the famous dancer.

After this fuss, the Bakst exhibition was soon sold out. Celebrities interested in the fine arts, from all over the world, who happened to be in New York, found their way into the gallery, and I had enjoyable conversations with them. Outstanding among my visitors was Walter Van Rensselaer Berry (1859-1927) who was a prominent non-resident American, connected with the Chamber of Commerce in Paris. Marcel Proust dedicated a volume of essays, *Pastiches et Melanges,* to this distinguished gentleman, and described him as *"avocat et lettré, qui depuis le premier jour de la guerre, devant l'Amérique encore indécise a plaidé avec une energie et un talent incomparables la cause de la France et l'a gagnée."* Soon after our meeting I had good reason for admiring Mr. Berry's taste, for although there were hundreds of examples to choose from, he elected without hesitation to purchase an "Odalisque," recognizing it as perhaps the finest of Bakst's water colors. Berry wrote a fine essay on La Societé Americaine et la Societé Francaise and his eloquence must also have been considerable and stirring, for Proust referred in one of his letters to a political address, "above the phrases of which thoughts rise very high singing like the skylarks of France." His tribute was elaborated in a series of letters* to the man whom he regarded as the creator of France's victory.

I arranged a second and still better Bakst exhibition in 1916, which was sent to various museums. It contained the large oil, Terror Antiquus and several portraits, including the superb water color of his friend, Mrs. John W. Garrett, the brilliant wife of our ambassador to Italy, who afterward helped me with my social problems when I took charge of the American exhibits at the Biennial International Exhibitions in Venice. I was asked to show Bakst's art and lecture about it at the Arts Club in Chicago, and it was with this second successful Bakst exhibition that I made my initial bow, in 1916, as the junior member of the firm of Scott and Fowles.

_____
* 47 *Unpublished Letters from Marcel Proust to Walter Berry.* The Black Sun Press. Rue Cardinale, Paris, MCMXXX.

III

Ten Years with Scott and Fowles

My association with the prominent firm of Scott and Fowles began quite unexpectedly. After six years, certain institutions began to take notice of my activities at the Berlin Photographic Gallery and directorships were hinted at. However, on the very day that I was contemplating the acceptance of such an appointment, which would have put an end to my commercial career, I met Sir Joseph Duveen, with whom I had already become acquainted on the ill-fated *Lusitania*. He was then leaving America incognito to avoid seizure by federal authorities who were examining his firm's import-tax evasions. In the course of our journey he offered me a position at what seemed to me an enormous salary. But I refused to join a firm whose import methods were just then undergoing unfavorable scrutiny by the government tax experts.

On learning that I was on my way to a meeting of the board of trustees of a prominent museum that was on the lookout for a director, Joe Duveen insisted that I first pay a visit to Stevenson Scott, who wanted an associate to take the place of his partner Fowles, who had lost his life when the Lusitania was sunk. In spite of my remonstrances and my insistence that I had no money to invest, Louis Levy shortly after this visit drew up a partnership agreement and I was persuaded to become Stevenson Scott's junior partner.

The Bakst exhibition, chiefly of maquettes for the Russian Ballet referred to in the last chapter, was my first effort in the firm, with which I remained associated until May 1926. The huge suc-

75

cess of the Bakst show led me to believe that the small illustrations of Rackham, Kay Nielsen and Edmund Dulac would be equally popular, and I was not mistaken. Each year before Christmas I planned to show the work of one of the above illustrators and of the earlier classical drawings by Flaxman, but having already published accounts of those successes, I need not repeat them here. My experiment with Dulac's work, however, resulted in an interesting experience outside of the art gallery.

It was at one of those memorable Friday night gatherings in the famous Lansdowne Road studio of Ricketts and Shannon mentioned in an earlier chapter, that I first met Edmund Dulac. Other visitors were Bosch Reitz, who was then in charge of the Oriental Department of the Metropolitan Museum of Art, William Butler Yeats the celebrated Irish poet, and Sturge Moore who afterward wrote admiringly of Ricketts. I had been asked to bring my violin, for although there were no pianists present Ricketts and Dulac were ardent lovers of music, and they were able to follow me with remarkable skill on a pianola. When it was suggested that we play the Cesar Franck Violin and Piano Sonata, Yeats immediately left the room, excusing himself on the ground that he did not like to listen to music.

When we finished playing, he came back, and the conversation took many interesting turns. Yeats told us that he had dozed off in an adjoining bedroom and had had a startling dream in which he made the astonishing discovery that "God" was an abbreviated form of Godfrey! Yeats's father, whom I had often seen in New York, had just written him a letter, warning him not to accept a Trinity College Professorship. He would have to spend his time explaining himself—a fatal procedure for an original thinker. A gentleman should never explain himself. Robert Louis Stevenson, according to the elder Yeats, had made that serious mistake and from that moment he ceased to write like a gentleman. Yeats's poetical drama *At the Hawk's Well or the Waters of Immortality*, had just been performed before royalty for a war charity. Dulac had made the masks for the narrators and had designed the golden setting. Michio Ito, the Japanese dancer, who was planning to visit America, acted the leading part of the Hawk, and since I had arranged to show Ito's large oil portrait by Dulac at Scott and Fowles, along with a hundred of the artist's illustrations, I suggested that a performance of Yeats's drama might be given in America immediately after the opening day of the exhibition. This proposal was greeted with enthusiasm. Yeats presented me with a manuscript copy of his play and left the arrangements in my hands.

With the help of Ito and John Murray Anderson, I undertook the production at the Greenwich Village Theatre. My Japanese friend Koscak Yamada wrote the incidental music. During the dress rehearsal, a few days before the *première,* I realized that no one in the audience would understand the poorly enunciated words uttered by an English actor who was entrusted with the role of The Chorus or leading narrator, while Ito and his mimes silently acted and danced. Anderson also agreed that the play would be a dismal failure if Yeats's lines were mumbled and distorted. He was at his wits' end until I volunteered to learn the part in two days.

I had all the words written out in large characters on a scroll, which I could unwind if my memory failed me. The performance luckily went off without a hitch. What is more, two of my personal guests in the audience, Maude Earl—who had painted King Edward's wire-haired terrier—and Somerset Maugham, never recognized me as the impersonator of the First Musician or Chorus, for my face was hidden behind Dulac's beautiful mask.

The play was a huge success, and was repeated the following summer in the open air on the lawn of a garden near Manchester, Massachusetts.

I regret that after his death no comprehensive memorial exhibition was held of Dulac's works, especially a group of portraits done from memory, and a long list of his inimitable caricatures. His finely designed English and French postage stamps, his bronze medals, playing cards, and more of the amusing figurines, as well as designs for interiors and stage settings, should all have been included. Dulac was enormously gifted and deserved such a tribute. It is true that an exhibition was arranged in London, but it was incomplete and quite unworthy of the artist.

In spite of our notable success with exhibitions like those mentioned, Scott never ceased to point out to me that such activities resulted only in reducing our bank account, for they prevented me from attending to what he regarded as our real business, which was to sell expensive works by the old masters. I had enthusiasm to spare, but I knew very little about intrigues and high prices, and Scott lost no opportunity to give me lectures daily on the ease with which masterpieces could be sold if one knew the right millionaire to approach. A fantastic price only made the item to be disposed of more desirable.

My senior partner took special delight in recounting the details of one fabulous transaction dealing with a famous portrait of King Philip of Spain, the patron of Velasquez, hanging in the Dulwich Gallery. This was supposed to be an original work painted to order as a gift to the Duke of Parma, a relative of the Spanish monarch. However, Beruete, the leading authority on the work of Velasquez, declared that the painting in the English gallery was merely an old copy by an unknown hand, and the authentic original picture was in Switzerland, in the possession of the descendants of the Duke of Parma. As soon as this became known; the firm of Agnew in London immediately bought it in spite of its high price, and Capt. Charles Williams, their engaging representative, told the story to Stevenson Scott while the two men were standing on the steps of the Metropolitan Museum. The price put on it was $450,000, and Scott, without seeing the portrait, did not hesitate to acquire it. He in turn offered a half share in the picture to the firm of Knoedler & Company, on acceptable terms and when these had been satisfactorily arranged the final disposition of the great picture was entrusted to Charles Carstairs, who then enjoyed the confidence of Mr. Henry Clay Frick. All the facts were laid before the famous collector, and he secured an option on the picture before seeing it. On its arrival in America he bought it, and the painting, which remains the finest example of a work by Velasquez in America, now hangs in a place of honor in the Frick Museum. It cost the purchaser well over the four hundred and fifty thousand dollars paid for it by Stevenson Scott.

Carstairs, however, did not long remain the sole salesman to Mr. Frick. After Pierpont Morgan's death, when his great Fragonards were on exhibition at the Metropolitan Museum, Carstairs began to negotiate with Mr. Morgan's son and heir for their purchase and he urged Mr. Frick to acquire them. Joe Duveen, on learning of this, had one of his scouts or employees patiently watch the museum entrance and report if Mr. Frick paid a visit with Carstairs to examine the panels. When this visit finally took place and was reported, Joe went at once to see the owner and offered to buy them. Mr. Morgan hesitated and said he was already negotiating for the sale of the priceless set. "But I am not negotiating," said Joe. "Name your price and I am ready to buy." Morgan quoted the price, over a million dollars, and Joe made out his check for the necessary amount. The Fragonards were now his. Next he went to see Mr. Frick, who, with some compunction, admitted that they had virtually been offered to him by Mr. Carstairs. "But they belong to me" was the surprising announcement by Lord Duveen. Mr. Frick, on finding that to be the case, bought them, to the consternation of Carstairs. Moreover, to win a fabulous client, this being their first transaction, Joe sold them to Mr. Frick for the cost to him without any profit whatever.

Stevenson Scott not infrequently followed in Lord Duveen's footsteps. A good example of my partner's honorable but shrewd methods will be of interest. The morning after Scott had bought Rembrandt's *Zeus in the House of Philemon and Baucis* at the Milliken sale, Otto Kahn paid us a visit. On being told that Scott and Fowles had purchased the picture as an investment for our stock and not as agent for any client, he asked Stevenson what price had been put on it. My partner explained that when we acted as agent in such cases, we received a commission of ten per cent on the price we had paid the auction company. However in view of the fact that the painting in question had been acquired only the night before, Scott suggested that the customary ten per cent advance would satisfy us. Kahn remonstrated, for he knew that an art gallery on Fifth Avenue could not be profitably conducted on such a margin of profit. He generously offered to pay twenty-five per cent on our purchase price but Scott firmly refused to accept Kahn's offer, and finding that arguments were of no avail, Kahn finally purchased the Rembrandt on Scott's terms. After the lapse of a few months, Kahn again called on us to tell

Scott that the small picture was lost on the large walls of the drawing room in his new Fifth Avenue residence and asked us to try to sell the painting for him.

When it was returned to Scott and Fowles, I showed the Rembrandt to Wilhelm Valentiner. He was so favorably impressed by its quality that he recommended its acquisition to Joseph Widener who promptly bought it for a sum considerably greater than Kahn had paid. Scott asked Widener to make his check payable to Otto Kahn as there was no point in having a record of the transaction on our books. Naturally Mr. Kahn on receiving the check wanted to know the details and Scott explained that his firm having realized a profit so recently on the sale of the picture, Kahn was entitled to the full amount Mr. Widener had paid.

It should be remembered that not all owners of valuable pictures are persuaded to sell their treasures, even for such fantastic figures. If I were commenting on our failures rather than on our successes I would mention Mr. Alexander of London, who refused to accept almost a quarter of a million dollars for the enchanting portrait that Whistler painted of his daughter Cicely. Actuated by patriotism, he preferred to present the masterpiece to the nation, and it now graces the National Gallery in London. In Holland too, the Six family, whose forbears sat for Hals and Rembrandt, rejected an offer of a million dollars for their Van der Meer and presented it instead to a national museum, where it will remain an inspiration for future generations of the painter's countrymen.

One of Lord Duveen's failures belongs in this category. The outstanding privately owned picture in Venice was the *Tempesta,* generally agreed to have been painted by Giorgione, although there is slight direct evidence of this. It was the gem of a vast group of less important pictures owned by the Venetian Prince Giovanelli. When he died, Lord Duveen at once began to negotiate with his son and heir for the small priceless painting. He is said to have offered a million and a half dollars for it, but as soon as Mussolini heard of this, the Giorgione was declared to be a national treasure which could not be exported. The inheritance taxes that the young prince was unable to pay amounted to several million dollars in our money, and the *Tempesta* was virtually confiscated by the Duce. It now hangs in the Accademia as part payment of the estate tax. Young Prince Giovanelli never received a lira in cash for his picture.

The sale of the Velasquez portrait to Mr. Frick had an unpleasant effect on my relations with another great patron of the arts. When a unique item like the Velasquez came into the possession of a dealer, he had to make a crucial decision and pick out the client who would surely buy it. If he made the mistake of offering it to a collector who for any reason whatever did not or could not acquire it, the painting, however great, would receive a black eye. For one thing, when other collectors learned of the rejection, their pride would be injured. In addition to their resentment because it had already been offered to a rival, they might suspect that something was wrong, not with the price, but with the picture.

Some time after the sale of the Velasquez portrait of Philip to Frick had been made public, we received a superlative example of the work of Goya. Since Goya was already well represented in the Taft Collection, I sent what I thought was a polite epistle to Archer Huntington, telling him something about the portrait and its special qualities. I did not have long to wait before learning that the thrill entailed in competing successfully and spectacularly against a rival collector was not to be lightly discounted. Time went by and there was no answer to my letter. Accordingly I wrote again, saying that the picture was really worthy of the Hispanic Museum, which was only one of Archer Huntington's many handsome public benefactions and that we were holding the painting in our vaults, offering it to no one until it could be submitted to him. My second letter also was apparently ignored. My senior partner then concluded that I had made some diplomatic blunder, or that Huntington, for some unknown reason, disliked me, so we sold the picture elsewhere.

I had almost dismissed the incident from my unpleasant memories, when Mr. and Mrs. Huntington came to the Scott and Fowles galleries for the preview of an exhibition of Paul Manship's work. The invitations had been sent out by the artist himself, and the members of the firm stepped aside, interfering in no way with our exhibitor and his guests. However, when Mr. Huntington was leaving the gallery, I greeted him formally and ventured to remark

that I had sent him a letter and, not having had a reply, I hoped
I had done nothing to offend him. Perhaps the matter simply did
not interest him. Mr. Huntington assured me that I personally had
done nothing wrong, but he added sarcastically that when Scott
and Fowles had something really important like a Velasquez to
offer, he was *not* informed, and naturally he took it for granted
that our Goya was not an outstanding item or we would have
offered it to some more important client.

There were other failures accounted for by my own sensitivity.
One of these, sufficiently amusing in retrospect, is perhaps worth
recording.

Mrs. Coburn, a kind-hearted widow in Chicago, had heard
favorable accounts of my activities and asked me to help her build
up a collection of nineteenth-century paintings that would be
eventually bequeathed to the Chicago Art Institute, in memory
of her husband. She already possessed a group of works, notably
some fine Renoirs, but I saw at once that there were many gaps
that it would be a pleasure to fill with pictures by salient masters.
I confided the situation to Mr. Harshe, at that time the director
of the Art Institute, and agreed to concentrate on acquiring works
by artists who were not already well represented in the Art
Institute's collections. Daumier was the name that first came to
mind, and since we had an appealing example in our gallery I first
submitted it to Mr. Harshe who urged its acquisition. I gave Mrs.
Coburn a short talk on the significance of the painter in the development of French art in the nineteenth century and left the
painting with her, trusting that its quality would soon convince
her of the advisability of adding it to her collection.

Weeks went by and finally Scott advised me to pay her another
visit and help her to reach a decision. To my surprise, she told
me that she did not like the Daumier and that a distinguished
expert had seen the picture and told her it was too dark and therefore not worthy of her collection. I was annoyed, but I did not
remind her that she had chosen me as her adviser, and that I held
myself responsible for the quality and authenticity of new acquisitions. Daumiers were not celebrated for the gay light pigments
Mrs. Coburn adored.

I asked her for the name of her new consultant, and she mentioned a name that I did not recognize. "But he knows you very well," she added, although I assured her that I had never heard of such an authority on Daumier. "Why," she continued, "he told me he was at one time associated with you!" Then slowly my clouded mind cleared. I recalled the name as that of a young fellow whom Scott had discharged. He had been working in our packing and shipping department for years. Before his departure he armed himself with a fairly complete list of Scott and Fowles clients, and with such an asset he had no trouble finding a job with a rival dealer. Despite's Scott's remonstrances, I refused to pay Mrs. Coburn any further visits.

Another lady whose patronage I lost had been a discovery of mine in Cincinnati. She had social ambitions and was anxious to join the list of collectors in that city, headed by such distinguished names as the Tafts, Mrs. Thomas Emery and Miss Mary Hanna. She was an ardent Catholic, and I thought I would make an auspicious start by hanging a lovely madonna and child of the Bolognese school over a Renaissance *prié Dieu* in her house. The picture had belonged to Joseph Widener. After holding it for some time, she returned it because her Irish maid disapproved of a naked Christ child and thought the painting indecent!

When Lord Duveen heard of the incident he went to see her and overwhelmed her with his convincing enthusiasm. How could a lady of such rare taste and accomplishments remain hidden from his sight in a city he thought he knew so well? Would she graciously forgive his stupidity? Soon the house was filled with his tapestries, furniture and rugs! I'm afraid that my ambition was not fired to rival great salesmen like Duveen and Carstairs. The incident of the Frick Velasquez had, in fact, had quite the opposite effect. It unnerved me. For a time I could hardly believe that pictures were sold for such huge sums; never having dealt in such figures, I began to regret having given up my former humbler position. Later, I was to learn how keen the rivalry between collectors could be, and in the meantime I began to realize that a Fifth Avenue firm could not exist on the profits to be derived from my favored activities. Nevertheless, I persisted in arranging modest exhibitions of artists from time to time.

One of these exhibitions was devoted to the celebrated classical drawings of the English sculptor, Flaxman, the engravings of which, by William Blake, were used as illustrations for Homer and other classical texts. Lord Hope, owner of a large diamond, who had inherited the Flaxman designs, had died, and these famous drawings were to be sold at Christie's just at a time when neither Scott nor I could attend the London sale. I advised cabling an unlimited bid to Sir Alec Martin, a member of Christie's well-known firm of auctioneers, and we secured the Flaxman collection for a surprisingly low figure because the drawings, instead of being listed in the sale of his art treasures, were sold in bound volumes with Lord Hope's library.

The entire set of drawings for Milton's Paradise Lost as originally bound in yellow morocco was sold to Mr. Grenville Winthrop, but the classical designs and the illustrations for Homer and the Greek dramatists were unbound, and we had each page beautifully mounted and framed for exhibition. I at once wrote about our acquisition to a few favored clients, among whom I may mention Martin A. Ryerson and Charles L. Hutchinson, pillars of strength in building up the Chicago Art Institute. They would have purchased the entire collection, but since that was no longer possible when they arrived in New York, they made an excellent choice of a large group of drawings that were later shown with Wedgewood porcelains in a beautiful room of the Chicago Museum. Similar letters were sent to Mr. John D. Rockefeller, Mrs. Radeke of Providence, Mr. Hunt Henderson of New Orleans, and others. Virtually all the persons to whom I wrote took advantage of my offer except Mr. Rockefeller, who, although we were his tenants and he lived only a step away, did not favor us with a visit until all the drawings that he seemed to like had already been disposed of. The Metropolitan Museum, represented by Dr. Edward Robinson, the director, and Bryson Burroughs, the curator of paintings, also waited too long before they came to see the exhibition, and then they surprised me by selecting some of the least significant items. When I showed Scott their choice, he was irritated; instead of accepting payment he sent the drawings to the museum with our compliments, and refrained from adding sarcastic comment.

Not all the exhibitions at Scott and Fowles passed off as pleasantly as the Bakst and Flaxman shows, or the remarkable group of portrait drawings by Sir Thomas Lawrence, and very soon I had good reason for recalling Stevenson Scott's warnings about the ingratitude and dishonesty of some artists.

In 1915, while still carried away by my determination to introduce new talent at the galleries of the Berlin Photographic Company, I had received a visit from a Parisian *marchand amateur* named Basler. He told me that I ought to look up a gifted sculptor who had just arrived in America from Paris and was searching for someone who would help to make him known. His name was Elie Nadelman. I promised to go to see him, but I forgot all about this until one day the artist himself walked into my gallery. He asked me how dealers expected artists to live if they took such slight interest in those who created their wares. I was struck by his romantic appearance and the justice of his remarks, and after humbly apologizing for my forgetfulness I dropped my work and accompanied him to an old dilapidated building on West Fourteenth Street. I climbed with him up the rickety stairs to the top floor. When he opened the door of the room that served as his studio I experienced one of the greatest artistic thrills of my career. Years before, André Gide in Paris had been impressed in the same way. As I entered, a French assistant, Albert Boni, was busy polishing a pedestal, and on every side lovely Hellenistic marble heads and more controversial works in wood and metal surrounded me. I realized at once that this artist, who spoke English and French with a marked Polish accent, had more than a spark of the divine fire. Almost immediately I promised to give him a show in the fall, after my return from a vacation, and urged him to continue working, but to show his works to no one. I hoped to startle New York with his show, which I intended to be one of my major efforts.

"But how can I live till you return?" he exclaimed. I had stupidly forgotten that detail, and now realized that he was practically penniless.

"Leave that to me also," I replied, "but remember, not a word to anybody in the meanwhile. This show must be like a bursting bomb when we open it, but give me a few months' time!"

The very next day I took Mrs. Gustave Radeke, the president of the Rhode Island School of Design, to pay him a visit, after telling her of the artist's predicament, and pledging her to secrecy. I shall have more to say of this noble woman, who had not only a great flair for art, but also for human character. Never shall I be able to discharge my many debts to her. She climbed to the top story of the filthy building and at once bought one of the marble heads, paying Nadelman enough to carry him along for a few months. It was, as far as I knew, the first item he had sold in America. Mrs. Radeke afterward confided to me that she was not too favorably impressed by the artist's personality or character and that certain traits were reflected in his work that aroused her suspicion! I kept Nadelman under constant surveillance. After I had announced the exhibition of an unheralded and unnamed genius to the press, I climbed night after night to his studio, staying with him until dawn and encouraging him in every way possible. Nadelman worked feverishly, like one possessed, and each time that I visited him I admired new facets of his remarkable talent. He knew how to flatter, too. "There is no one in America with an eye like yours, Birnbaum," he exclaimed, and I, in turn, fed him with genuine praise.

When I returned from a brief vacation, my mind full of plans for making his exhibition a great success, I was bowled over by a little news item. It announced the first exhibition of Nadelman's work at Alfred Steiglitz's gallery at 291 Fifth Avenue. I was not merely surprised; I was enraged and outraged. When I faced Nadelman, however, he merely smiled blandly and insisted that Steiglitz would show only drawings and a few unimportant experimental works that would not attract many people, whereas mine would really be his first important American exhibition. Mrs. Radeke's words came back to my mind, and I notified Nadelman, in no uncertain terms, that I was not playing second fiddle, and that there would be no further relations between us.

May I say that the paragraphs that follow and in which there are elements of humor, should not obscure the fact that Nadelman was a genius? I tell these stories with a certain diffidence, since the artist is now dead and there isn't the slightest danger of his reading my remarks. One does not like to offend against the principle of saying nothing but good *de mortuis.*

The First World War was on. The Steiglitz show did pass almost unnoticed. The Berlin Photographic Galleries had closed their doors, and I had taken up my duties at Scott and Fowles. Not long after my work had begun there, I received a visit from a kindly middle-aged gentleman who introduced himself as Mr. Bernays, the brother-in-law of Sigmund Freud. The publicist Edward Bernays is his son. The elder was quite a diplomat. He soon announced the purpose of his visit. He had heard of my quarrel with Nadelman, whose work he had been purchasing for the past few months, and he invited me to come to see him at his residence. He admitted that I had good reason for severing relations with Elie, but after all I was intelligent enough to realize that we were dealing with a naive, ill-advised man, and must make every allowance for the eccentricities of genius. The Steiglitz exhibition, he added, was an unimportant venture and was entirely forgotten. Surely I was too liberal in spirit to harbor ill-will against a man who realized with sincere regret that he had made a grievous, inexcusable mistake, and was ready to make amends on my own terms.

I relented, and went to see Nadelman's recent works which exerted their usual spell. Despite Scott's misgivings I agreed to give the exhibition, believing that Nadelman had learned his lesson.

Thanks to Mr. Bernays' generosity, the artist was now temporarily economically independent. Nevertheless, as soon as I had a group of his works in one of our storerooms, I began to sell them in quick succession to visitors like Mrs. Walter Dillingham and Mrs. Chauncey Blair, and I secured important commissions for him as soon as I found that he was a born portraitist. Mrs. Crocker's children, Francis Neilson and Miss Jane Barger Wallach were among his many sitters, and the busts he made of Mrs. Fagan and of Mrs. Stevenson Scott are indeed among the most beautiful marble portraits I know of, and can hold their own with any works in their category. The mahogany heads of little Marie Scott and of the niece of Mrs. Haggin were compared with the works of

Houdon. When a collection of items created by Nadelman was finally shown on gray pedestals in a room whose walls were hung with gleaming dark-blue satin, many visitors declared that it was the most beautifully presented art exhibition they had ever seen.

I already knew that the artist compromised his artistic virtues by violent exhibitions of egotism, but for once he seemed satisfied with my effort, and he certainly had no reason to complain of the financial results. Shortly after the exhibition, as soon as he had a respectable bank balance he began to ride horseback in Central Park with his fine head of hair oiled, perfumed, and carefully dressed. A little later, he went to Virginia to mingle with the idle rich at Hot Springs. Not long after that, his marriage to the charming widow, Mrs. Flannery, was announced.

Soon after Nadelman's successful debut at Scott and Fowles, I learned that although we had an exclusive verbal contract with him, his works were being secretly offered in the back room of a rival gallery. When I questioned him, he nonchalantly told me that he could not waste time discussing such trivial matters. His art needed no dealer whatever, his works sold themselves, he said; in fact, he was informing my acquaintances that his genius was already making Birnbaum rich.

To find out what truth, if any, there was in such claims, I ordered our employees to leave Nadelman's sculptures severely alone on their smart pedestals. No one was to call the attention of visitors to their admirable qualities, but if anyone asked about them the prices were, of course, available. I wanted to find out whether, generally speaking, the public purchased works of art without encouragement or persuasion. The results were what I thought they would be. Not a single sculpture by Nadelman was purchased, and soon he came in to ask me why he was not receiving any checks from us at the end of the month, as theretofore. My answer was to the point.

"Surely, Nadelman, you are not in need of funds. Other art dealers, I hear, are attempting to sell your works, now that we have created a market for them."

He knew that the jig was up.

I studiously avoided him after that, but he carefully cultivated Scott's society, and when the Nadelmans opened their handsome new residence off Fifth Avenue, a host of admirers, including the Scotts, went to the housewarming. I, however, was conspicuously absent. The friendship with the Scotts ripened and resulted in the superb bust of the beautiful Mrs. Marie Scott, and other portraits of Scott and his lovely daughter. After his frequent visits to the artist's studio Scott would tell me of Nadelman's latest creations, which he now effusively admired. My partner continually reproached me for bearing the sculptor a grudge.

I knew what Scott expected of me, and finally I swallowed my pride and went to see these works myself. Nadelman again began to flatter me, and although I paid little attention to his remarks, which I now quietly scorned, to please Stevenson I again agreed to give an exhibition at our new premises.

"But remember, Nadelman," I added, with the air of a dictator, "the responsibility for showing and disposing of your works is mine. You will furnish me with the necessary material, but you will have nothing whatever to do with the installation or other details."

Nadelman agreed abjectly to all my conditions. I collected his sculptures in a basement room long before the exhibition and at once began to dispose of them. This time, however, I told Nadelman nothing. When I had almost worked myself into a sick bed with the preparations for his show, I again foolishly relented. I called him up the night before the opening after every item was in its carefully allotted place and Scott had just congratulated me on the way I had arranged everything in the small rooms I had at my disposal. I felt it only fitting that the artist should be the first to see his works as I planned to show them. The problems of harmonious disposition were far from simple, and I mistakenly thought that my share in the work would meet with his approval. The preview would not be held until the afternoon, so there was ample time to make any minor changes that the artist might suggest. The next morning, a few minutes after Nadelman had passed alone through the door leading into the exhibition galleries, Pastorini, my head man, came out greatly excited. "Mr. B.," he exclaimed, "that man is crazy. He is upsetting the whole show, and there will be no time to move the heavy marbles from one place to another before the opening. Please stop him."

Only a gifted writer of tragicomedy like Frank Wedekind could

do justice to the scenes which followed. When I went in to find out
what Nadelman was doing, I discovered that all the pedestals
had been moved and were standing, almost touching one another,
in the middle of the small first gallery instead of near the walls.
It would not have been possible for a crowd of visitors to avoid upsetting them. I was aghast.

"What are you doing, Nadelman?" I inquired.

"Do not ask me," he replied. "I am the artist who created these
works, not you! My sculptures must have air! You must be able
to walk all around them! They must not stand in front of a wall!"

"But, Nadelman," I rejoined, "these rooms are very small. There
will be no place for the many visitors we expect. Moreover, you
agreed that the success of this exhibition is solely my responsibility, and I invited you here only as a matter of courtesy."

He became frantic. Flushed and trembling with rage, he began
a violent harangue to which I refused to listen, and I left him
standing in the room surrounded by his works, drawing the curtains that closed the entrance to the first gallery behind me. A few
moments later, Scott arrived. Seeing the curtain drawn, he asked
me what was going on inside, for the work of installation had
already been finished the night before. It was now Scott's turn
to receive the habitual Nadelman kick in the pants.

"Where are the men?" Scott inquired.

"Inside with Nadelman," I answered quietly, "rearranging the
whole show."

What followed may sound like a fantastic scene in an uproarious
farce, but Nadelman did not think it was the least bit funny. Scott,
drawing aside the portières, passed into the room, and I heard him
yell: "What's going on here?"

"Naturally, I am arranging my exhibition!" was Nadelman's
answer.

"But Birnbaum had already finished doing that last night, and
he did a damn good job."

"I do not care what you or Birnbaum think. I am the only man
living who understands this work, and I know how it should be
shown."

"Is that so?" was Scott's reply. "Well, get out of my gallery and don't cross this threshold again! You are a damn fool. You ought to go down on your knees and thank Birnbaum for what he has done for you! Leave these premises at once!"

John Pastorini and the other workmen were the sole witnesses to this devastating scene. Scott, with those parting words, shut himself up in his private office.

The pale artist, at first speechless, now came out gesticulating and screaming, "Birnbaum, did you hear him! Never was a great artist like me insulted in such a way. You understand me! You have eyes and a mind! What shall I do?"

"Obey him!" I replied calmly, ignoring the fact that he was again flattering me and paying me fulsome compliments. "Take my advice, Nadelman. Go and don't come back. Remember you promised to allow me to answer for the results of this exhibition."

Nadelman left. The pedestals were hastily put back in their original positions. In the afternoon, the guests for our preview arrived, and the exhibition was a tremendous success. The newspaper criticisms, however, did not appear for several days because the opening day was a Saturday and there was no time to print the reviews in the Sunday editions, which go to press several days in advance. This disturbed the artist, and ignoring Scott's orders he came back a few days later, suggesting that we advertise the great event. He seemed to have forgotten what he once told me, that he was not interested in publicity or the comments of journalists and art critics, and furthermore claimed that he never read what they wrote. He seemed, however, to be deeply interested in the financial success of our venture, and I enjoyed teasing him for weeks by holding back the news that so many important items had been sold, even before the opening day.

Years went by before our quarrel was patched up, but when we met after my retirement he never lost an opportunity to urge me to start a new gallery. After his untimely death, Mrs. Nadelman and her friend, Mrs. Stewart Walker, approached me hoping I would take charge of a memorial exhibition, which the Museum of Modern Art was planning. However, I was merely an ordinary member of that institution and had no official connection with it. The work was entrusted to Lincoln Kirstein, and the catalogue he wrote was admirable. It contained many interesting biographical facts new to me. The arrangement was really a fine original achievement, but for some unaccountable reason, many of Nadelman's outstanding works which I had painstakingly called to Kirstein's notice were deliberately omitted. The exhibition did not have a very salutary effect upon the artist's reputation, nor did it create the notable sensation expected. None of his great portraits was included, the best Hellenistic heads were not shown, and one searched in vain for the fine kneeling dancer, the group of bronze deer, and above all, the Femme Drapée, an important analytical work, now in the Philadelphia Museum, which was considered by Nadelman to be the embodiment, or epitome, of his theories. The lame excuse that only controversial works were shown had no weight, for there was ample room, and works that would have added lustre to his reputation were passed over in favor of dozens of small plaster figures, some of them, it is true, breathing the very air of Hellas, like antique Tanagras, and tastefully arranged in wall vitrines. I wonder what hysterical outburst would have greeted the museum officials had the shade of Elie Nadelman walked into those pretentious halls.

Nadelman reminds me of another Pole, Stanislaus Szukalski, who once called to see me, at the suggestion, if I remember rightly, of a well-groomed Chicago critic, Count Monteglas. Szukalski, who was a sculptor, showed me some remarkable drawings that impressed me immediately, and so strongly in fact, that I told him I would gladly introduce his work to New York if he had enough of it as original and interesting as the drawings he showed me. Rightly or wrongly, I assumed that he was in need of funds, and even offered to buy the sheets he had submitted to me. To my astonishment he told me he had plenty of material—sculptures as well as drawings—but he would not sell any. He intimated that the world was not yet prepared for an artist of his stature. My partner Scott, who lost his patience when I suggested that it would be interesting to exhibit the work of an artist who refused to sell any of his creations to an unworthy public, intimated that I often showed signs of idealism, bordering on business madness. I did not hear anything further about Szukalski until I read Ben Hecht's interesting autobiography in which he wrote that the life work of this Polish genius was entirely destroyed by a Nazi bomb that fell in Warsaw on the studio presented to the artist by an appreciative Polish government.

Another artist who spurned mere commercial recognition was the Englishman, the late Eric Kennington, whose work is known to Americans only through reproductions in books written about him.

A remarkable war painting, *The Kensingtons at Lavenie,* in reverse on a sheet of glass was the first original work of his that I saw. It was a distinguished technical achievement, besides being a fine piece of draftsmanship. I lost no time in looking Kennington up in London, and he entered with enthusiasm into my plan to give an exhibition of his work in New York. Money was never mentioned. We spoke only of the ways and means to present his work in the best possible way. But when I introduced him to my partner, Scott began to question him about any previous financial successes he might have enjoyed. When he was asked whether he knew any of the influential art collectors in America, Kennington became rigid. He did not insult Scott, but fearing that he would, I hastened to bring the discussion to an end, and Scott left me with an indignant artist who informed me that he would not allow a single item to be exhibited in a gallery controlled wholly or partially by a commercially ambitious dealer who obviously did not sympathize with my idealism.

Stories like the Nadelman and Rothenstein episodes could be repeated until many pages would be filled with accounts of the dishonesty and ingratitude of artists. There are elements of comedy in such situations, but I shall content myself with only one or two more examples of what some people have charitably described as artistic naïveté. One is obliged to mention the names of those involved, otherwise the stories would hardly be believed.

Paul Manship, whose exhibition under my auspices made my name familiar to many artists, would often generously call my attention to the art of his friends. He was particularly eager to have me take an interest in the work of Hunt Diederich, whose playful greyhounds, fighting cocks, weather vanes, and fire screens I already admired.

I knew that the tall collateral descendant of Hunt, the distinguished painter who made the Barbizon masters so popular in America, was what the French call an *original*, but I thought highly of his talent and soon persuaded Stevenson Scott to add Diederich's name to the list of contemporaries whose works were a feature of our gallery. Scott did this reluctantly, for without any really good reason he suspected the artist, as well as my old rival "Putzi" Hanfstängl, of being German sympathizers, and possibly spies. We were to be the artist's sole agents, and the edition of each of his bronzes was to be strictly limited. Knowing that the artist was in financial straits, Scott, in spite of his vague suspicions, agreed to buy outright some of Diederich's works, on the retail price of which we were to receive a commission of twenty-five per cent.

One quiet morning Mrs. William Murray Crane, whose interest in art and flair for original talent were well known, walked into our gallery, and her keen eye was immediately attracted by a bronze door knocker, realistically modeled by Hunt Diederich in the the shape of a squirrel. To make the point of this *petite histoire* more telling, I should state that the selling price of this item, fixed, of course, by the artist, was $250, and we had already bought it from Diederich for $187.50. Mrs. Crane, on being told the price and on being assured that the bronze was to be limited to six casts, purchased it and drove away, taking the squirrel with her.

Some weeks later I received a polite letter from Mrs. Crane that stated in substance that in our past dealings she had never had any reason for doubting my word, and accordingly she felt obliged to tell me that a "squirrel" exactly like the one she had bought from us was offered for sale by another art dealer for $100, although I had stated that Scott and Fowles were the artist's sole representatives. Naturally, her letter upset me, remembering Scott's advice to have nothing whatever to do with the artist. I wrote to Mrs. Crane without an instant's delay, offering to return the purchase price to her, and begging her to tell me the name of the art dealer who offered her the replica. I could only think of one reasonable defense. The artist might have sold a cast of the squirrel before he had entered into the agreement with Scott and Fowles, and the purchaser, tiring of it, might have sold it for a small sum to the other dealer. Mrs. Crane, for some unknown reason, refused to part with the bronze but she gave me the name of a prominent decorator whose premises were a few steps from Fifth Avenue, several blocks from our gallery. Early the next morning, as soon as the doors were open, I hurried to the decorator's premises and found a young girl in charge. Many examples of Diederich's work were in the display room, but the squirrel was not among them. The inexperienced salesgirl did not know me, and in answer to my inquiries she said that she believed such an item could be had. She looked into the stock books which listed works held on consignment, and told me that the price would be $100. I then asked whether I, as a dealer would obtain a discount from the retail price, and she replied that since they received only thirty-three and one-third percent from the artist I could not expect very much! I would have to arrange that with her employer.

To say that I was furious and disheartened would be an understatement and I wondered and dreaded what outburst would greet me after the facts became known to Scott, who had warned me not to take Diederich under our wing. I rushed back to my office and called up the artist on the telephone, hoping to reach him before Scott's arrival. I ordered Diederich to drop anything he might be doing and come to the gallery at once. He realized that I was unduly excited and wondered what was the trouble.

"Come at once, Hunt," I answered, "or you will not find any of your works in this gallery."

He arrived shortly afterwards, smiling quizzically and asked, "What is the matter?"

"Hunt, are we your sole dealers?" I questioned.

"Of course," he replied without hesitation.

"Then why is a collection of your work being shown and offered at Miss C's?"

"Oh," he said laughing, "she is not an art dealer; she is a mere decorator."

"Indeed!" I countered. "And you authorize her to sell your bronze squirrel for one hundred dollars, besides allowing her thirty-three and one-third percent discount, whereas we, believing ourselves your sole agents, receive only twenty-five percent, and are obliged to sell it for two hundred and fifty dollars? Furthermore, we bought your work for cash to help you out financially."

Now Diederich laughed more heartily than ever!

"Is that the cause of all this fuss?" he queried. "Why, I can go to Third Avenue and buy a cup of coffee for five cents, but if I want to patronize a Fifth Avenue restaurant I would have to pay fifty cents; Miss C's premises are not on Fifth Avenue."

White with scorn and disgust, I shouted, "Well, take your works at once to the Bowery or Third Avenue, where they belong, for if Scott arrives before you leave, you will find them, as I warned you, in the gutter."

Hunt Diederich was obliged to take them away in a taxi, but Mrs. Crane, I regret to say, never graced our threshold again, nor did she acknowledge the receipt of my letter. I am afraid that she still holds me responsible for the artist's dishonesty, although she must long since have heard that before his death he was obliged to give up his seat as an Associate of the American Academy because of conduct unbecoming a member.

Fortunately for me, even before the experience I have just described, I had not been tempted to give Diederich a one-man exhibition, but there were other artists with whom I had the friendliest relations. One of them was the late Maurice Sterne, whose works I had shown twice at the Berlin galleries, and again at Scott and Fowles. I shall always remember him with pleasure, and his successes may be soberly described as almost incredible.

A partial, inadequate account of my first relations with Sterne has already appeared in a very early book of mine, but one or two additional incidents may be appropriately added here. During Sterne's first show, devoted chiefly to works produced in Bali, a man walked into the gallery and correctly assuming that I was in charge, introduced himself with the terse statement, "I am Doctor Barnes." I bowed politely, but it must have been obvious that the name did not register and meant nothing to me. "Don't you really know who I am?" he questioned, rather annoyed. I confessed my ignorance, and told him hesitatingly that I was a comparative newcomer in the art world. "But I have the greatest collection of modern art in America!" he continued, and again I was obliged to tell him that I was ashamed to admit that I had never heard of it.

He was irritated, but quickly got down to business. "Are these pictures for sale?" he inquired.

"Yes, indeed," I answered. "But the ones marked with gilt-paper stars have already been sold." I then let him consult my private price catalogue, and with it he made the rounds of the gallery.

To my surprise the great collector stopped before a Balinese drawing of no special importance.

"How much is this?"

I looked at the catalogue that he held and answered (if my memory still serves me rightly), "Eighty dollars, sir."

"Oh, I can read! But how much will it cost *me*? It is an honor for an artist to be represented in my collection."

"Doctor Barnes," I said, "these works all belong to the artist, and I am not free to change his prices. Only in the case of public galleries does Sterne allow a discount of ten percent. I would have to submit any offers to the artist and abide by his decision."

"Do that," he added, " and if he agrees to give me the discount, [which amounted to eight dollars] you may send me the drawing."

I regret to add that Sterne accepted the millionaire's offer. In his place I would have refused it. I afterwards learned that A. C. Barnes had amassed a fortune from argyrol, a patent medicine, and he seemed to be just another millionaire, who probably suffered from an inferiority complex which he nourished by refusing to allow prominent collectors like Sir William Van Horne of Montreal or Paul Sachs, one of the directors of the Fogg Art Museum, to visit his collection. I never attempted to visit his museum near Ardmore, Pennsylvania, and never saw him again.

When I saw Sterne a second time, it was at Anticoli Corrado, the fascinating hill town not far from Rome, and I was the guest of Edward Bruce and his charming wife, Peggy. Our other companions were my chum Alfred Potterton, the young peasant Mario Topi who painted delightful religious pictures, and Leo Stein, whom we all regarded as a profound philosopher and a

man of original taste. He was even then not on the best of terms
with his sister Gertrude. Although Leo was not particularly com-
municative, I managed to draw him out and learned with satisfaction that some of our aesthetic judgments, especially on
abstract art, coincided. Color and tone he regarded as abstrac-
tions, but cubes, circles and parallel lines were, he said, not more
abstract than landscapes or human figures, only far less interesting and not emotionally moving. The whole company enjoyed
dancing and gay repasts under the starlit Italian sky, or we
listened to the bagpipers who crossed the valley separating us
from Anticoli Roviano, led by the handsome brigand Gigi il Moro,
who was one of Sterne's models. My genial host Bruce had been
a football player in his Columbia College days, but when his
banking interests took him to Pekin, he became a serious student
and lover of Chinese art. His outstanding collection was for a
time shown at the Metropolitan Museum, but the best items were
eventually sold to Mr. Grenville Winthrop. After he became a
professional artist, Bruce was the leading official in the Government's attempt to help artists during the war and to create an
art movement in America. He was chiefly responsible for the
many commissions given to our painters and sculptors to decorate public buildings in Washington and elsewhere. Sterne's monumental bronze which I named *The Awakening* was on Bruce's lawn
overlooking the country surrounding Anticoli Corrado, and Sterne
insisted that it be shipped to Scott and Fowles where it would be
the dominating item in his next exhibition.

I had already recognized Sterne's talent for sculpture when we
showed his bronze head of an Italian peasant, now in the Metropolitan Museum and catalogued there as *The Bombthrower*. It is
my recollection, and I am sure it serves me rightly in this instance,
that I pointed out the artist's natural bent for sculpture to Mabel
Dodge Luhan, who became Sterne's first wife after she visited his
exhibition at the Berlin Gallery, although in her published revel-
ations she claims that it was she who called my attention to his
special talent. In any case, he was shortly afterward given an important commission to make the group of Puritans, which stands
at a crossing of two roads near Worcester, Massachusetts. Unfortunately, the soft-grained Italian stone that the artist used for this

monument was already crumbling when I last saw it. I wonder whether a coating of paraffin, applied in the same way in which my old professor, Ogden Doremus, treated Cleopatra's Needle in Central Park, to preserve it, would save Sterne's work from eventual disintegration.

When the huge bronze *Awakening* arrived at Scott and Fowles for Sterne's second American exhibition, my senior partner again lost patience with me, for it was with the greatest difficulty that it was moved into one of the galleries which it almost completely filled; Scott made me promise to have it removed immediately after the closing day of the show. As was my custom, I sent a few letters to clients who might be particularly interested in such a bronze, and the first of these to call at the gallery was the late Walter Hayden Crittenden, who was president of the Brooklyn Museum, which owns a notable group of contemporary sculptures. Crittenden paid his visit to us early in the morning, and to my delight his reaction was obviously favorable. He agreed to acquire *The Awakening* on condition that there would be only two other replicas, and that neither of these would be offered to the Metropolitan Museum. I agreed to all this, congratulating myself secretly on the effect this sale would have on Scott—as well as on Sterne.

But wonders never cease! Hardly had Mr. Crittenden left, and before my satisfaction had time to cool, when Ralph Pulitzer came in to see the bronze and Sterne's paintings. He was quite overwhelmed when he walked into the small room in which *The Awakening* was being shown, but questioned how such a huge figure could be utilized. Having been a frequent visitor at his beautiful Long Island home, where a string quartet entertained his guests on Sunday afternoons, I suggested that if *The Awakening* were resting on a pedestal hidden just under the surface of a rectangular pool of water beyond the large picture window of his music room, it would have an ideal setting. This inspired solution of the problem appealed to him, for now his guests would have something besides a broad sheet of water to admire, and Ralph ordered the bronze replica without further hesitation.

Another hour went by while I could hardly wait for Scott's arrival to announce my vindication, when Galen Stone, the well-known banker and stockbroker, walked in. He had received not only my letter, but another from his bosom friend, Ned Bruce. When he saw the bronze he turned to me and said, "I dare say it's very fine, but I dislike bronzes."

"But you can't have this bronze, Mr. Stone," I replied. "It has already been sold to the Brooklyn Museum. However, Sterne has the right to make just one more replica and I am sure that if you ordered him to make one of marble, he would even improve on this bronze, and your example would be virtually unique. You could have it placed on the summit of a hill on your estate in Massachusetts, and your guests would have a special reason for climbing to the top."

"Well! You have something there! Tell him to go ahead."

Even then my excitement had no time to cool, for other selected clients came in and acquired many of the paintings. When Maurice Sterne and his wife, Vera, who had been one of the Isadora Duncan dancers, strolled in to get a first view of the exhibition, he seemed worried, although he was pleased with the way his works looked.

"But where," he asked, "shall I store this figure? Already I owe Ned Bruce a large sum, which he advanced for shipping expenses."

I then broke the news to him piecemeal and tantalizingly. Almost overcome by the news of the first sale, he was speechless when I told him that Ralph Pulitzer's replica would have to be cast and that he must go at once to take measurements of the pool. And then, when I broke the news of Galen Stone's order and told him that this marble was already paid for, he was completely overwhelmed. Vera was in tears, and Sterne's own eyes were not quite dry.

Sterne's pictures at this exhibition were also popular. The late Sam Lewisohn not only bought a number, but his favorable attitude, I believe, carried much weight in the decision to hold a large exhibition of Sterne's work at the Museum of Modern Art, some time later.

Unfortunately, Galen Stone died before the marble was delivered, and his widow was shocked when she saw the nude figure her husband had ordered to decorate their estate. She would not accept it, but was finally persuaded to give The Awakening to the Boston Museum of Fine Arts. I wonder what her reaction would have been had she witnessed one of her husband's sumptuous stag parties which my friend Arnold Genthe, the famous photographer, vividly described to me.

Still another incident in connection with Sterne should be mentioned here. When the exhibition at the Scott and Fowles galleries was at its height, a slender young visitor, after examining it, asked me whether the artist had created many other works that were not included in the current exhibit. On being told that there were a considerable number in Sterne's studio that had never been shown because space was lacking, he told me, to my surprise, that if a suitable price could be agreed upon he would buy a collection of the unsold works, including those still unsold hanging on our walls. The young man's name was Carl Hamilton. He was a Yale graduate who had made some financial "strikes" in the copra market and was beginning to surprise the art world by indulging in what seemed to many to be daring transactions.

The purchase of the large block of Sterne's output that he negotiated was by no means the most sensational of Hamilton's activities. Joseph Duveen, who had already discovered him, found to his sorrow that Carl Hamilton was a very courageous collector and one who could not be trifled with. Some Renaissance items that Hamilton had acquired, including a Piero della Francesca, were put up for sale at the Parke-Bernet salesrooms, and Joe Duveen went to the exhibition held prior to the auction. Duveen expressed himself too loudly while adversely criticizing some of the finest items. Naturally, intending bidders were frightened by Lord Duveen's audible remarks, which put them on their guard. However, on the night of the sale, Duveen bought the Piero for a relatively small amount and to ingratiate himself with Mrs. John D. Rockefeller he then sold the picture to her without making any profit whatever. Carl Hamilton started a lawsuit against Lord Duveen, but their quarrel was settled out of court, against the advice of Hamilton's attorneys who would have claimed very much higher punitive damages.

The Sterne group was hardly in Hamilton's hands when he began to arrange exhibitions of his Sterne collection and offered to sell single items at a considerable advance over the prices he had paid. Sterne resented this, although I tried to explain to him that

Hamilton was doing him a very good turn. He was establishing a high value on the painter's future output, assuming, of course, that Sterne's powers would not wane. The first purchasers of a gifted artist's works, like Hamilton Easter Field, Sam Lewisohn and others, deserve to make a profit on their investment in the field of art and the artist himself is ultimately the gainer when the value of his works is boosted by such fearless spirits. Carl Hamilton is still active and was until quite recently an artistic adviser to the North Carolina Museum of Art in Raleigh. Sam Lewisohn, who died in 1953, bequeathed the larger part of his collection, which contained several Sternes, to outstanding American museums including the Metropolitan.

Maurice Sterne's exhibition was not the only one that was quickly sold out, and again it was Galen Stone who helped to make Maxfield Parrish's debut a legendary success. The name of the artist, a personality as charming as his works, was already almost a household word in America, and with the appearance of Kenneth Graham's *The Golden Age*, Parrish's illustrations aroused the spontaneous enthusiasm of Professor Hubert von Herkomer, the prominent English painter and an influential critic. He hailed the new star, praising his uncompromising realism, his excellent draughtsmanship, his meticulous technique and phenomenal finish, and he hoped that Parrish would paint and not lose himself for the world of art by merely doing illustrations. John Singer Sargent had also praised Parrish's talent and had singled out the artist's remarkable tree trunks as extraordinary.

Parrish had never had a one-man exhibition, and I went to his studio in Windsor, Vermont, to persuade him to paint some fairly large canvases. His home was fascinating, for virtually the whole abode was furnished by the artist. He had made the household furniture, the lamp shades, the garden ornaments, the toys for his children, and almost everything needed for the decoration of his home. Japanese artists could hardly have improved on a grasshopper with movable joints which his little son played with. Beautifully painted roadway signs in the region were other pleasant surprises for the visitor. Parrish would be a hermit when

Windsor was literally buried in deep snow, and did not come to New York even to see the exhibition of his work. Almost every item was sold in a few days. Over a hundred thousand dollars was realized and when he received what he regarded as a fabulous check, he sent me one of his many exquisitely written letters. His handwriting was so beautiful that I begged him not to reply to my letters on a typewriter, and my request was usually granted. "During the war," as he put it, "no extra charge is made for this."

Unfortunately, he did not study the chemistry of his pigments with sufficient care, and many of the beautiful colors—except an azure which he made of precious powdered lapis lazuli—have faded or turned black. However, future generations will always delight in the color reproductions of his works which do not fade.

Parrish's success did not change Scott's attitude or interrupt his warnings and when I realized that I could not continue indefinitely to ignore my senior partner's business methods, I succumbed and began to pay closer attention to his counsel. Soon I had won my spurs and showed considerable ability in a field new to me. I found out that earlier in my career I had had more difficulty in selling an etching for ten dollars than I now had when I sold a painting for many thousands of dollars. One instance must suffice.

In the course of my visits to London, I was invited to lunch with Charles Carstairs, then a member of the firm of Knoedler & Company. On entering the dining-room directly above the firm's premises in their Bond Street gallery, I was immediately fascinated by a picture over the mantel. It was a magnificent portrait of Mlle. Gonin by Ingres. She was the daughter of the celebrated French artist's patrons, in Florence, and to show his gratitude for their many kindnesses Ingres painted this enchanting portrait, which was afterwards rather too enthusiastically described by Lapauze. The leading authority on Ingres said it was the finest portrait of the most beautiful woman in the world by the greatest of all painters. I urged my partner, Stevenson Scott, to acquire this item, as Mr. and Mrs. Charles P. Taft of Cincinnati, whose entire collection was virtually assembled by Scott and Fowles, had no work by Ingres at the time, and I felt certain that they would buy it. Mrs. Emery, another remarkable collector in Cin-

cinnati and their friendly rival, already possessed a version of
Ingres' portrait of the composer Cherubini.

I was such a frank admirer of the painter, however, that I was
not entrusted with the task of bargaining for it, so Scott shrewdly
acquired the portrait for our firm and shortly after it arrived from
London I was off to Cincinnati to submit it to Mr. and Mrs. Taft.
They did not know that I was coming, and I arrived early one
winter morning, greeted by a terrific sleet and snow storm. When
I rang the doorbell at their beautiful house—built by the architect
of the White House in Washington for the Sintons, the parents of
Mrs. Taft—I heard that they had already left for the office of the
Cincinnati Enquirer, a newspaper that they owned. I loitered a
few minutes in the reception room where a portrait by Rembrandt's famous pupil Ferdinand Bol was hanging, and I decided
that the space between the windows there filled by the Dutch
portrait would be an ideal setting for the Ingres. After preparing
the hooks and wires in case it had to be hung quickly, I drove off
to the newspaper office. When the charming sprightly Mrs. Taft
saw me, she exclaimed, "Why, Mr. Birnbaum, what are you doing
here at such an early hour? I hope you are not here to submit any
art works to us. We have absolutely no money to spare. I have
just been obliged to pay last season's symphony orchestra lia-
bilities."

Before this visit I had already won her good will by playing
sonatas for piano and violin with her friend Professor Ogden, in
the drawing-room hung with a superlative group of the Barbizon
School paintings, sold to the Tafts by my predecessor Mr. Fowles.
I now told Mrs. Taft the purpose of my visit, and said I wanted
to be sure that she and Mr. Taft should see the Ingres before
anyone else, for I regarded this painting as a truly great prize.

She said again, "But we have no money!" To prove her point
she brought out her checkbook and showed me a check for over a
hundred thousand dollars that she had just made out to pay for
the deficit of the Cincinnati Orchestra. In spite of her remonstrances, however, both she and Mr. Taft finally agreed to return
to their residence to see the picture before I took it back to New
York. I hurried ahead of them in a cab before they reached their
home to hang the portrait so that it would show to the best ad-

vantage. The dear old couple insisted on following me on foot, in spite of the heavy snowstorm that still raged, for Mrs. Taft quoted the Bible and said, "This is the day the Lord hath made; rejoice in it." When they arrived and opened the door of the reception room, the picture was already hung, and they stopped in the doorway and caught a first glimpse of its uncommon beauty. "Oh, Charles, it is really lovely!" Mrs. Taft exclaimed. "I think we must have it."

After one look, Mr. Taft added, "Yes, my dear, I agree with you."

Without further comment, Mrs. Taft left us, to return immediately to the newspaper office, and only then did Mr. Taft ask the price, which ran into six figures. Without raising an eyebrow, he said, "Very well. I hope you can wait a month or two before I pay." Needless to say, that was entirely satisfactory to Scott and Fowles, for in the past he had made out single checks for one million dollars each payable to the firm, and these impressive canceled souvenirs of his former purchases hung in Stevenson Scott's private office, neatly framed.

The whole transaction did not take more than a few minutes. The Tafts, like Mr. Grenville Winthrop, had the true spirit of great collectors, and did not think in terms of columns of figures or possible profits and losses. The only question that concerned them was the permanent artistic value of the item they were acquiring. They would have heartily agreed with the Moorish architect of a fine Medersa, in North Africa, who, when his royal patron protested the price demanded by the artist for his work, tore up his book of accounts and wrote, "A thing of beauty is never too costly, and one never pays too much for what pleases man."

The Ingres was only one of many treasures that I acquired for Mr. and Mrs. Taft. One of the two full-length portraits Sargent painted of the thin Robert Louis Stevenson in his baggy trousers is now an outstanding item in the collection. The other version belonged to the late Mrs. Harry Payne Whitney. I was also pleased when I persuaded the Tafts to acquire a large and exceptionally fine Bonnington. Not infrequently I would exchange an item like a small Gainsborough landscape sold to them by my predecessor, Mr. Fowles, for a far more important example we had acquired subsequently. When Lord Duveen got wind of the fact that this costly painting in which he had a half interest was sold by me, his enthusiasm for any talent I may have had as a salesman noticeably waned, and henceforth he introduced me grudgingly as a student of modern art, repeating and emphasizing the word "modern" until he was satisfied that he had impressed his listener with the conviction that contemporary pictures should be the sole field of my commercial activities.

In due course I shall give an account of a transaction that turned out disastrously for me. It relates to a Whistler, a master not represented in the Taft collection, but this seems an appropriate place in which to mention the acquisition by Mrs. Semple, the daughter of Mr. and Mrs. Taft, of the famous early painting by Whistler, *At the Piano*. This had once belonged to Sir Edmund Davis of Chilham Castle, and at the sale of the Davis pictures Stevenson Scott and I, no longer partners, were both bidding for that painting. Acting as the agent for Mr. Winthrop and later for Thomas Cochran, I had once offered Sir Edmund over a hundred thousand dollars for it, but each time Sir Edmund demanded considerably more, whereas at Christie's it brought only half the sum I would have been willing to pay. At the Davis sale I was also bidding for the late William H. Donner, who sat next to me, and for whom I acquired the Whistler nocturne, *Battersea Bridge*, a lovely Alfred Stevens, a number of drawings, and Winterhalter's portrait of the youthful Queen Victoria, without knowing that the late Queen Mary was an underbidder for this last-mentioned item.

The Tafts were not the only great collectors in Cincinnati. Their friend, the gentle Mrs. Emery, had superb paintings ranging from Mantegna and Van Dyck to Ingres. Mrs. Emery seemed to have no faith in the quality of a picture unless it was very costly, and furthermore it had to meet with the approval of her Negro butler. Lord Duveen had an ample supply of such treasures, and he knew how to win over the butler. Eventually the collection was bequeathed to the Cincinnati Museum.

Miss Mary Hanna was another devoted follower of the Tafts, and she could always be counted on to buy a pretty child by an English master, no matter how high the price. I know of one instance when she exchanged a fine example by Raeburn for a sweet Romney figure of a child, paying a large additional sum to secure the pretty girl's portrait. The discarded Raeburn became an outstanding item in the collection of Judge Harding.

The collections just mentioned obliged me to pay annual visits to Cincinnati and I would occasionally show a group of old masters in a local gallery hoping that the exhibit would arouse the interest of some visitor who might develop into another ambitious collector. Count John McCormack, whose golden voice I had first heard at Covent Garden would usually be giving a concert in Cincinnati just when I was there and he would occasionally buy some of the finest items in my exhibition before returning to New York. The famous tenor was a great lover of art, and with his friends the Scotts I had enjoyed his hospitality in England at Lord Esher's home which McCormack then occupied. It was filled with paintings of exceptional quality, and undoubtedly inspired the great singer to gather together a small but distinguished group of works some of which he acquired after he saw the fine private collections in Cincinnati.

The record of an even more exciting commercial incident than the sale of the great Ingres may find a place here. I do not consider such transactions as achievements and this book will, I hope, not resemble a textbook on methods of salesmanship. However, the sale deserves to be described in detail because it has a certain bearing on the manner in which collectors of works of art sometimes begin and the transaction resulted in the initiation to the pleasures of collecting of a man who might have developed into one of the outstanding figures in the field had he lived long enough.

One of Stevenson Scott's most sympathetic friends was Ashton Knight, son of Ridgeway Knight, who amassed a respectable fortune painting sentimental pictures of pretty French peasant girls standing on the banks of rippling streams or in gardens, and bidding adieu to their lovers who were not in the picture. The sun-flecked brooks, the thatched cottages, the gardens ablaze with flowers and the mossy river banks, were often painted by the artist's son, Ashton, who soon began to produce similar landscape settings independently. He owned the manoir de Chante-reine, a picturesque estate in France, at Beaumont le Roger (Eure), where he lived with his family, entertaining his friends and painting an interminable series of pictures that appealed to unsophisticated tastes. Often he was seen standing in midstream, in high boots, painting the surrounding scene on a canvas tied to an easel that was securely propped up in the shallow water. The pictures had obvious attractiveness and the amiable Ashton Knight often persuaded Scott and Fowles to display one of his works in their beautiful show window. When I objected on the ground that the pictures were not distinguished paintings and had no place in the window of a dealer who dealt in great art, I was always overruled and told that I had no experience and that Charles P. Taft, our most important client, had begun his famous collection by purchasing an Ashton Knight!

My resistance was invariably broken down and one evening, when a horizontal panel by Knight was on display in solitary splendor in our window, a tall, gaunt, intelligent-looking man walked into our premises and asked the faithful John Pastorini the price of the painting, which was a particularly showy example of Knight's work. The visitor was referred to me, and I confess I was ashamed to answer his question. However, with as much non-chalance as I could muster, I told him that the price was three thousand dollars.

"I'll take it," he replied laconically. "If you have a blank check, I'll make one out to your order, and you can deliver the picture at my home, after you satisfy yourself that my check will be honored."

I was not unduly elated.

"Would you care to examine the painting at closer range in our gallery?" I inquired.

"Oh no," he answered, "I know exactly what I need, and I am sure it will fit over my fireplace above the mantel, in my entrance hall."

We had an ample supply of blank checks and after he had filled one out I asked him whether he wanted the long reflector which lit up the painting.

"Will it cost anything extra?" he asked.

"No sir, nothing extra," I answered.

"Well, then, send it along," he said.

Something about the assurance of the man impressed me, but I merely added, "Very well, sir. At what time do you want me to hang the picture?"

At this he smiled and replied quite sarcastically, "Young man, I am not an art collector. Don't waste your valuable time on me. I merely need this one painting, and I have plenty of men who can hang it properly for me. Moreover, I live in the country near Port Chester, and you would be merely squandering precious energy and time to take such a useless trip. You might even be missing a really important client while you are serving no useful purpose whatever by driving to my home."

"Nevertheless, sir," I persisted, "I like to feel that every picture coming from our gallery is hung and lighted to the best advantage, and if you have no objection I really would prefer to have our man hang it."

"Oh," he answered, in a bantering tone, "I have no objection whatsoever. But I hate to see a clever young fellow waste his time."

He then handed me his check signed Edward F. Price, told me how to reach his residence, and left.

Next morning my men left with the picture on a van and I followed them on a train to Port Chester. From the station I reached the Price residence in a taxi, driving through beautiful gardens past a magnificent dairy. My men had just finished hanging the Ashton Knight in the entrance hall and were awaiting my arrival for approval. Seated on a winding stairway leading from the hall, where she had been watching the men at work, was a lady simply dressed in a morning gown, and I subsequently learned that she was Mrs. Price. She answered my greeting by asking, "Did you sell this picture to Mr. Price?"

"No," I answered without hesitation.

"Well, who did?" she queried.

"No one," I replied.

"But he bought it at your gallery, didn't he?"

"Oh, yes! He bought it! I was in the gallery at the time, but I did not sell it. The gentleman happened to pass our window, saw the picture, walked into our premises, asked the price and made out his check for it. He did not ask me for my opinion or for any particulars regarding the picture or the artist who painted it. I was not obliged to make any effort whatever to persuade him to acquire it, and therefore I cannot rightfully be accused of having sold it."

"Why, you sound as if you don't like the picture," she interrupted.

"You are quite right. We have many pictures costing less that I prize far more highly. This painting is not even our property, and if it were returned to us before we paid Mr. Knight for it we would gladly exchange it for something better, or even refund the purchase price."

I had barely finished when Mr. Price entered the hall. After our mutual greeting he smiled and said, "Well, well! I see you do not value your time too highly. You came all the distance from New York to take a look at my estate and see if I might need more pictures. Now you can see for yourself that I don't. This comfortable house and its furnishings are good enough for anybody, and I am not the kind of damn fool who pays ten thousand dollars for the picture of a cow, when I can buy a living champion Jersey for that amount."

I felt that I had nothing to lose by arguing with him, so I ventured to remark that judging by the size and beauty of his estate I knew that he was an extraordinarily successful man in some field of business endeavor.

"But I assure you, sir," I continued, "I come into contact with many intelligent men, and some of them buy prize cattle for more than ten thousand dollars a head, and at the the same time they buy pictures of cattle by such masters as Troyon for even greater sums."

At that point he stopped me and said, "Who among your clients buys such fine cattle?"

"To mention only one," I answered, "I have been told that Mr. Ames has paid as much as forty thousand dollars for his famous champion Jersey bull."

"The bull of Mr. Ames," Mr. Price now informed me, "is no longer the champion. If you have more time to waste, come with me and I will show you the present world champion, which is none other than the son of Mr. Ames's bull."

Naturally, I accompanied him to his dairy where he showed me what was said to be the finest existing herd of Jerseys, and his magnificent bull.

"I like you," Mr. Price added, "and some day I shall call to shake your hand when I walk down Fifth Avenue. But if you ever try to sell me any oil paintings, our friendship will cease."

He loaded me down with as much delicious cream and butter as I could carry, before I left for New York.

I really never expected to see Mr. Price again, but one day he walked into the office and surprised me at my desk.

"You see, I am a man of my word. I came in to tell you how pleased I am with my picture."

Then his eye fell on a small graceful gilt bronze dancer by Mario Korbel, who had left it with me on consignment a few days before.

"Where have I seen that bronze?" Mr. Price inquired.

"I am quite sure you have never seen it before, Mr. Price," I answered.

"Don't say that," he retorted rather angrily. "When I say I have seen a thing, you may be sure I have seen it."

"But, Mr. Price," I informed him, "it was not here at the time of your last visit. There are only three of these bronzes in existence. Besides this one, another is in a western museum, and the third is in a Washington collection, in a house crowded with works of art."

"Yes," asserted Mr. Price, "it is on the mantel in James Parmelee's dining room."

I really was surprised.

"Mr. Price, you amaze me! You claim you are not interested in art, yet you remember a tiny object like this which is hidden and buried, so to speak, in a house containing countless items of greater importance."

"Well, just remember that I do not make vague statements. Is this little figure for sale?"

I told him the value put on it by Korbel, and before he left the gallery he asked me to send it to his wife at Port Chester.

The very day after the little bronze was delivered, John Pastorini, as usual who, was at our door and thought he could correctly estimate at a glance the wealth and social importance of
any woman driving up to our entrance, warned me that a lady
wearing a fine "string of rocks" had just stepped out of a Rolls-
Royce and was coming into the gallery. A charming, attractively
dressed woman whom I recognized as Mrs. Price, the lady who
was present when the Ashton Knight was hung at Port Chester,
entered the gallery. When I arose to greet her, she said, "I came
back to thank you for that graceful little *objet d'art* delivered to
our house yesterday."

I invited her into our main gallery, hung with crimson cut velvet, in which we were then showing a fine collection of English
portraits ranging from Hogarth to Lawrence.

"Oh, what a beautiful collection!" she exclaimed, "Why don't
you show it to Mr. Price?"

"I dare not," I replied. "He warned me that if I valued our
friendship, I must not show him any pictures. If, however, you
can persuade him to tell me that he has changed his mind, I
shall be only too happy to invite him to see our current exhibition."

"You know," Mrs. Price said, "he can acquire almost anything
his heart desires, and it is ridiculous that our home should be the
repository of mezzotints by Arlent Edwards and such a picture
as that Ashton Knight."

"Nevertheless, Mrs. Price, I shall not take the first step. Your
husband is not a man to be trifled with when he has made up his
mind, and he seems determined not to acquire fine works of art."

The next morning Mr. Price was my first visitor! I could see at
once that he was not in the best humor.

"Good morning," he said with a dangerous twinkle in his eye.
"I just dropped in to tell you that you are upsetting the tran-
quillity of my home. Mrs. Price does not like it as much now as
she once did."

"Oh, come, Mr. Price," I replied with an answering twinkle,
"it is you who are disturbing her. She is a woman with excellent
taste, and naturally she would like to have her home surroundings
as beautiful as possible, and while your residence is obviously a

comfortable abode, fitted by a capable commercial decorator, it is not, if you will pardon my saying so, filled with items of which Mrs. Price has reason to be particularly proud. Determined as you seem to be to leave it furnished as it is, I am bold enough to tell you that I could soon transform one of your rooms into a far more attractive place, if I could rearrange it and add a few luxurious items that I believe the owner of the world's champion Jersey bull can afford. It would cost you nothing to let me try to prove this. My effort may indeed meet with your disapproval, but why not put me to the test?"

"I know," he answered. "You would like to fill the house with costly oil paintings."

"Not at all," I remonstrated. "The room would have less in it than at present, and the pictures which I would add need not be great masterpieces! Naturally, however, if I had sufficient wealth at my disposal, I would want the finest works available. Just let me waste my time, as you put it, and allow me to experiment with one of your rooms. You may then have the satisfaction of telling me that my efforts have failed to meet with your approval, in which case I will undo what I have done and arrange the room exactly as it was before I entered it, down to the minutest detail."

As a result of this conversation and over the protests of my senior partner, I went up to Port Chester with a vanload of our choicest portraits and landscapes by the greatest English masters of the eighteenth and early nineteenth centuries.

I chose a nicely proportioned Adams room, which I emptied after making a diagram showing the exact location of every chair, table, rug, vase, or *objet d'art*. Then I selected my pictures from a group of works by Gainsborough, Reynolds, Raeburn, Romney, Hoppner, Lawrence, and Richard Wilson, and when my decisions and arrangements were final, and a few vases of flowers rounded out my day's labor, the result even exceeded my sanguine expectations.

When Mrs. Price walked into the room she was thrilled. "Oh, it ought never to be disturbed and spoiled!" she exclaimed.

I informed her that the pictures, of course, were among our best and costliest, and that good results could also be obtained by retaining the genuine old carved frames and substituting less valuable but still attractive works for the rare items I had hung. If, for example, a pretty woman's portrait by Coates were to take the place of the fine Reynolds, or the portrait of a handsome woman by Gainsborough were replaced by one of his bust portraits of a man, the price of the group would be considerably less. I then left, promising to return after I had seen Mr. Price, and agreeing if need be to return the room to its original state, exactly as it was before I had disturbed it.

Early the next morning, Mr. Price again paid me a visit. This time his greeting was cordial but briefer than ever.

"You win! How much do I owe you?"

I was not prepared for such a decision.

"Mr. Price, the pictures now hanging in your home are among our finest and are not cheap. As I already explained to Mrs. Price, the old frames are all of a standard size, and I can substitute attractive works by other less important masters for those I left. Superficially the effect would be just as harmonious, and you would still own paintings that would give you pleasure, even though they would not be masterpieces of the greatest English masters. The average visitor to your home might be as agreeably impressed by my substitutes as they would be by the group I left with you."

"But if I am going to have any, " Mr. Price answered, "I want the best. Let us negotiate on that basis."

The pictures were never removed, and he then began leisurely to acquire paintings for other rooms, the first change being a magnificent Israels to take the place of the Ashton Knight. Mr. Price had, without suspecting it, a real flair for quality, and before his untimely death I had many opportunities to be astonished by his inborn taste and judgment. Had he lived longer, he might have become one of our most discriminating connoisseurs.

Occasional attacks of rude or bald frankness like my first interview with Mrs. Price when I told her that I did not like the painting of Ashton Knight her husband had purchased, resulted not infrequently in winning the confidence of a new client.

During the winter of 1923, while examining a collection of American portraits offered for sale at the auction rooms of Parke-Bernet, a grime covered painting of a woman attracted my attention. It was attributed to Gilbert Stuart and for a long time had hung in the Boston Museum of Fine Arts. It had been withdrawn by the owners and subsequently sold, after it was found that the last will and testament of the former owner, who bequeathed it to the museum, was not a valid, enforceable legal document.

Stevenson Scott and I went to see the pictures in the Clark Collection at the Parke-Bernet auction gallery several times, and we concluded that this Stuart had all the earmarks of a fine work, but needed cleaning. When Stevenson Scott decided on acquiring a picture at an auction sale, he usually succeeded, and the Stuart was knocked down to us for a very small sum. We were delighted to find, after the dirt on its surface had been removed by Dr. De Wild, a famous Dutch restorer who had settled in New York, that it was not only one of the few signed pictures by the American master, but actually was a very attractive portrait of Betsy Ross, the creator of the American flag. It was therefore a work of historical interest.

Scott, whose experience as a dealer was highly respected by all his rivals, warned me to show it to no one, for although the picture had great value it might be recognized as the Clark picture, which had been sold for a song. Eventually when the auction sale was forgotten, we might make a handsome profit on it, but for the present it would be wiser to put it away, and wait several years before we offered it. The painting would ultimately rank with the best George Washington portraits by Stuart and bring a very high price. Shortly afterward, Scott sailed on his annual visit to London, after ordering the picture to be carefully stored in the vault underneath our premises. One day Mrs. Nicholas Brady drove up to our gallery with a titled English lady. After my greeting she asked me to show her friend some of our finest treasures. She added casually that she was also searching for a picture to grace the small dining-room of her stately residence on Long Island, but she wanted an American portrait, not an English one, and she knew that we did not specialize in American works. I immediately thought of the Stuart in our vault, and in spite of Scott's warning I ordered a porter to bring it up. When I showed the lovely picture to the ladies, they expressed their admiration enthusiastically. Would I reserve the item and show

it to Mr. Brady? Of course I would. The next day, accompanied
by her husband, Mrs. Brady returned to Scott and Fowles and I
showed the Stuart again. Mr. Brady liked it very much, asked
me the price, and then, turning to his wife, said, "My dear, if you
like it I will buy it for you as a gift."

I said to Mrs. Brady, "Please do not decide so quickly. Let me
try it in the room where you intend to hang it, and you can reach
a wiser decision."

Accordingly, I hung it in her small paneled dining-room and
satisfied myself that it was admirably suited for its new environment. Mrs. Brady agreed that nothing much finer or more appropriate might ever be found to embellish that particular room.
I left, convinced that it would remain there permanently and
cabled the news to Stevenson Scott. Weeks passed, however, and
no confirmation of the sale was made by Mr. Brady. At last
Scott cabled to me and asked what was the reason for the delay.
Almost at the same time I received a rather rude telephone call
from Mr. Brady's secretary, asking me to come to see him in his
office on lower Broadway. Of course I went. I was not too politely
received. The secretary said something to the effect that Mr.
Brady was no fool, and that although he liked the portrait he
would not pay the fantastic price I had demanded.

"What makes you think the price is fantastic?" I replied rather
testily. "Are you an expert in this field?"

"Well, this will explain Mr. Brady's attitude," he said, handing
me a priced catalogue of the auction sale and adding, "Don't you
think you are expecting an extraordinary profit on your investment?"

"Certainly," I replied, "and I think I recognize the handwriting
of the dealer to whom that catalogue once belonged. He was
present, along with almost every New York dealer at the sale,
but only Scott and Fowles realized the quality and importance
of this picture. The owner of that catalogue should be ashamed
to admit that he had allowed such a prize to slip through his
fingers when it was being offered. Having once recognized its
value, Scott and Fowles would have gone on bidding to a much
higher figure, if anyone else present had fully appreciated the
picture's value and had bid against us. If Mr. Brady thinks we

are asking too much, let him return the portrait without delay; but let me tell you something. Had Mr. Brady bought a vacant lot in Texas or California for a pittance, and had afterward discovered an oil well on it, would he consider selling the land for a few thousand dollars, instead of perhaps several millions?

"You may tell Mr. Brady that we will give him a letter promising to take the picture back at any time within the next ten years, and give him a ten percent profit on his investment, in addition."

With that parting thrust, I left the office, but the Gilbert Stuart was never returned. In the course of my conversation with the secretary, I noticed that the door leading into Mr. Brady's private office was slightly ajar.

Scott had never been wholly in sympathy with my desire to introduce living artists to the public, and after my discouraging encounters with Nadelman, Hunt Diederich, Mario Korbel, and others, I reluctantly succumbed to his pressure and began to pay more attention to the activities of Lord Duveen. Besides being the man who was directly responsible for my partnership agreement with Scott, he was held up to me as the outstanding example of a brilliant salesman. There is much information about Lord Duveen in S. N. Behrman's admirably written book, but, unfortunately, Behrman did not know Joe, as his intimates called him, and the impression created by the book is not quite fair. Lord Duveen's attorney, the late Louis Levy, who furnished many of the facts, resented Behrman's version. Lord Duveen was more than a shrewd salesman. He was an engaging, vivid personality, and a lively raconteur. He could hold wealthy clients spellbound and really win their hearts. They enjoyed his company and his conversation so keenly that they were willing to pay dearly for such entertainment in spite of the rumors current about his business methods.

If Joe was present at a dinner party, it was almost impossible for anyone else to get a word in. He might start for instance with the story of a Gainsborough which a gentleman who was connected with the royal household wished to bequeath to Queen

Mary. After his will had been witnessed and signed, Joe persuaded his lordship to change his mind and sell the picture. Then
he had an excellent copy of the painting made, and framed it in
the original frame so that the painting was never missed by visitors, and in due course Her Majesty became the owner of the
substituted copy which was comparatively worthless. No one
ever suspected that the original was already in an American collection. Joe could tell a story like this in the liveliest manner,
following it up with others equally entertaining, and not only
were the guests—among whom Colin Agnew and Count Sala were
prominent on the occasion I have in mind—fascinated, but no one
would venture to interrupt his chain of stories, although others
at the dinner table might perhaps have matched his amusing
anecdotes.

My own acquaintance with Lord Duveen began on the ill-fated
Lusitania, when he was traveling incognito on account of the
sensational lawsuit then in progress in which his firm was charged
with smuggling art objects into the country without paying import
duties. A disgruntled employee who had been refused a raise in
salary, had given damaging evidence to the United States Government as a profitable act of vengeance.

As an example of the questionable but certainly clever methods
used by the firm and revealed at the trial, a Renaissance *cassone*
was shipped to the New York branch from London, accompanied
by an invoice stating that its value was, let us say, a few thousand
dollars. This document was sent to the New York office of the
firm for Custom House purposes. At that time, John Quinn, the
famous lawyer and collector of contemporary art, had not yet
succeeded in getting removed the Federal import tax of twenty-
five percent on antiques. To avoid possible injury to valuable
fragile items at the Custom House, while being unpacked for
inspection and repacked for ultimate delivery and also to save
in the cost of handling, reputable firms could persuade the officials to open cases containing precious imports on the dealers'
own premises. When the examiner opened the case in the cellar
of Duveen's beautiful Fifth Avenue galleries and saw the bulky
cassone, he would probably not even ask the workmen to lift it
out for further inspection. A superficial glance at the object would

be sufficient to satisfy him before departing, that the invoice and valuation were in order and correct. Had he troubled to open the *cassone*, however, he might have found that it contained a priceless set of tapestries worth several hundred thousand dollars! If the examiner, by a remote chance, had discovered the contents, he would also find that the firm had protected itself in advance against punitive damages for attempted smuggling, by a very simple method. A few days after shipping the case, the London office had sent a letter to New York saying in substance that through the carelessness of a shipping clerk in London, some tapestries stored in the *cassone* had not been removed and were sent to America by mistake. Since they had not been ordered by the New York branch, the letter requested that they be returned to London without delay. As a matter of fact, if they were not discovered they would not be shipped back nor would any import duty be paid on them.

Similar methods were pursued for some time, and items of great value had been smuggled into America. After a long, costly litigation conducted by Stanchfield and Levy, Samuel Untermeyer was called in as consulting attorney. He shrewdly advised the firm to plead guilty. The whole affair was blamed on a junior member of the firm. The government's suit was settled on payment of one and a half million dollars cash as damages, but the scapegoat, a young member of the Duveen family, never came to America thereafter. It is said that Henry Clay Frick, a devoted friend and admirer of "Uncle Henry" Duveen, at that time a senior partner in the firm, offered to advance the sum needed to preserve the firm's existence, but the Duveens had sufficient funds.

The brilliant attorney, Samuel Untermeyer, whose advice was followed, was himself a collector of note. He owned Greystone, a magnificent estate on the Hudson, whose famous gardens had been decorated by Paul Manship. One of Mr. Untermeyer's pictures was the Whistler Nocturne that was the chief subject of dispute in the celebrated suit brought by the painter against Ruskin. Untermeyer wanted to have the painting cleaned, but I advised him not to make the attempt, for the bitumin used by the painter had already begun to run and the picture might have been completely ruined by a restorer. However, I urged him to engage David Rosen, now a recognized expert in this field, to attend to other pictures in his collection, and I recall that when Rosen began work in my presence on what were supposed to be two Siennese primitives, we found that these were painted on panels over two typical eighteenth-century works by the interesting Venetian Magnasco.

I do not know what fee Mr. Untermeyer received from the Duveen firm for helping to settle the government's lawsuit, but it must have been a considerable sum, for the cost of maintaining his greenhouses and giving lavish outdoor concerts at which celebrated stars performed was enormous. One of Untermeyer's clients was the celebrated oculist and surgeon, Dr. John Wheeler, who successfully performed an operation that restored the eyesight of the King of Siam. Probably no other surgeon would have dared to undertake it, and the eminent specialist appealed to Mr. Untermeyer for advice when the time came to demand a fee from the fantastically wealthy oriental potentate, who, with his entourage, occupied entire floors of the hospital. Dr. Wheeler had made out a bill, leaving the amount due, blank. When he asked Untermeyer to suggest an adequate but not too great a sum, the lawyer took the slip of paper and in place of figures, wrote: "A king can do no wrong." It was then sent to the Siamese ruler, who returned it to Dr. Wheeler with a check for $250,000! The surgeon, in turn, not only gave a large portion of the money to the Harkness Pavilion where the operation was performed but sent his check for $50,000 to Samuel Untermeyer. From the Duveens, the distinguished lawyer must have received a comparatively handsome retainer.

We had ample opportunities for studying Joe's amazing methods, and although the story of the wrought iron gateways on the Stotesbury estate in Palm Beach has already been partly told by an anonymous writer in *The Nation,* I may be forgiven for outlining it briefly here.

It was generally known in trade circles that Lord Duveen had experienced dealers and experts to assist him in his activities. Tolentino, an Italian whom I once knew well, was engaged to attempt to corner the market in genuine "Savanarola" chairs, and after he had collected as many as were available they were described as excessively rare. Several of them were put up for sale at public auction and were bought in by Joe at excessively high prices to establish a market value for them. Only then were they offered to collectors of Italian pictures at still higher prices, to help furnish the harmonious environment that their pictures demanded.

Similar methods were used by dealers of etchings made by talented nineteenth-century masters. After the publication of a new print, one example would appear in a sale at Christie's or Sotheby's, where it would be bid up to a figure far beyond the published price. The news of such a sale spread like wildfire among collectors, and before long the remainder of the edition would become exhausted and the print for some time afterward, almost unobtainable. Furthermore, the problem of selling entire editions of the artist's future works was simplified.

When Lord Duveen was helping the Stotesburys to spend their great fortune and decorate their Palm Beach winter residence and its surrounding gardens, he employed an expert agent to travel about and secure the finest items in the market. On one of his visits to the Florida resort Lord Duveen was amazed to find that the gardens boasted a pair of magnificent Spanish gates that he had not furnished. Unknown to Joe, his agent had become acquainted with Mr. Stotesbury, and realizing that he would make a far greater profit for himself by selling items directly to the millionaire than by letting his lordship act as a middleman, he had sold the gates in question to Joe's client. He was soon to learn something new about his lordship's powers. Joe sought out Mr. Stotesbury and demanded to know who was ruining his labors in the garden by permitting such forgeries to be erected among his authentic items. On occasions like this, Joe's daring was really incomparable. When Mr. Stotesbury divulged the fact that they were acquired from Duveen's own agent or protegé, that unfortunate man was asked to come to Florida at once and defend himself. In the meanwhile, the agent had been instructed to admit Joe's supremacy as an expert and remove the gates, but he had also been assured that his own interest would be taken

care of. The gates were removed and sent to New York, but to
Mr. Stotesbury's surprise, a few weeks later, they were again
erected in the Florida gardens.

Joe's explanation was astounding! When he had first observed
these masterpieces of metallurgical art, he was convinced that
they were forgeries because he had never before seen any gates
so fine! On studying them more carefully, however, in New York,
and tracing their provenance, he was amazed to find that they
were indeed genuine priceless treasures, and he humbly had to
admit that for once he had been mistaken. Naturally, he immediately secured them for Mr. Stotesbury. The financier swallowed
Joe's subterfuge hook, line and sinker, and Joe continued to supply the Stotesburys with pictures and garden ornaments for vast
sums.

Still another example of Joe's shrewdness, daring, and clever
showmanship began with his theatrical entrance at Christie's
rooms just as the great Oppenheim sale of drawings was about
to start. Every seat was occupied, and there was not an inch of
standing room. However, a chair prominently placed in the first
row, was being held for him by a messenger boy, and when he
strode toward it and took the seat the boy vacated, all eyes were
instantly focused on his lordship. The outstanding item at this
sale was a fine, small portrait drawing by an unknown master,
but it was attributed to Fouquet. The Countess Behague of Paris,
whose notable collection of drawings ranged from Durer to Ingres and Whistler, had crossed the Channel for the express purpose of acquiring this excellent French drawing. She sat not far
from Lord Duveen, and when she began to bid against him it soon
became apparent that salesroom fireworks were about to ex-
plode. She held out bravely until ten thousand guineas was
reached, but she gave in when her rival bid that sum, hitherto
unequaled at the public sale of a drawing. Joe told me that it was
really a bargain at that price, for the news of his victory was
heralded all over the world, and the publicity he received was
worth much more. In turn, I told him that the amount paid for
the Oppenheim Fouquet was perhaps exceeded centuries ago
when the almost legendary Shah Jehan paid the greatest Persian
miniaturist Bihzad, three thousand gold rupees for an illustrated

manuscript, a sum in our money far in excess of the price Joe paid for his acquisition. In any case, it was cheap compared to the sums occasionally paid for a rare postage stamp or a black tulip. Another high-priced drawing, Michelangelo's study for one of the sybils on the ceiling of the Sistine Chapel, was offered us by Signor Beruete for ten thousand dollars, but my senior partner did not care to embark on the field of old-master drawings, the authenticity of which had to be endorsed by the opinion of experts. Fortunately, the Michelangelo drawing subsequently became one of the gems in the collection of the Metropolitan Museum of Art.

The stories of the Fouquet and the Michelangelo drawings call to mind my experience with another old-master drawing sold at the memorable Strauss sale in Paris after I had retired from Scott and Fowles. Lady Mendl, George Blumenthal and other European and American collectors of like prominence were in the crowded salesroom to bid for the choicest items. I had little hope of competing with such rivals, and I decided to concentrate on a single item. This was a very fine drawing by the French sculptor Houdon, on the reverse of which was pasted an original letter by the sculptor explaining the meaning and purpose of his design. Some of the great Fragonard drawings, each bringing over a half-million francs, were sold just before the Houdon was reached, and there was such a buzz of astonishment after the sale of each Fragonard that when the Houdon was put up on the easel, apparently no one but I paid any attention to it. I sat immediately under the eyes of the auctioneer who recognized and accepted my modest initial bid and then rapped for order. When he was ignored, and the commotion in the audience became even more disturbing, the irritated auctioneer, to my amazement and delight, first knocked down the Houdon to me for my unchallenged first bid, and then made a speech demanding quiet. However, I was already the fortunate owner of the one thing I wanted in that sale, and I left the salesroom in high spirits soon afterward.

I had seen this remarkable item in Versailles, at the Centenary Exhibition of the great sculptor, who had made the well-known portrait of Washington in marble. When I visited the Versailles exhibition I learned that only one other drawing by Houdon was said to be known, and that it was not comparable to my prize.

Never having dreamed that this all but unique item would ever come into my possession, I decided then and there that my friend Mrs. Gustave Radeke (born Metcalf), who was president of the Rhode Island School of Design, would be the person to whom I would offer it, for Grenville Winthrop was not buying eighteenth-century art.

Very early on the morning of the day following the sale, Richard Owen, a dealer on the Left Bank, called to see me. Without any preliminary explanation he said he had come to buy the Houdon and would pay me a good price for it.

"But Owen," I replied, "I am not offering the drawing for sale."

"Oh," he said, rather disdainfully, "everything is for sale at a price. Besides," he added rather insolently, "you would not have acquired it had not Elsie DeWolfe (Lady Mendl) been talking to me and had I not been distracted by the noise following the sale of the Fragonards. In short, I did not know that the Houdon was being sold."

"You were unfortunate," I said, "since the drawing in question is no longer in the market."

"Well," he replied in a peevish tone, "I see that I must lay my cards on the table. I had an unlimited bid from an important client of mine for that drawing, and I must have it, even though you will demand an exorbitant price."

I was becoming irritated by his manner and said with finality, "You are wasting your time and mine. I am not demanding an exorbitant price. You simply cannot have the drawing. It is even now in the hands of Pottier, my *emballeur,* or perhaps already on its way to America."

He left me in anger, but sometime later he asked me to come to his shop to look at some very important nineteenth-century drawings that he knew I was searching for and which he did not really want, for he was known as a specialist in eighteenth-century masters. I accepted his invitation, and he first showed me two works by Ingres, very beautifully mounted in blue eighteenth-century-style mats and appropriately framed in finely carved gilt frames in the style of the period. I at once recognized the subjects because lithographs of them had been disposed of at the recent Lapauze sale. Owen told me he had obtained these drawings from the descendants of the subjects. I asked him to permit me to remove them from the frame so that I could examine them without a covering of glass.

"But why?" he questioned. "The drawings are protected by *passe partout* mounts, and surely you don't doubt their authenticity."

But I insisted that I would not consider buying such expensive items—he demanded over six thousand dollars for one of them—unless I could examine them without their glass covering. At last he carelessly permitted me to unframe the drawings, and I soon found that they were lithographs, lightly touched up with *mine de plomb*.

I told him all this, and that they were worth only a few dollars each! I also remarked that the lithographs naturally could not be erased. Would he try erasing them? In his anger and embarrassment he quite forgot that he had told me he had bought them from the descendants of a distinguished family. Now he said that he had acquired them from a total stranger who had walked into the gallery, and that he had bought them without careful examination. He evidently had ignored the fact that the new mats and frames would arouse suspicion. He even thanked me for my discovery, for he might otherwise have offered them to some innocent amateur, he said. "But now," he calmly continued, "I will show you something you really want. I will let you have them because, as I have said, they are nineteenth-century items."

He then showed me some vulgar, erotic watercolors, and another item, obviously a forgery, a line of heads of lawyers, all attributed to Daumier. While he was commenting on their wonderful quality I suddenly realized that one of the heads was a copy of a head reproduced by Fuchs, in his *catalogue raisonnée* of Daumier's work. It did not take me long to conclude that all of them were by some dishonest copyist or imitator. I did not want to argue with Owen, but he insisted on my opinion. Did I think they were not right?

I then said, "Owen, I assure you they are not right, and I advise you not to offer them to anyone."

"Why," he shouted angrily, "you are ridiculous! I was told you are an authority on nineteenth-century drawings. And here you are questioning works which the celebrated Forain assured me were great Daumiers."

I looked him straight in the eye and said sarcastically, "Too bad—surely you have read the sad news in today's papers that Forain died yesterday morning. But even if he were still alive and stood here, and would tell me that these are by Daumier, I would contest his statement and advise him to continue making his brilliant journalistic drawings and not to try to pose as an art expert. These drawings are obviously not by Daumier."

We saw no more of each other, but a few months later Philip Hofer, then connected with the Morgan Library went into Richard Owen's gallery and turned down these same drawings. The dealer, knowing that I had formerly advised Mr. Hofer on certain occasions, wrongly jumped to the conclusion that I had warned him against these particular forgeries, and he became my bitter enemy. I believe it was Professor Paul Sachs of the Fogg Art Museum who about this time, innocently introduced Owen to Oscar Strauss, our American ambassador. Mr. Strauss bought a number of forgeries of eighteenth-century drawings from the dealer at very high prices. He invited experts to admire them, and when they told his excellency that he had been defrauded, he demanded a refund from Owen, but the dealer claimed that he had already spent the money. As a result of the unsavory transaction, Owen was forced to close his shop, and left France for New York and Hollywood, far richer fields than Paris for his activities.

While I was traveling in Europe, Lord Duveen, always on the lookout for lesser fry who might be of service to him, was completely taken in by this pretentious dealer and allowed him to arrange an exhibition of drawings at the building, now demolished, on the corner of West Fifty-sixth Street and Fifth Avenue. I was in Europe at the time. Mr. Winthrop was persuaded to visit the exhibit, and he bought a watercolor that was sold as a Barye. It was such an obvious fake that Harold Woodbury Parsons, who had introduced Owen to Winthrop, insisted that Owen return the purchase price. The dealer again claimed that he had no cash on hand, but would give a fine Delacroix drawing in exchange. The drawing in question was a genuine tracing from the Delacroix studio, on *papier calque*, and was worth a few dollars at that time. I felt keenly chagrined that my friend Grenville Winthrop, who had paid several thousand dollars for the false Barye, could still be fooled by such a poor imitation although he already owned a magnificent group of watercolors by the great *animalier* and had feasted his eyes on genuine masterpieces.

After Charles Ricketts, trustee of the National Gallery in London, had seen the Winthrop Collection, he complimented us because he did not find a single doubtful item at 15 East 81st Street, with the possible exception of a fine dramatic composition that might be a Fuseli, not a Blake.

Ricketts did not know that ordinarily when Mr. Winthrop found he had been imposed upon he did not hasten to return the questionable work. He preferred to suffer the money loss and keep a forgery, regarding such a transaction as a costly but useful lesson, and he gradually accumulated quite a number of such not altogether worthless curiosities. In fact, he enjoyed confusing so-called experts by submitting his false Chinese jades—which were difficult to distinguish from genuine antiques—to such visitors. He had secured some false items made of actual antique material, and I remember one great Chinese authority who, in the course of his visit to 15 East 81st Street, studied the incomparable Tomb Jades and declared that one was a modern copy, after shutting his eyes and passing his sensitive fingertips over the surface of the work in question. Mr. Winthrop was not often victimized, and it was he who discovered that a large collection of questionable material was being impressively shown at the American Museum of Natural History, the gift of a benefactor of the institution who had been imposed upon by unscrupulous dealers. Volumes have, of course, been devoted to the subject of forgeries, and we could add many interesting pages, but this book is not the place for them. Besides, the false examples of the work of Ingres and Daumier already referred to, my associates and I discovered many forgeries of Whistler, Beardsley, Renoir,

Rodin and Goya, which from time to time were offered to us or were put up for auction.

New compositions created by copyists of Daumier and Beardsley and false imitations of Bakst designs actually reproduced and published in journals during Bakst's lifetime were among my finds, and I was indeed fortunate never to be caught by such criminal methods. One danger against which collectors should be on guard are original works by artists whose works resemble those of greater contemporaries. The paintings of the talented Eugenio Lucas, for instance, might be passed off as the creations of the genius Goya, whose works they superficially resemble, and in a somewhat similar category many watercolors offered as *instantanées* by Rodin were imitations by a dishonest person in the great sculptor's entourage. False pastels by Whistler have often been sold at public auction, and I know of one such group that was described as having been the property of Henry Irving who of course was dead at the time of the sale. Lastly I may mention a large group of false small unfinished works offered as having come from Renoir's studio, which were withdrawn from sale by an auctioneer after my protests.

I did not set myself difficult problems in detection but relied chiefly on swift intuitions and my familiarity with an artist's calligraphy.

While engaged in building up Mr. Winthrop's collection I was haled into the Special Customs House Court that handles importations and taxes, because a costly portrait of Paderewski by Burne-Jones was unsigned. I had offered no proof that it was an original work by the artist, and it was claimed that the portrait was subject to a duty of twenty-five per cent. When the case was called I asked the Judge whether I might act as my own attorney, and talk freely on the witness stand. Permission being granted, I began my defense by saying that undoubtedly there were days on which the judge received several hundred letters, advertisements and requests from charitable organizations in his morning's mail.

"Naturally," I continued, "Your Honor runs through this correspondence rapidly, throwing much of it into the waste basket without even opening some of the envelopes. Finally, let us as-

LEOPOLD AND MARY BIRNBAUM, THE AUTHOR'S PARENTS
From a painting by Joel Levitt

MRS. ANNIE BERTRAM WEBB

MRS. LEONARD WEBER

NORMAN DOUGLAS IN FLORENCE
Photo by Martin Birnbaum

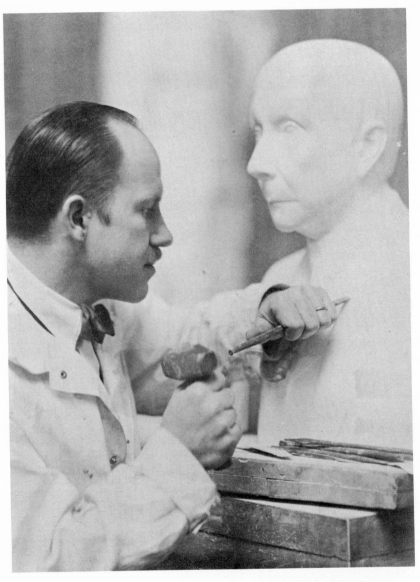

PAUL MANSHIP WITH HIS BUST OF JOHN D. ROCKEFELLER

BARTLETT ARKELL
*From a painting by
Leonebel Jacobs*

THOMAS COCHRAN
*From the bust by
Paul Manship*

133

SIR WILLIAM ROTHENSTEIN
Self-portrait, Metropolitan Museum

to Martin Birnbaum
a friendly memento
Edmund Dulac

LÉON BAKST 1921

G Edmund Dulac

LEON BAKST
Caricature by Edmund Dulac

135

Bernard Berenson

136

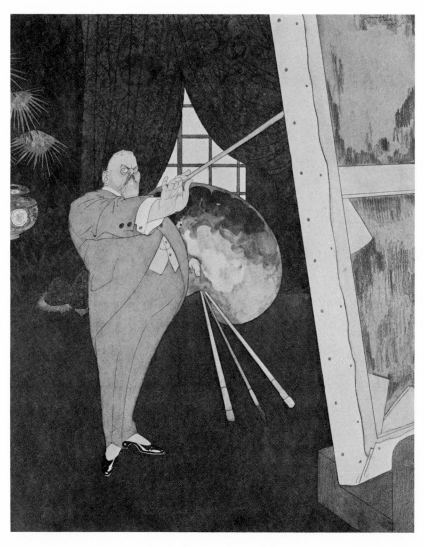

JOHN SINGER SARGENT
Caricature by Edmund Dulac

MAURICE STERNE, ALFRED POTTERTON, MARTIN BIRNBAUM,
EDWARD BRUCE, AND LEO STEIN IN ANTICOLI CORRADO

ELIE NADELMAN

Lord Joseph Duveen

Stevenson Scott

GRENVILLE LINDALL WINTHROP

Edmund Dulac

AUGUSTUS JOHN
Photo by Arnold Genthe

143

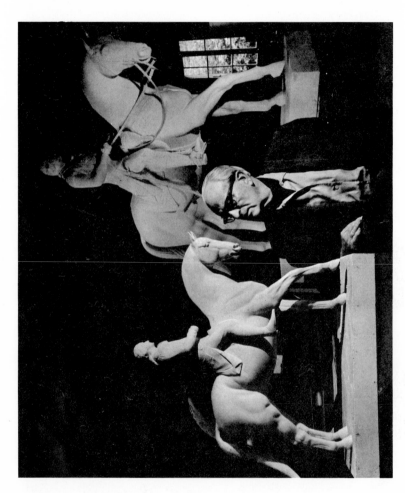

HERBERT HASELTINE WITH MODELS OF HIS GEORGE WASHINGTON

144

CECILIA BEAUX

145

GARI MELCHERS

ROBERT CHANLER

146

ALBERT STERNER

147

DESPIAU IN HIS PARIS STUDIO

148

HERBERT CROWLEY
From a Bas-relief by Mowbray Clark

ALEISTER CROWLEY
From a drawing by Augustus John

Mrs. Gustave Radeke

151

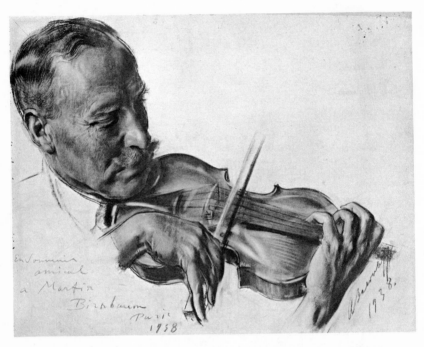

MARTIN BIRNBAUM WITH VIOLIN
From a drawing by Alexander Jacovleff

sume you came to a letter addressed in a handwriting that you recognize at once as your wife's. You did not see her write it, yet you would be ready to stake your life on the correctness of your assumption. Unquestionable familiarity with your wife's handwriting is the sole reason you are able to give for your conclusion, yet it would probably be quite a simple matter to copy or forge your wife's style of handwriting and its mannerisms. Now, for many years I have studied hundreds of drawings and sketchbooks of Burne-Jones. These works are in his inimitable handwriting, far more difficult to forge or imitate than your wife's script. So thoroughly has my eye absorbed the qualities of Burne-Jones's most casual drawings that I am prepared unhesitatingly to pay thousands of dollars for an unsigned masterpiece like this portrait of Paderewski, although I was not present when the artist made it. A forged copy of his monogram would be the easiest thing to add, but I can instantly pick out a genuine work of his from among thousands of unsigned drawings."

The case was decided in my favor and dismissed.

When I joined the firm of Scott and Fowles, such modern masters as Manet, Whistler, Sargent, Winslow Homer, Ingres, Degas and Renoir were rarely handled by the firm. I continually pestered my senior partner to find great examples by these painters, and one day Stevenson asked me whether we ought to acquire a large full-length portrait by Whistler, for our stock. It was known as *The Pink Girl* in England.

Although it was not one of my favorite pictures by the "Butterfly," I was willing to take the risk of handling it. Lord Duveen knew the owner, and when Scott suggested that he acquire the painting for us, his interest in the financial possibilities of the transaction was aroused. He agreed to purchase it, but he insisted on having a half share in the picture. I should explain that it was frequently the custom for two or even more dealers to purchase a notable canvas in common. In the first place, it testified to the good reputation, importance and quality of the painting, a comforting assurance to the rival owners. Moreover, the dealer who sold it would get the larger share of the profits. Lord Duveen

had been taking careful note of my enthusiasms, and when he
learned that I too could sell a Gainsborough for a price running
into six figures, his praise of my ability began to grow lukewarm,
even when he owned a half share of the painting I had sold.

One morning, Stevenson informed me that the Whistler had
finally arrived in America but that Joe was holding on to it, thinking he could sell it without difficulty and make a handsome
profit. Scott, who had slight respect for my business instinct, had
kept the purchase price to himself, fearing that my enthusiasm
would fade when I found I was expected to sell an item for what
I probably would think was an exorbitant price. Not long afterward, I read with astonishment on the front page of the *New
York Times,* that Lord Duveen, whose taste and genius were
extolled, had sold *The Pink Girl* to Mr. Henry Clay Frick for
"about" two hundred thousand dollars! The vague, fictitious price
surprised but did not sadden me, for I assumed that the huge
profit would help to make me economically independent.

When I saw Scott at the office, he warned me that not everything in the *Times*—especially a picture price—was correct, and
I had better not spend my share of the profits on this particular
painting in advance.

The sensational account of the sale was cabled to the *London
Times,* and naturally caught the eye of the former owner. When
he read the amount the picture was said to have been sold for and
calculated the profit, he was enraged. He immediately dispatched
a letter to Frick, telling him the actual low price for which he had
been persuaded to sell *The Pink Girl* by Lord Duveen, and pointing out the enormous profit the shrewd art dealer had made on
the transaction, for of course the former English owner assumed
that the amount quoted by the newspaper was correct. On receiving this letter, Mr. Frick, who had not yet paid any part of
the purchase price, telephoned to Joe and asked him to come to
see him. Suspecting nothing, Joe went to the Frick residence immediately and was handed the embarrassing epistle without
delay.

I was not a witness to Joe's defense, but he actually boasted
of it to Scott, who told me the whole story. It is easy to quote
Joe's extravagant vocabulary and to hit off the tone of his voice.

What follows therefore, is not an entirely imaginary conversation between the two men, invented by my senior partner; Joe thought it would vastly amuse his bosom friend, Scott, to learn how brilliantly he turned the devastating situation to his own advantage, for after all, Frick was his client and Birnbaum was still too young and inexperienced, as Joe put it, to be entrusted with the handling of such important collectors.

On reading the incriminating letter that Mr. Frick handed him after greeting Joe in a bantering tone, surprise is too feeble a word to express Joe's state of mind, but like a flash his genius rose to the occasion.

"My dear friend," he exclaimed without hesitation, "I am simply delighted that the former owner sent you this letter, for now I can tell you the real facts, which until this moment, you will readily understand, I was not at liberty to do." Beaming at Frick and working his favorite adjective, he continued without pause. "This *marvelous* picture was not altogether mine. I only owned a share in it, and Martin Birnbaum wanted to sell it to Mr. Charles P. Taft. But I had it in my possession and was determined that such a masterpiece would grace no collection but yours. Birnbaum, however, claimed that he would obtain several hundred thousand dollars for it, and that nothing less would be accepted by Scott and Fowles. I was, therefore, obliged, against my will I assure you, to demand this sum from you. Now, however, we have Birnbaum where we want him. If you were to return this picture, no other collector would buy it, for it has been widely reported as your recent purchase. Prospective purchasers would assume that there is something wrong with the picture if it is unworthy of your collection, and since you have not paid for it, all you have to do now, my friend, knowing what it cost us, is to name what you think is a fair price, no matter how small an advance on our original cost, and the masterpiece will remain yours."

The picture, of course, never left the Frick collection, and Scott and Fowles' one-third share of the profit was not epoch-making. But Mr. Frick never bought anything from Martin Birnbaum after that episode.

To show further how impudent Lord Duveen could be and how

strong a hold he had on the affections of Mr. Frick, an amusing but authentic story of their relations is current. I repeat it at the risk of earning a reputation for frivolity but it is certainly entertaining.

Duveen's firm did not send a bill to Mr. Frick immediately after each purchase, they waited until the end of each year and then submitted a statement of their annual transactions. The amount often ran into millions, and on one occasion a dispute arose between the two men about the correctness of the sum due. The amount in question was one hundred thousand dollars, and their polite arguments ended only in heated irritation. Finally, to put an end to the disputation, Joe, with colossal impertinence, smiled at the financier and with perfect composure said, "Why, my friend, I wouldn't kiss your ass for a mere hundred thousand dollars!"

"Indeed, Sir Joseph," replied Mr. Frick turning the tables on his lordship. "Well, what *is* your price?"

The story of *The Pink Girl* calls to mind Whistler's biographer, the excellent etcher, Joseph Pennell. Many were the tales he told me when I visited his studio overlooking London and the Thames, while we sipped vermouth, Pennell's favorite beverage, of which he consumed extraordinary quantities. He rather resented my publishing in one of my earliest essays a Conder-Whistler anecdote that he had till then never heard, and which he claimed could therefore not be true! But it appeared without credit, in later editions of his *Life of Whistler*. He was guilty of a much more curious and serious error when he came to see me in New York and I showed him the second nocturne of the Cremorne Gardens, now in the Winthrop collection at Harvard. The bitumin used by the painter had made ugly streaks in parts of the painting, and I showed it to Pennell, hoping he would suggest some way to save and restore this interesting example. To my amazement, Pennell asserted that it was not painted by Whistler at all! My arguments did not prevail until I brought out a copy of his own standard book on the Butterfly and showed him a full-page reproduction of the picture and its unassailable provenance, proving that Pennell himself had alluded to it as an important item in the great memorial exhibition held in London after Whistler's death! I should add that during this strange interview, as far I could see, Pennell was not under the influence of vermouth.

While Duveen was still able to rise from his sickbed in London, he asked me to accompany him to the British Museum to see the fine marble building he had given the nation in which to house the Elgin marbles. With Gisela Richter, the gifted honorary curator of the classical division of the Metropolitan Museum, I had already seen one of the divine fragments, which had been cleaned in accordance with Lord Duveen's instructions, and we both felt that the marble was greatly improved. At last one could imagine how beautiful the Elgin marbles had been when they were created by Phidias and his assistants.

As a matter of fact, the field of Hellenistic art was not one in which Lord Duveen could boast of any special knowledge. He was responsible for the loss of the great seated goddess, which I went to see with Wilhelm Valentiner and Paul Manship shortly after it was shown to the public in the museum at Berlin. It had first been offered to Lord Duveen, but he turned it down because small unimportant pieces of the fifth century B.C. marble had been chipped off and lost!

When I paid my visit to the noble structure in London with the donor, some of the sculptures from the Acropolis were already in place, and Duveen asked my opinion of what had been accomplished. Naturally I had only words of praise for the beautiful building and his lordship's generosity, but to my way of thinking none of the fragments except the bas reliefs should be permanently attached to the walls; the marbles belonged originally to the Athenian Acropolis and with a few exceptions, they should be shown in London with the walls of the new building as a mere background. Students could then use their imagination and reconstruct the glorious original setting. Joe at once agreed and had the curator called into the great hall. His lordship was already too weak to stand up, but he rudely criticized the niche in which one of the sculptures rested, and repeated some of my phrases almost verbatim. Later, I learned that the director of the British Museum had resigned in protest against Duveen's dictatorial interference. Bitter controversies arose about the methods used to clean the marbles, and it was whispered that the resulting scandal would prevent the King from opening the building, at the dedication. The museum was bombed during the war and repairs had not yet been completed when I paid my last visit. It was a keen disappointment for the dying man. His illness grew steadily worse, and he died in May 1939.

Colin Agnew and I went to the funeral services held in an orthodox synagogue filled with lords and ladies. The former were obliged to wear their silk toppers, in accordance with Jewish orthodox ritual, and after an extravagantly fulsome and panegyrical eulogy, which bordered on the ridiculous, Joe's body was followed to the cemetery by a throng of titled aristocrats with whom he had loved to associate. His father and "Uncle Henry" and their respective wives already rested under huge slabs of jet-black polished marble, on a perfect velvety-green English lawn. He was buried beside them in quite the most dignified and beautiful cemetery enclosure I have ever seen.

Lord Duveen's death and the advent of high income taxes brought a temporary end to the epoch of high prices in the history of art collecting. A new generation of buyers, however, carried away by the persuasive powers of dealers are now paying very high, even vertiginous sums for the works of Cézanne, Van Gogh, Picasso, Renoir, Seurat, Matisse, Rouault, Gauguin, and other artists of the nineteenth and twentieth centuries.

Before we moved from the west side of Fifth Avenue I had undertaken to arrange a small salon of contemporary American art which I hoped would become an annual feature at the Scott and Fowles galleries. I wanted to prove that the Academy exhibitions were unnecessarily dull. They were regularly damned, or almost ignored, by the sprightly critic of the *New York Sun*, my venerable friend Henry McBride, who had begun his journalistic career on the *Sun's* staff, as assistant to Sam Swift (at my suggestion).

My plan was to visit the salient figures in our artistic community and ask them to let me choose one or more of their works that had not yet been publicly shown. When I had collected more than sufficient material, I decided to exhibit only those items that would hang harmoniously together in our intimate rooms, before returning the rest to the artists. A considerable stir was created when my plans were announced and I was brought into touch with men whom I knew till then only by name. For example, I wanted a screen by Robert Chanler, an abstract flame-like wood carving by Robert Laurent, new candlesticks by Manship, a large meticulously painted portrait by Cartotto, a newcomer, a still life by Henry Golden Dearth, a flower piece by Maurice Sterne, and of course, examples of the art of Alden Weir and Gari Melchers, the presidents of the two rival groups of painters. Scott, as usual, had doubts about the wisdom of such an undertaking, for a great deal of time would be wasted paying visits to studios and little if anything could be expected in the way of financial returns. He also warned me that I was looking for trouble, for I might make powerful enemies if I took no notice of some popular academicians. As usual, he was right.

My first visit was paid to Alden Weir, who offered me a charming flower piece. My second call was on Gari Melchers, at his Beaux Arts studio, where I interrupted him while he was painting a head of his favorite red-headed model. He was suffering from gout and one of his feet rested on a low chair in front of his easel. He already knew the purpose of my visit and asked me to pick out anything from among the many paintings that were stacked against the walls. I decided on a large, unframed brilliantly colored still life of fruit and flowers. The main color note was struck by a slice of ripe, crimson melon, and the canvas would hardly have been recognized by the admirers of Melchers' popular, ably painted figure pieces. He was delighted with my unconventional choice, and promised to send it on after he had it framed fittingly. When all the offered works were assembled, I found, to my embarrassment, that I could find no room for this large item, and furthermore the powerful crimson in the composition was entirely out of key with the more subdued tones of the other pictures. I tried vainly to choose adjoining pictures that would at least make one wall a harmonious unit, but I finally gave up the attempt and decided not to hang Mr. Melchers' offering. I returned it hesitatingly, with as profound an apology as I could muster. In due course, the little salon was favorably

reviewed, especially by Frank Crowinshield in *Vanity Fair,* and
soon passed from my memory. Mr. Melchers never acknowledged
the return of his picture, and Scott reminded me that I had succeeded in making another powerful enemy. Fortunately he was
mistaken.

Some years later, Melchers, as chairman of the committee that
was advising Mr. Mellon when he was contemplating the foundation of a great museum, recalled my honesty, taste and courage
when I refused to hang his still life and wrote a letter to me which
I shall always treasure with pardonable pride.

Washington, April 3, 1930

My dear Birnbaum,

This is only a hasty note that I am writing between two sittings
of a portrait. The Secretary of the Treasury, Mr. Mellon, has just
left me—and will be here again in an hour.

First let me thank you for the card you sent me from Egypt
some time ago—and I am so glad that you are having such a really
fine time!

Last evening I dined with my good friends the Parmelees, and
from Mr. Parmelee I learn that he has kept you informed on just
what the situation is here. I refer to the National Gallery of Art.
Dr. Abbot has confided to me that the actual realization of the
new building is very near—and that the question of the new director is not to be pressed at the present moment. However, let me
say to you right now that you are now, as before, the one candi-
date for this position in my mind—and I honestly believe Abbot
feels exactly the same way. In fact, no other names are being
mentioned, and nothing is being said or made public, about this
whole business. Dr. Abbot is out of town and returns here in a
week, when I will see him. My portrait of Mr. M. is only begun.
We started yesterday, but it is quite possible that before we finish
he will have something to say—as yet only impersonal matters are
the subjects of our conversations, and he, of course, is very de-
sirous not in the slightest way to have anybody know or discuss
his plans—and naturally I will never even mention the word National Gallery—unless he does so first. Now, just sit tight, as I
am, and let us wait. Mr. Parmelee tells me that he has just had a
nice letter from you, in fact he read it to me—and the thought of
your buying a home in Greece must not be even considered by
you for a single moment, no indeed, nothing of the sort can be
thought of now. But wait, and stick by me, as I am going to stick
by you, in this most important question.

This hasty note you must forgive—but I wanted to send you hearty greetings, good wishes, and all sorts of good things.

Always faithfully yours,
Gari Melchers

In due course Mellon made his own admirable choice without further consulting the above-mentioned committee.

In the meantime I was innocently getting into hot water with another artist, and Scott had good reason for concluding that at last I would be taught an unforgettable lesson and thereafter would devote my time to old masters, or at least to artists who were dead and who could not torment me with their artistic temperaments and sensitiveness. Here again I am telling stories about a highly gifted man now deceased, and I hope I shall not be misunderstood for recording these facts.

One of the artists whom I was anxious to include in my salon was the Bulgarian-born Parisian, Jules Pascin, whose works I had shown at the Berlin Photographic Gallery. I already knew that Pascin was a man with delicately adjusted nerves, and that one could not be too careful in dealing with him.

The first breach between us had occurred shortly after his arrival in America. As a total stranger to our shores, he was treated by me with what I thought was marked cordiality. To discuss the details of his coming exhibition I invited him day after day to lunch at the excellent restaurant managed by the Bustanoby brothers in the Beaux Arts building at West Fortieth Street and Sixth Avenue. One morning, when unsuspectingly I again suggested luncheon, the storm burst. "Do you take me for a hungry, penniless beggar, always asking me to eat with you?" he angrily exclaimed, and he left me abruptly without giving me an opportunity to proclaim my innocence.

A more serious rupture now occurred when I was arranging the little salon that is the subject of these paragraphs. Knowing that he was never guilty of perfunctory platitudinous performances, I paid a visit to Pascin's studio, and after I had explained my needs, he handed me a folio and I chose a group of his watercolors of half-dressed or nude girls, lolling about in careless or expectant attitudes on a chaise longue or in bed. The watercolors were unframed, and I promised the artist to attend to that detail. While I was busy hanging my exhibition on the morning of the day set for the opening, two women, who I afterward learned were Pascin's intimate friends, strolled into the gallery. After a survey of all the works already hung, they walked out again. At the time of their visit I was still awaiting the arrival of Pascin's drawings from our framer, and they did not reach me until an hour before the public came streaming in. Spaces on the walls had been left vacant for these items, however, and hanging them just in time was a simple problem.

The next day, Scott received a rude personal note from the artist beginning, "That fellow Birnbaum came and took my time and asked me for some of my works, which I am told he has not hung in your exhibition. I want them returned to me immediately."

Scott was delighted, for he was eager to have me learn a few business lessons. He removed the works in question without consulting me, and sent them back, accompanied by a letter saying that the artist had been misinformed. The drawings had indeed been hung, but in the writer's opinion the exhibit would not suffer if they were removed and pursuant to his wishes they were being returned with Scott's letter. As a matter of fact, in the interim the critics and reviewers had seen them in their allotted places on our walls and had commented in print on the works of Pascin, who must have been mystified, but I never learned what his reaction was on learning the facts.

Not long afterward this richly endowed artist committed suicide by hanging. I have never ceased to admire Pascin's gifts, and I never bore him any ill-will. It was perhaps my fault that I did not weigh every detail of our personal encounters with greater care, for I always knew that, besides possessing unique powers, he was a human being sensitive to a fault.

Sometimes the sensitiveness of an artist, real or assumed, was sufficiently discouraging to prevent my entering into any relation with him. My difficulties with Diederich, Nadelman and Pascin were enough to hold me back from exhibiting another remarkable figure with whom I came in contact during the First World War, when continental artists took refuge in England. The failure of my negotiations with George Minne I shall always regret, for he has never been adequately introduced to America.

Lady Davis, whose husband, Sir Edmund, owned beautiful Chilham Castle, helped many of the refugees, and Ricketts persuaded me to go to see some of them in the country homes she had generously provided. One of these artists was Van de Woestyne, a talented meticulous Belgian painter with an aristocratic taste who had almost nothing to offer me, but the other was the celebrated sculptor George Minne, about whom Meier Graefe has a good deal to say in his *History of Modern Art*. Minne and his wife lived next door to their countryman, Van der Woestyne, but the two artists in exile did not even exchange polite greetings when they met.

Almost immediately after my arrival at Minne's temporary home, he and his wife complained bitterly that Lady Davis did not supply them with enough coal, although fuel was at that moment almost unobtainable and Chilham itself was far from comfortable. Minne had countless drawings scattered about, often made on odd scraps of paper. Many of them were slight original ideas, but I was pleased at the thought that there was ample material for an exhibition. I also planned to purchase a number of them outright and thus relieve the temporary obligation the Minnes were under to Lady Davis. An important autobiographical manuscript, written in French, was entrusted to me, and I promised that if I could find a publisher for a translation all the proceeds would go to the artist-author. To my astonishment, when I hesitatingly broached the subject of the price of some pencil drawings I had chosen from literally hundreds that covered every available shelf and table, the artist and his wife feigned surprise. Surely, they said, I would not separate the artist from these works, which he regarded as his children, his very flesh and blood! Naturally, I left without any further bargaining.

On the day set for my return to America, a registered parcel arrived by mail at my London address. It contained all the drawings I had set casually aside, and a letter from Madame Minne telling me that she had at last persuaded her husband, with the greatest difficulty, to part with these, his favorite "children." The price list enclosed was staggering. The cost of a single drawing was more than I was prepared to pay for the entire lot. Shannon and Ricketts had a good laugh at my expense, and I returned the drawings with a polite apologetic note, saying that I should have known that such unique treasures were beyond the reach of a modest collector like me.

Minne's austerity and surprising comprehension of monumental form were notable. His native talent, like Maeterlinck's and Verhaeren's, was the product of his Belgian environment at Gand. It is a pity that no American institution has ever exhibited his works.

Another artist whose work was prominently shown in the Scott and Fowles salon was Robert Chanler, one of the most picturesque figures in the art world at that time. The scion of an old American family, he lived a bohemian life, free from all inhibitions and social conventions. His screens, ornamented with themes inspired by his studies of undersea life, were known only to comparatively few people, although he had already decorated the ceiling and the walls of Mrs. Payne Whitney's bathroom in such a way that when she was in her tub she thought she had dived into the sea and was bathing in azure waters surrounded by the strange denizens of the deep.

I was anxious to secure one of Chanler's panels for the salon, and my first visit to his studio on East Nineteenth Street as an interested acquaintance soon ripened into genuine friendship. His collection of fresh-water aquaria which were to be seen in almost every room of the two adjoining houses he lived in, both owned by Mrs. Whitney, was one of the bonds between us. One of the first things he showed me was a graceful prize fantail goldfish. He had named it Lina, after his former wife, the lovely diva, Lina Cavalieri.

Bob Chanler, even when he was not quite sober, was a genial, lovable giant, and we got on famously together. His particular girl friend at the time, known to us only as "Redhead," seemed to like me, and the three of us went together to see a troupe of excellent Spanish dancers performing at a theater on Columbus Circle. Bob created a sensation in the crowded audience as well as among the performers, by standing up in the orchestra pit, gesticulating and shouting wildly, "Hola, Hola, Hola!" and throwing his hat at the gypsy girls on the stage as though he were at a bullfight in Spain.

I shall never forget his New Year's Day luncheon party to which I was invited, and asked to bring my fiddle. The front door of his home was open day and night, but I rang repeatedly until I was finally admitted by his Chinese butler. It was already well after one o'clock in the afternoon, but the Oriental, instead of announcing me, merely said, "Mr. Chanler upstairs in bed." Bob, who was not asleep and was evidently expecting me, called down, "Birnbaum, come up." I found him reclining in his bedroom and he told me that his guests were still sleeping after the New Year's Eve orgy. Many of the girls who had been there refused to leave until they were warned that the wives of all the men present would soon arrive and have everybody sent to jail!

In due course, the house guests as scantily arrayed as Pascin's models in a Polly Adler house, finally collected for luncheon in the dining room. John Gregory the talented sculptor, Aleister Crowley the wicked magician, and I, were the only guests properly dressed for a midday repast. Amid the screams of the gaudy blue-and-yellow macaw and Chanler's shouted orders, champagne was served in unlimited quantities, and I can recall no other course.

A few years later Chanler and I occupied adjoining studios in Paris in a building near the famous *Café du Dome* and we were patients at the same time in the American Hospital in Neuilly, where I underwent an operation under the hands of the brilliant surgeon, Dr. Thiery de Martel, who committed suicide when the Nazis invaded his beloved Paris. It was while Bob was being carried on a stretcher from the hospital that I last saw him alive.

Physically and in many other ways, Chanler reminded me of Seraphin Sudbinin, a handsome Russian giant who made a commercially unsuccessful debut in America a few years before

I came to know him. Although his talents were recognized, his fine work in lacquer and his highly original bronzes and marble busts failed to attract purchasers, and he was having a difficult time financially. One afternoon, the beautiful Minnie Ashley Chanler insisted that I go with her to Sudbinin's studio to see a recently completed heroic bust of John Barrymore as Hamlet. It was no ordinary achievement, and recalling my success with Paul Manship's portrait of John D. Rockefeller, I made arrangements to show the Barrymore bust in a room by itself, in a Renaissance setting.

Stephen Carlton Clark, one of our most discriminating collectors, was the first visitor to see Sudbinin's work. He was obviously impressed by the huge marble head, but wondered how one could use such a work of art. "Mr. Clark," I ventured to reply, "your distinguished father [Alfred Corning Clark] would never have asked that question. When he felt that a genuine artist needed encouragement whether he was a painter like Robert Blum or a prodigy like the pianist Joseph Hofman, he would buy his work or supply funds for the musician's support, without weighing the problem of their future." Mr. Clark evidently agreed with me, and bought the portrait of Barrymore.

Sudbinin was naturally gratified by Mr. Clark's purchase, but an even greater stroke of good fortune came his way. Andrew Mellon, accompanied by the genial Carman Messmore of the firm of Knoedler and Company, also came to see the bust, and the visit resulted in a commission to create a whole series of handsome heads and bas-reliefs of Mellon which I assume ultimately found their way into the various institutions in which Mellon was interested. Later, I saw the artist in Paris, stripped to the waist, working on those portraits in the open air. The tide of Sudbinin's fortunes had certainly turned. He received a tremendous commission to decorate the gardens of the Guggenheim estate on Long Island and then quite suddenly, after he was economically independent, he abandoned sculpture and became an outstanding ceramist. When I last saw him in his modest Parisian home, he was seriously ill, poisoned by the fumes from the ovens in which he baked his ceramics.

My relations with Stephen Carlton Clark did not begin with

the sale of Sudbinin's Barrymore. Back in the days when I had charge of the Berlin Photographic Company, I had given an exhibition of the works of Robert Blum, many of whose most important works were inherited from their father by Mr. Clark and his brothers, Ambrose and Robert Sterling Clark. Robert Clark was not only an independent collector of note, and founder of the fine museum at Williamstown, Massachusetts, but before his death he attracted attention as the owner of the winner of the English Derby. The taste of his brother Stephen, as I had occasion to learn, was not only catholic but kept changing and developing. He bought works by Sargent and Matisse, Delacroix and Cézanne, Segonzac and Ingres, then unexpectedly he would tire of an item, sell it, and experiment with the lasting qualities of an entirely novel phase of contemporary art. We went together to see the memorable exhibition of Delacroix in the Louvre, and on finding that a large picture of children playing with a strangely elongated horse was privately owned, he commissioned me to purchase it for him. However, it did not long remain in his collection. Even a masterpiece by Degas—the bronze dancer dressed in a real cotton costume with bows of silk ribbon in her hair—was sold to Grenville Winthrop, who also bought a watercolor by Ingres which Stephen Clark had at one time lent to the Metropolitan Museum. It was obvious that Clark had fallen under the spell of Cézanne and Matisse and had grown tired of traditional classic styles. Segonzac, with whom I wandered around Paris till we found Jacovleff's studio, sold me his best landscape for the Stephen Clark collection, and I think it still holds its place there.

In the course of my visits to Paris I learned that Jacques Blanche, who painted many English celebrities, owned a famous Manet, *The Girl with a Glove,* which hung in his large studio on the Rue du Docteur Blanche, a street named after his father. I was told that the picture was for sale and I cabled the information to Stephen Clark. Before deciding to acquire it he sailed for France expressly to see the picture and I arranged with Blanche— who had left Paris for his summer home on the coast—to have the valuable painting brought up from an underground vault, so that it would be ready for Clark's inspection. In spite of the painting's high price, it did not take Clark long to reach a decision, and

he returned to America immediately after authorizing me to purchase it.

I called up Monsieur Blanche on the long-distance telephone
to tell him the news, but the connection was very poor and we
could not understand each other. Accordingly, I took the early
morning train, intending to pay for the picture at once and then
return to Paris. To my surprise, my arrival was greeted almost
with tears by Madame Blanche. She had persuaded her husband,
after I accepted his offer, to refuse to sell the picture on the
ground that their friends knew that the Manet was bequeathed to
France in Blanche's will, and he would be disgraced if he sold
the picture to an American. Nothing that I said would now persuade them to change their minds, even though I pointed out
the moral and legal side of our controversy. Needless to say, I
regretted my failure and the trouble to which I had put Mr.
Clark, but I did not want to take legal action to enforce the contract. On my return to America, I found that Blanche had, after
all, sold the picture to an American dealer, using my name and
my accepted offer to secure a higher price than I had agreed
to pay.

Having already acquired a fine Rodin bronze and other small
items from Blanche for Mr. Winthrop, the visit to his summer
home was my last encounter with the artist. Besides a delightful
luncheon, I was rewarded with a sight of his wall decorations in
the local church, and a gift of some inscribed copies of his literary
works which are more interesting to me than his paintings. I still
read them occasionally with mixed emotions.

A number of other incidents reflecting credit on Mr. Clark's
relations with artists come to mind. When Augustus John was
exhibiting his work at the Scott and Fowles galleries, I was asked
to arrange sittings with John for a portrait of Mrs. Clark, one of
the most gracious and attractive American matrons. She had already sat for Orpen, but that portrait was a failure. I warned
Mrs. Clark that John after many sittings had slashed his portrait
of the wife of our Ambassador to Mexico because it failed to
satisfy him, and I also reminded her that Suggia's famous portrait
was not quite finished after seventy sittings. However, Mrs.
Clark braved all hazards; she bought new costumes and acces-

sories to meet John's demands; and the long series of sittings began. One day little Miss Clark met her mother at the studio, and John, struck by the child's charm, interrupted Mrs. Clark's sittings and insisted on painting her daughter. This painting turned out to be an unqualified success. The same cannot be said of Mrs. Clark's portrait. John remonstrated to me that she was "too beautiful"; he even threatened to destroy it and begin again, but Mr. Clark accepted it as a fine example of John's technique, although it certainly did not do the subject justice. With characteristic generosity, Mr. Clark remarked, "After all, I have the admirable portrait of my daughter."

Another typical incident in the course of my relations with Mr. Clark took place when I was collecting items for the retrospective exhibition of nineteenth-century European and American portrait painters for the Biennale at Venice. One of the pictures I was eager to secure was a full-length portrait by the great American realist Eakins, of Prof. Henry A. Rowland the physicist, who had once been a student at Phillips Academy in Andover, Massachusetts. This painting had been acquired by Mr. Clark from the artist's widow, and when Thomas Cochran, an outstanding benefactor of the school, heard that I was showing the picture in Venice, he asked me to try to buy it, so that it would become a part of the permanent collection in the fine building he had already given to Phillips Academy. I broached the subject to Clark but he refused to sell it, saying that Mrs. Eakins had once offered it to Cochran, but for some unknown reason the banker had refused to buy it. However, Clark added that if at any time in the future he should change his mind, he would offer it to Cochran for the original sum paid, plus the interest on the cost. Not very long afterward, when the fine gallery at Andover was opened to the public, one of its outstanding treasures hanging in a place of honor, was the Eakins portrait of Prof. Rowland, the gift of Stephen Carlton Clark.

Thomas Cochran's gifts to Andover were many, and some were princely benefactions. Cochran was also responsible for changing the location of the Arch of Constantine in the Tuileries Gardens of Paris, so that the view through the archway to the distant Arc de Triomphe, at the Etoile, would be in an unbroken unobstructed straight line. For this costly artistic gesture he was decorated by the French Government. I recall with pleasure a day before his last illness that Paul Manship and I spent with him at Chartres, studying the famous sculptures and the marvelous windows through our opera glasses, and ending the visit with a perfect luncheon at Chartres' most celebrated restaurant near the Cathedral. He envied our activities in the field of art, and told me that the day was one of the happiest in his memory.

After repeated failures and disappointments, Marchant, one of the most progressive English art dealers, finally arranged to have me meet Augustus John. I was relieved to find that the artist did not wear earrings like his friends the gipsies, with whom he enjoyed intimate associations. He was not anxious to meet an American art dealer, and I felt that he had accepted my invitation to lunch with considerable reluctance. After a drink or two, however, he began to thaw, realizing that I was a genuine admirer of his work, and not just another merchant bent on becoming a little richer at his expense. My arguments finally won the day, and he agreed to let me arrange an exhibition. That was in 1916. For a long time, however, we made little progress with our plans, although we corresponded quite regularly and discussed the matter in our letters.

Our relations became more and more friendly, and the details of his exhibition began to crystallize. One day John wrote me: "If Thursday will suit you and your fiddle, to come again, *I will be here.*"

Both my violin and I accepted this invitation and spent an interesting evening there with some of his friends and admiring young disciples. It developed into a memorable bohemian experience.

While I was playing some Hungarian *czigány* (gipsy) folksongs Guevara, a handsome young Peruvian artist, left the gathering. In a short time he returned accompanied by a woman who, to my amazement, entered the room in which we had gathered, completely nude. At the moment I was playing one of my brother's favorites, a wild gipsy air entitled "The Bagpipe Player" and the naked dancer started cavorting and gesticulating in a vain attempt to interpret the rhapsodic Magyar rhythms. She was none other than Lady Constance Richardson. Her high-kicking and astonishing performance only proved that Prince Troubetskoy's familiar little figure, a clever sketch in bronze, was indeed a faithful portrait of her, but as a dancer, as far as I was concerned, she was a ridiculous failure. Her nudity in a room filled with conventionally clad men and women was embarrassing, but John relieved the tension by executing some remarkable standing somersaults, evidence of his superb physical condition. He was then in his prime, handsome and vigorous and looked like a cross between Christ and Guy de Maupassant. The fine etched portrait of himself, known to collectors as *L'Homme Farouche,* was made a few years before I met him, but it was still a striking likeness.

I saw a good deal of John in London one summer. Once we met at a bar on Great Portland Street, where he wanted me to see the decorations of Wyndham Lewis, already known as a painter as well as a talented writer. There were no customers there except ourselves and a pretty young model who never uttered a single word in the course of the entire evening. The proprietor stood by to take orders, holding a tiny kitten in his arms. A magnum of champagne, already partly consumed, was on the table. I was hardly seated when I was startled by a meow of pain from the kitten. This was repeated at short intervals, and I soon discovered that the man was pinching the helpless animal's tail. I remonstrated, but the cruel fellow continued to amuse himself by torturing the kitten. I threatened to leave, but the brute only laughed, and another "meow" enraged me. Then John suddenly jumped to his feet and yelled at him, "Get out!" He fled from the bar, leaving us to examine the decorations. They were interesting, but the elongated designs reminded me of the Austrian genius Gustave Klimt, a leader in the Secession Movement, who was apparently unknown to John. By this time the magnum had been consumed, and John, visibly annoyed by my lack of appreciation, merely said, "Birnbaum, you know too damn much!" The evening was not a success.

At last, toward the end of 1922, all details for his show were agreed upon.

The exhibition was all I had hoped for. It contained many su-

perb drawings and portraits of Lawrence of Arabia and of the
strange Aleister Crowley, and was dominated by the fine portrait
of Suggia, at one time the wife of the incomparable cellist Pablo
Casals. Homer St. Gaudens, at that time the organizer of the international art exhibition held in Pittsburgh, was among the visitors.
That year he invited John to be on the jury and he also asked
us to send the painting of Suggia for the exhibition in Pittsburgh.
The portrait not only won first prize, but Lord Duveen promptly
purchased it from the owner, Mr. Clyde, and had it sent back
to London, a gift to the Tate Gallery.

It always reminds me of a portrait of myself playing the violin—
the last work of my lamented friend Jacovleff, made just before
his untimely death after an unsuccessful operation. The Russian
genius, however, finished his sanguine drawing in a single afternoon, during which I never stood still while improvising on my
Gottfried Hamm violin, whereas John demanded more than seventy sittings from Suggia and claimed that the painting was
never finished. When the Suggia arrived in London, the art
students in Chelsea carried it in triumphant procession through
the streets, imitating the religious worshippers of the Madonna
during the Renaissance.

On arriving in America, John, the gifted Ambrose McEvoy,
Pascin, and other European artists, as well as the Mexican painter
Diego Rivera, whom I once entertained in a Negro cabaret, became very enthusiastic about the stimulating exhilarating atmosphere of New York. John was especially excited after his frequent
visits to Harlem. About this time his health began to run down.
A large carbuncle—fortunately not maligant—formed on his brow,
and my nephew, the late Dr. Jerome Martin Ziegler, removed it.
The artist afterward presented him with an attractive, though
rather academic, portrait of a pretty Harlem Negro woman.

I felt it my duty, when not otherwise engaged, to show John
something of the city, and I recall how keenly he enjoyed our
first luncheon, at which I introduced him to New England clam
chowder and an avocado pear. I also advised him to read Mel-
ville's description of a chowder in *Moby Dick*.

Together we went to see the successful dramatization of *Rain*,
which rather bored John although he was a great admirer of

Somerset Maugham's short story. A more successful evening was spent at the Ringling Circus. The simultaneous performances in three rings confused him but the side show of freaks in the basement fascinated him and he gazed silently for a long time at a giantess whose face Rowlandson would have compared with that of a placid unattractive horse. After we left our places in front of the platform on which the unfortunate exhibit stood, John muttered, "There are men who would love that woman." The American exhibition which interested him most was one of native American Indian art at the Grand Central Art Galleries. He loved the dancers, and sat as if hypnotized by a demonstration of the remarkable powers of the Indian sand painters, who filtered colored sand between their sensitive fingers to make beautiful, magical designs on the floor of the gallery.

John would not rest until we found a shop where fine Indian watercolors, silver beads, strings of wampum, woven baskets, Navajo blankets, and polished black earthenware were sold, and he acquired a good collection to take back to England. When I later became the *Commissario* in charge of the American Building designed by Delano and Aldrich for the Venice Biennale, an exhibition of these same Indian arts won instant acclaim.

Before John returned to England, Stevenson Scott secured a commission for him to paint a portrait of Joseph Widener. The artist was then strongly under the spell of El Greco, and the remarkable Widener portrait is a tribute to the great art of the Greek painter who became the pride of Spain. John was then occupying a studio in the old Beaux Arts Building, on West Fortieth Street, and when the portrait was finished I persuaded Mrs. Gustave Radeke to go to see it. I hoped that she, too, would pose for a portrait by John, which would some day grace the halls of the Rhode Island School of Design of which she was both president and chief pillar.

I chose an unfortunate time for our morning visit. John must have spent the previous night in Harlem, and when he appeared on the balcony of his duplex studio and looked down on his visitors I knew that he was suffering from a more than mild attack of *Katzenjammer*. Nevertheless, he was quick to recognize the simplicity, charm and intelligence of that rare woman, although I dreaded presenting him when he was in a morose rather than a talkative mood. Widener's large portrait, which now hangs in the National Gallery of Art at Washington, D.C., was on an easel, and after it was unveiled Mrs. Radeke examined it quietly and sympathetically. She seemed impressed and even fascinated by the painting. After an interval of respectful silence, she hesitatingly remarked, "Mr. John, I am puzzled by the textile which you used as a background for your subject. The design suggests a series of flickering flames."

John slowly came to life.

"You are quite right, madam," he replied almost savagely. "Those are flames to which I have consigned the sitter!"

After recovering from the shock of his reply, I told John that Mrs. Radeke thought of posing for him.

"Madam," he said, "I would consider it an honor to try to paint a portrait of you."

However, when I explained that the sittings would have to be arranged in Mrs. Radeke's Providence home, he declined the commission. I suspected that he was reluctant to leave Harlem and its primitive charms. He enjoyed our unbleached Americans so much that he went off to the West Indies, where he painted a considerable number of pictures that I afterward saw at the Arthur Tooth Galleries, in London. Only a few of them, however, seemed to me to be worthy of his remarkable talent.

I saw him a few years later in Venice when he was there on a visit with his attractive daughter, and I asked him why he was not inspired to paint the beautiful Queen of the Adriatic.

"How can you expect me to paint," he replied, "when I am surrounded on every side by such beauty?"

Before John left America, the debonair Frank Crowninshield gave a luncheon in honor of John and me at the Coffee House Club. The *Tribune's* distinguished critic, Royal Cortissoz, introduced John with one of his graceful speeches, but when the artist was called upon to respond to the complimentary address, John merely arose and said, "Gentlemen! an artist should be seen, not heard! Thank you!"

Then the witty Frank Crowninshield addressed the guests, "I need not introduce Martin Birnbaum to any of you New Yorkers, but I must tell you of one of his latest exploits. Recently, a lady from the Middle West walked into the gallery of Scott and Fowles and asked, 'Can you tell me where I can find Saks' store? I want to buy some rayon stockings.' Martin, without difficulty, sold her a costly Rembrandt instead!" The story, was not true, but it served Frank's purpose.

Crowninshield, besides being the editor of *Vanity Fair*, was renowned as a brilliant conversationalist. Like most human beings, he had his weaknesses. I hope I shall not be called the devil's disciple by divulging that Frank was guilty of practices for which he should have been called to account. He ordered articles from me for *Vanity Fair*, and printed them without giving me credit. When I sought a reason for this, he patted me patronizingly on the shoulder and said, "Why, Martin, the article is so short! Surely you would not want your name to appear in connection with anything so slight." Worse still, incorrect changes would be made in an article without asking the writer's permission, and sometimes a fictitious name would be used instead of that of the author, who was not even paid for his piece.

Crowninshield was certainly a witty ornament to society, but I never knew him to laugh at the brilliant remarks of any other talented man, and if he favored a person's joke with a smile, his face wore an expression of gentle mockery. In spite of all this, he was enormously popular, and I always assumed, or hoped, that he was my friend, although he repeatedly gave me reason to suspect that his friendship was spiced with a kind of jealousy that amounted to a mild brand of hostility, especially if any respect or deference was paid in his presence to my estimates or opinions.

The exhibitions of works by John, Sterne, Manship and Nadelman were among the last that I arranged at Scott and Fowles.

It had taken me ten years to realize clearly that I must not stand still amid the circumstances in which I was living. I knew that I would never be really happy selling costly masterpieces to rich people, with most of whom I had little in common outside our business relations. My way of life suddenly seemed contemptible, although it had resulted in my becoming modestly independent economically. My beloved parents, after sixty years of married life, had passed on. I felt that the time had come to break the ties that bound me to the commercial world, and follow the almost irresistible yearnings in my heart and the promptings of my spirit. The hopelessness of my point of view ever being understood by Scott or Lord Duveen made unnecessary any attempt at explanation. Hoping that my life would acquire more breadth, I secretly determined to do some singular thing, and reach for wider horizons. The year's notice I gave Scott was not taken seriously until I showed him my steamship ticket from Los Angeles to Tahiti. On May 26, 1926, the chain was severed, and my zest for living could now be enjoyed to the full. I was free at last!

The examples of Bob Flaherty and of Frederick O'Brien, author of *White Shadows in the South Seas,* may have given me the necessary courage—or was it what Thomas Hardy called the waggery of Fate? In any case, there was something compelling about the beauty of Bob Flaherty's experiences, first in the Arctic and then in the South Seas, among simple natives who were happy because they were ignorant of the quandaries in which so-called civilized people constantly find themselves. I often accompanied Bob when he was photographing New York scenes from such strange vantage points as the roof of the old Flatiron Building, and he was the man I most envied at that time. In 1925 he had returned from Samoa bringing with him Fiala Lei, a charming native girl who had acted as his interpreter when he made his famous picture *Moana of the South Seas,* and in 1926 I started on my prolonged quest for a little more wisdom and happiness instead of greater affluence, by sailing for Papeete.

A few outstanding adventures on my subsequent travels are described in earlier books, and the lessons I learned were not altogether unwholesome. Eventually they entitled me to membership in the pleasant Explorers Club.

However, one cannot entirely rid oneself of the habits of a good portion of a lifetime. When I confided my plans to several of my clients, in particular Grenville Lindall Winthrop and Mrs. Gustave Radeke, they asked me to keep in touch with them, and especially to inform them if I saw any items that I thought might interest them. One product of this continuing connection was the collection that Mr. Winthrop bequeathed to the Fogg Art Museum. A more detailed account of our friendly intercourse, which now became closer than ever, is the subject of the next chapter.

IV

Building the
Winthrop Collection

In the course of his only trip to America in the late thirties, Charles Ricketts, artist and trustee of the London National Gallery, paid a visit to 15 East 81st Street, New York City, the last home of Grenville Lindall Winthrop. When he left the Winthrop residence, after a luncheon at which we feasted only on the choicest products of the vegetable kingdom, Ricketts exclaimed: "This visit has been my most exciting experience in America. I had expected to see collections like those of Frick, Morgan, Widener, Mrs. Havemeyer, and other millionaires, but I would never have believed that America could boast of an assemblage of art works like this one. There is nothing quite like it anywhere in the world."

Since this collection was the one that I had more to do with than with any other, I shall comment on it, and on its owner, at greater length because, in a sense, the Winthrop Collection typifies the main subject matter of this book of reminiscences, and Winthrop's death virtually ended my active career in the field of collecting art works for others, although naturally I shall never cease to take an interest in the subject.

Grenville Winthrop did not purchase and collect works of art to acquire social prestige, nor was he obliged to indulge in the custom of certain Americans who attempt to bestow posthumous nobility on their ancestors. He had traceable forebears in plenty, chief among whom were the first Governor of Massachusetts and his son John, who became the first Governor of Connecticut.

Groton, their birthplace in England, served as a name for Mr. Winthrop's estate at Lenox, Massachusetts, as well as for the country home of his younger brothers, Beekman Winthrop, at one time Governor of Puerto Rico, and Frederick Winthrop, of Hamilton, Massachusetts.

At the beginning of the eighteenth century, Daniel Defoe quaintly describing Groton and its neighborhood, wrote that "Its beauty consists in the number of gentry who dwell in and near it, the polite conversation among them, the affluence and plenty they live in, the sweet air they breathe in, and the pleasant country they have to go abroad in." Mr. Winthrop, who had visited the charming English town about 1911 attempted to reproduce its atmosphere at Lenox. With infinite patience he drew plans of his grounds to scale, and never tired of planting trees, laying out attractive paths, constructing fountains on his spacious lawns, restoring the old buildings and otherwise beautifying the town that he had selected as the seat of his residence. So well did he succeed at Groton Place that in 1934 the Massachusetts Horticultural Society awarded him the H. H. Hunnewell gold medal for one of the finest private achievements of landscape gardening in the country.

While it is not my intention to dwell on the history of the family no one who knew Mr. Winthrop could forget that he was proud of his long, high lineage and that he emphasized the English strain in his blood. Family and good breeding were perhaps too highly stressed, for, after all, the distinction they confer is an almost indefinable quality, which loses first grace, and then value when its importance is emphasized. He avoided the trivialities of social existence but in his study he had a framed copy of his family tree. It was of such vast ramification that on it one might safely claim that the sun never set on the Winthrops. Their English armorial bearings with the motto *Spes Vincit Thronum* decorated his bookplate, the colonial doorway of his residence, and the fireplace of the dining room at Groton Place. He surrounded himself, in the halls and dining rooms of his residences, with portraits of the early Winthrop worthies and he was pleased to find that some of his progenitors had had the good sense to be painted by Gilbert Stuart and such respectable later artists as Huntington, Eastman Johnson, and Healy.*

Otherwise, the Winthrop annals down to his own day reveal no outstanding ancestral addiction to art, if we except Governor John Winthrop of Connecticut, who was a distinguished scholar and member of the Royal Society. John Winthrop had spent years among the classical treasures of Italy and as a founder of Ipswich and New London he invited good English architects to emigrate and settle in New England. I never had the pleasure of knowing Mrs. Winthrop, who was born Mary Tallmadge Trevor, and the artistic temperament may indeed have been secretly hidden in other members of their line, for it blossomed out recently and is living in the person of Mr. Winthrop's elder daughter, the poet Emily Winthrop Miles, who donated her collection of American Glass to the Metropolitan Museum. The Brooklyn Museum was more recently enriched by a superb collection of Wedgwood and of Tassie medallions, as well as a notable group of early silhouettes. She is not only a gifted sculptress and draughtsman, and a distinguished photographer but also shows vital interest in the interrelation of all the arts.

Grenville Lindall Winthrop was born in New York City on February 11, 1864, the third of the seven children of Robert C. Winthrop and his wife, Kate Wilson Taylor. He first attended Everson's Collegiate School in New York, and later went to Groton. There was little to distinguish him from the other well-bred, irresponsible American boys who went to school in winter and enjoyed long vacations in summer. When he entered Harvard (Class of 1886) he was a pleasant enough youth, not too grave in demeanor, with the proper background in the Harvard sense, and a fit aspirant for admission into the Porcellian, the Hasty Pudding, and other clubs, which play such an important part in a student's social life. He received his Bachelor's degree *cum laude* in 1886, after having taken courses under Professor Norton in Ancient Art, Florentine Art and Venetian Art. He must have known that a remunerative career was destined to be his reward, either in his

---

* These portraits and many others are now in the possession of his nephew, Robert Winthrop, the son of the late Frederick Winthrop.

father's bank or at a desk in the law firm of the family solicitors. His sense of loyalty to the family traditions would indeed have prevented him from rebelling at the thought of becoming a lawyer or banker, but who can foresee the conditions that mold a young man's life? A fateful meeting with a persuasive, sympathetic personality, an accident to which one attaches slight significance when it takes place, changed the ultimate course of young Winthrop's career. Whether it was the scholarly and benevolent Victorian Professor Charles Eliot Norton, or Professor Norton's nephew, Francis Bullard, one cannot be quite certain, but after enjoying friendly association with these two men, young Winthrop no longer strained after the complacently aristocratic or conventional American ambitions of most of his classmates.

The late Professor George Santayana, who was also at Harvard in the Class of '86, remembered him but never spoke to him. When questioned about their student days, Professor Santayana sent the first of his charming letters to me from his ivory tower in a Roman convent, where he died. Winthrop, he wrote, "moved just behind the scenes, when I watched the play, as an exemplary person that everybody knew and admired; and in later years I heard of him, no doubt at the Bullards, as a collector. But both he and I seemed to have cared little for miscellaneous society, and our particular circles only touched at the circumference, in the persons of our common friends."

Without further investigation into the influences that colored his future and the tenor of his ways, we know that banks and downtown law offices, with their dry atmosphere and dull routine, became forever afterward stifling enclosures in which he would never find inspiration. Genuine freedom of action, was, however, held back throughout his life by inherited instincts of which he could not rid himself. An ancestor obsession undoubtedly played a role in his reaction to life. A natural privacy surrounded him, and his aristocratic courtesy kept strangers at a distance. This reserve or cloak of breeding, combined with his stubbornness, became at times hard, intimidating, and almost awe-inspiring.

He would have regarded a revelation of his more intimate ideas or deeper meditations as almost indecorous, but no ambiguous ring could ever be discovered in spirited statements that he made verbally, or in writing, and he expressed himself not only clearly but at times bluntly. He disliked artistic jargon, and modestly exaggerated any lack of information about his possessions. Often he could tell from the fact that a visitor paused admiringly before an obvious or unimportant item whether it was worth devoting any time to that person, and as a token of disapprobation his manner would change subtly after his appraisal of a visitor's dullness or pretentions. He could rebuff in no uncertain fashion. Even so, under that superficially cold exterior and Puritan poise there was hidden, perhaps even nurtured, a spiritual hunger for beauty, and a tenderness of spirit that he could not always conceal.

I have seen him deeply moved at a symphony concert, or when we read some poem written by his elder daughter, Emily. No appeal to aid some deserving artist remained unheeded, and all ironbound rules were cast aside to help a friend. I must not forget to mention his attitude of respectful hospitality toward enthusiastic young students. The needs of a stray mongrel dog or the welfare of the birds in his aviaries were also matters of real concern. Shy chipmunks braved imaginary dangers to eat from his hand. At Groton Place his pheasants—"living jewels," he called them—would perch on his knees and shoulders and demand to be fed the nuts which he always carried in his pockets, and they were sure to receive other friendly attentions while he sat under the great pines, musical with unseen oriental bells, when gentle winds swayed branches from which they hung.

By the time I came into contact with Winthrop, he had begun to collect modestly. He had already finished the beautiful catalogue of prints from Turner's *Liber Studiorum*, which was a tribute to his deceased friend, Francis Bullard.* The quiet tempo of his life, which settled into certain grooves, was only broken when he moved between New York and Lenox, from one of his two houses to the other. Both Groton Place and his home on Thirty-seventh Street in New York contained some Barbizon

---

* A Catalogue of the Collection of Prints from the *Liber Studiorum* of Joseph Mallard William Turner, formed by the late Francis Bullard of Boston, Massachusetts, and bequeathed by him to the Museum of Fine Arts in Boston, privately printed in 1916 by the Merrymount Press.

pictures, many fine proofs from Turner's *Liber Studiorum,* and a number of pre-Raphaelite drawings, admired and no doubt recommended by Professor Norton, who had been a friend of Burne-Jones. There were also excellent examples of old English and French furniture, Wedgewood ware, a remarkable group of Nini terra cotta portrait medallions, and a miscellaneous group of *objets d'art.*

It may be fairly claimed that it was Professor Charles Eliot Norton who first inspired Grenville Winthrop to collect art treasures, and one day—it must have been in 1914—this naturally courteous man walked into the little exhibition gallery of the Berlin Photographic Company on Madison Avenue. Without my knowledge, Mr. Winthrop had been following the exhibitions I was in the habit of arranging there, and now he explained that he thought of really starting a collection, but he did not want to compete with wealthy American amateurs who gathered costly groups of paintings by Dutch, English or Italian old masters under their roofs. He wanted virgin fields to plow, and although plans were only vaguely entertained it was clear that he did not wish to collect in a mere desultory way. Quite naturally, I suggested one of my personal enthusiasms—the collection of drawings by the salient figures of the nineteenth century.

The field of original drawings had not yet been cultivated in America, and I loved them because these spontaneously created products, as Berenson described them, often not more than preliminary scrawls, eventually developed into priceless finished masterpieces. The drawings I liked most were not examples of mere virtuosity or academic exercises, but were like series of pages from an artist's sketchbook, his confession, so to speak, in a diary revealing the germination of his ideas, the secrets of his temperament and his development. If a drawing is remarkable for the economy of means employed and the sharpness of the artist's improvisation, so much the better. By restricting operations to contemporary and recent periods, many of the pitfalls of attribution and expertising were avoided.

After he once began to acquire items, Mr. Winthrop's activity became an endless search for the beautiful. From modest beginnings his projects and purposes broadened and eventually he developed a critical sense of a high order. Although certain art dealers and even a few museum curators were already among his cherished antipathies, our relationship ripened first into reserved *camaraderie* and then into friendship. Fortunately his tastes coincided with mine at frequent points.

Neither of us had any patience with modern trends in perverse art criticism, pseudoscientific analyses of paintings, and the new fads in music and poetry. I recall how irritated he was when Carroll Carstairs, a perhaps too ardent admirer of the unfortunate Modigliani, tried to justify the long neck of the portrait of a young girl by arguing that if the neck had been shorter the picture would have been different! Such absurd pronouncements as well as the uncritical adulation bestowed on naive children's drawings or the too serious consideration given the scrawls of criminals and the insane, foster the confusion that now prevails among so many laymen when they are shown ugly or quite meaningless distortions by incompetent men. However, his quiet mirth rarely failed him even though he had no faith in the exuberant creativeness of many so-called moderns. He could not tolerate the monotony of their ugliness and he refused to overlook the frequent offenses they perpetrated against his standards of taste and beauty. For Mr. Winthrop a picture gained in value if it expressed a moral quality of noble intellect, and reflected a great soul.

I think I may fairly claim to favor new ideas, for I was probably the first person in America to purchase or exhibit the works of such men as Lehmbruck, Kokoschka, Gargalo, Feininger, Klee, Pascin, Ensor, Munch, and others, but I also viewed, and still view certain current trends and formulas, which reflect anarchy and chaos, with suspicion and even positive dislike. Men who disdain competence which they cannot boast of, are particularly boring.

Again and again when discussing contemporary art, I have pointed out that the immortal Greek artists never tried to shock with novelty. Their aim was to improve on earlier standards of beauty. A stiff primitive stone figure of Hermes created in the fifth century B.C., would be a favorite subject to inspire generations of sculptors and would develop swiftly into the divine figure at

Olympia by Praxiteles. The whole problem has been profoundly discussed and unanswerably settled by Berenson in his admirable essay, "Seeing and Knowing," which ought to be compulsory reading for all teachers, critics and art students.

A real masterpiece of painting or sculpture requires so little explanation, if any. It is always beauty as seen through the eyes of love. What Robert Frost wrote about inspired poems is equally true of all other art forms—they begin in delight and end in wisdom. A similar statement might easily be made about music and although Mr. Winthrop did not show any special interest in Paul Verlaine, the opening line of the French poet's *Art Poetique*— "Music first and foremost of all!"—might well serve as our collector's most important measure of a work of art. Mr. Winthrop seemed always to be seeking fleeting suggestions of music in his beautiful possessions.

Love of music was indeed one of the bonds of our mutual understanding. Mr. Winthrop particularly enjoyed the quiet evenings at Groton Place when I played classical airs for him on my violin, without accompaniment. Furthermore, he overlooked the fact that I was then a merchant, for he agreed with Alfred Stevens, the distinguished Belgian painter, that *"les bons marchands de tableaux"* had their uses. They did not merely raise artists' prices, but explained their virtues, created connoisseurs, and saved the artist from the embarrassment of singing his own praises.

Accordingly, when I retired from active business in 1926, Mr. Winthrop asked me to be a kind of special agent for him, thinking that if I accepted his offer he could overcome the self-imposed obstacles of a sedentary life and share *in absentia* or vicariously a collector's adventures. I was primarily responsible for drawings, sculptures, and paintings. C. T. Loo, the late Joseph Brummer, Bahr an expert on oriental art, Messrs. Miya and Tanaka of the Japanese firm of Yamanaka, and other men were on the lookout for outstanding examples of pre-Columbian, Chinese, Near Eastern and Renaissance art, although many of the items in these and other departments were also found by me. Some dealers took advantage of my absence to persuade him to add items that are not worthy of his collection, but this is no place to air such grievances.

Here one should emphasize the fact that although many objects in Mr. Winthrop's collection were only seen by him after their actual acquisition, they were always chosen by me, aside from their fitness and importance, with his taste and leanings in mind. Very often the desirability of a purchase was carefully discussed by correspondence; if possible, the final decision always rested with him, although he was very modest and exaggerated his lack of expert knowledge regarding his treasures. Important artists not particularly well represented in American collections were favored, and when we discovered items that showed the influence of one artist on another—as for instance Rowlandson on Gericault and Daumier—every effort was made to secure such related drawings.

Neither his dreams nor mine seemed fantastic or even very ambitious when we entered into our agreement, for we did not realize how swiftly the program would develop and how it would spread into channels unthought of originally.

The keen search did not really start and our plan cannot be said to have approached fruition until we had opportunities to acquire the keystone of a nineteenth century group of drawings in the form of a number of items by the celebrated Ingres and his master, David.

By that time—in 1916, to be exact, after Joseph Duveen had recommended me to Stevenson Scott—I had become Scott's junior partner, taking the place of Mr. Fowles, who had been lost when the *Lusitania* was sunk. One of my first minor triumphs on a business trip to Europe had been the discovery of a large pencil version of Ingres' *Martyrdom of St. Symphorien*—evidently made for an engraver, since it was made after the artist had finished the large painting at Autun. Although we had intended to restrict our field to nineteenth century drawings, the provenances of which were rarely in doubt, I felt that the interest and authenticity of the Winthrop collection would be further enhanced if specialists on certain masters would fortify my opinion. Accordingly, on the very eve of my departure from London for America, a friend in London flew to Paris with the drawing to show it to

Lapauze, who had written a large monograph on the master. My messenger returned by plane the next day with a written confirmation of my opinion, and then I hurried to Tite Street to share my excitement with John Sargent who was an Ingres enthusiast. Years afterward, two painted studies of details for Ingres' great religious picture were purchased from the Countess Behague.

Then we secured a still greater prize—a drawing of the Forestier family, showing the first Madame Ingres before her marriage, in the bosom of her family. It had once belonged to Degas, who literally worshipped the Master of Montauban, and the drawing had figured in the memorable Degas sale at which the Metropolitan Museum acquired its famous portraits of Monsieur and Madame LeBlanc by Ingres.

Ingres had made three versions of the Forestier family—one in the Louvre, another now in the museum at Biarritz acquired by Bonnat from the Lapauze collection, and the Winthrop example, which Ingres had always kept for himself. Degas obtained this drawing directly from the artist's family. It has always been my fond belief that Degas felt its special quality and I thought that Ingres would have retained the original and best version for himself. The Winthrop collection was its fitting final resting place.

Ingres drew many of his incomparable portraits with hard *mine de plomb* on paper tightly stretched over a frame of wood, making a rectangular drum. The first Mrs. John D. Rockefeller once owned two portrait drawings on such original mounts, but unfortunately they were removed from the wooden frames to clean some unimportant foxed spots from the paper before I could interfere. Ingres' method demanded a firmness of touch and steadiness of hand never surpassed nor even equaled. The exquisite delicacy of the drawing of the figure about to leave the room at the extreme left of Winthrop's drawing of the Forestier family is another ground for my opinion that this is the first version, because in the other replicas, all of which I have carefully examined, this figure seemed to be drawn a shade more coarsely. Its discovery and acquisition for Mr. Winthrop gave me a pleasant emotion. Perhaps we were already adding something to the artistic heritage of America, for Royal Cortissoz, our friend in common, in one of his reviews of the collection, reminded us that not so long before it had been impossible for an art student in America to examine an original work by Ingres. Soon that deficiency no longer existed.

Ingres, an artist touched by the wand of beauty, was a particularly appealing figure to Mr. Winthrop, and he was not satisfied until he had examples covering the artist's entire career. The acquisition of some of these masterpieces was often a complicated transaction, and occasionally I was obliged to resort to a subterfuge recommended by Sir Joseph Duveen. The reluctance of an owner to confess to his family and friends that a treasure had been sold was overcome by replacing the original with a carefully executed copy. This method of persuasion was resorted to when I bought the *Femme a l'Ombrelle* by Ingres from Madame Marot, the daughter of Gerome and widow of Aimé Marot, at one time the teacher of Herbert Haseltine, the enormously gifted American sculptor who recently completed the great equestrian statue of the youthful George Washington, which stands near the entrance to the Cathedral in Washington. A fine Ingres drawing of a gentleman in a silk hat promenading through the streets of Florence, which I found later, has always seemed to me to be the pendant of the lady carrying an umbrella.

The earliest Ingres item in the Winthrop Collection came from the aged Baron Joseph Vitta, a well-known French collector who became my good friend. He adored Ingres and was so pleased with my enthusiasm that he presented me with a charming *Academie* dating from Ingres' student days, which the master had once given to a talented pupil. I in turn gave it to Mr. Winthrop, long before he secured the beautiful head of an Italian girl, showing strongly the influence of the divine Raphael. The master's later drawings, which are not as delicate as the incomparable portraits of his middle period, were the last items we acquired.

In the meanwhile, after repeated efforts, we came to know Madame Ramel, the surviving sister of the second Madame Ingres, and this meeting eventually resulted in the acquisition of unique gems that had been left to Madame Ingres under the will of her husband. She, in turn, left them to Madame Ramel. These included not only many drawings, but the only existing complete version of the *Age d'Or* from which Ingres had worked for years on the great wall decoration at the Chateau de Dampierre. Annoyed by the comments of visitors to the Duc de Choiseul, owner of the domain, Ingres finally abandoned the work after five years of labor, and the famous painting remained unfinished. Like many other easel pictures by Ingres, Winthrop's *Age d'Or* was painted on thin paper and mounted on a wooden panel, which was then carefully cradled. This was only one of several treasures acquired from her heirs after Madame Ramel's death. Her sons were rather unpleasant to deal with. They insisted that until I paid in cash for the *Age d'Or* they would not deliver it, and even after I had complied with their wishes in the presence of witnesses, they counted the sum paid several times and refused to give a receipt, obviously thinking that such a document might oblige them to pay French inheritance taxes on objects inherited from their mother.

Perhaps the finest item of all those acquired from the family, and surely one of the master's most delicate works in watercolor, was a superb small version of the *Grande Baigneuse*, a painting which now hangs in the Louvre. Another preliminary study in the Ramel apartment—a large grisaille study, in oil, for the Grande Odalisque—was turned down in favor of other items, but fortunately it is now in America, for it was eventually acquired by the Metropolitan Museum in New York. One of the finished versions of this painting (formerly in the collections of Carroll Tyson and Mr. Walters of Baltimore) was later added to the Winthrop Collection. The rejection of the remarkable self-portrait, on the ground that it was unfinished, was advised by Professor Sachs and another member of the Fogg Art Museum faculty, when I took them to the modest Ramel apartment on the Rue de la Boetie. A few years later, however, it was acquired through Mr. Wildenstein, who unfortunately had had it cleaned and retouched. Lapauze, in his monograph, incorrectly stated that this portrait was the work of Ingres' pupils, although at the time when he wrote his well-known book, Lapauze had not even seen the original picture. The painting which differs in many details from the version at Antwerp and is obviously not a copy, appealed strongly to me just because it was unfinished, and I felt convinced that Lapauze was wrong. After a long search, I located Ingres' original holographic will in Paris in the archives of his attorneys, and found to my triumphant delight that the artist had bequeathed the portrait to his widow, describing it in his testament as his last work, "painted by my own hand." Lapauze must have realized his error, for after the publication of his book—a fine work, although it contains many blunders—he invited this portrait to form the *clou* of several Ingres exhibitions which from time to time he helped to organize.

Not satisfied even with the possession of such gems, Mr. Winthrop acquired the original version of *Raphael and the Fornarina* from the family of the deceased Baroness de Rothschild. From this same source came the watercolor version of Ingres' sole experiment in Romanticism, *The Poems of Ossian*, said to have been a gesture to find favor with Napoleon. Several masterpieces among Ingres' portrait drawings were found in Russia, and two of these important examples were added by the firm of Wildenstein. A series of life-size studies of hands of some of Ingres' most famous sitters were acquired from the Comtesse Behague and still others and paintings as well were added from the collection of Baron Vitta who was purchasing priceless early printed books with the proceeds of his sales of art works. The public auctions of the Oppenheimer and other noted collections were drawn upon from time to time, and before Mr. Winthrop died Ingres' works covered all the available wall space of a hallway and a sitting room to which it led on the upper story of 15 East 81st Street.

With the collection bequeathed by Bonnat to Biarritz, this became not only one of the two finest private collections of the kind —surpassed only by those of the Louvre and the Ingres Museum at Montauban—but one of the most remarkable artistic shrines in America. It became commonplace to describe the collection as unique. The last important work by Ingres, purchased from Knoedler's, was the large hitherto unknown family group of Jerome Napoleon—not nearly as fine, to be sure, as the Forestier family, but nevertheless a rare document and a remarkable achievement. We can only hope that at no distant date the entire Ingres group will be rehung in a room at the Fogg Art Museum dedicated to the master of Montauban, in the beautiful building designed by Ronald Pearce and approved by Grenville Winthrop. Professor Paul Sachs has repeatedly and solemnly promised that such a wing will be built on the vacant ground adjoining the old building, but thus far we hear of nothing being done.

The works of another great artist, Jacques Louis David—who was Ingres' master and who today is considered to be the real pillar of nineteenth century French art—were far more difficult to find, and we had to wait more than a decade before authentic examples reached the collection. As so often happened, a curious chain of circumstances surrounded their acquisition. For a long time, only forgeries or questionable attributions were offered us, and we had grown rather pessimistic. One disappointment followed another. For example, we waited impatiently to be present at the dispersal of the celebrated Strauss Collection with its wealth of Fragonards and Watteaus only to find that the sole example by David was an attractive drawing attributed to him, but which might well have been the creation of one of the large group of his highly talented pupils. Naturally we passed the questionable David by, but our patience was finally rewarded.

The longed-for opportunity presented itself when I was living in Venice, acting as one of the foreign *commisarios* at the biennial exhibition. In the course of my official visits I met Mariano Fortuny, the Spanish representative at the Exhibition. Son of the immortal Mario Fortuny, he was himself a talented painter, but better known as a stage decorator and a designer of rich textiles, as well as the discoverer of a special kind of paint that has some of the qualities of cool tempera. His spacious studio in the Palazzo Orfei was filled with treasures, including some drawings by Ingres, and many of his father's works, which he refused to part with. While examining them I casually commented on the scarcity of David's works and Señor Fortuny went on to tell me that Madrazo, his maternal grandfather, had been a favored David pupil. The French master had given Madrazo a large drawing that was now the property of his grandson, Señor Fortuny's cousin.

Armed with a letter of introduction, I called on this gentleman, who was a portrait painter, as soon as I returned to Paris. He was living on the top story of a typical Parisian apartment house, and I was shocked to find him an incurably sick man, and his rooms in wild disorder. Here Balzac would have found concrete material for one of his great romantic descriptions. Choice drawings by many masters, dedicated photographs of contemporary celebrities, and quantities of sadly neglected artistic souvenirs were strewn in all directions, covered with layers of dust.

When I told Señor Madrazo the special purpose of my visit, he showed me the David drawing, and my excitement grew when I recognized it as a large preliminary pencil study for the *Serment du Jeu de Paume*. Where it had been folded, the lines had begun to wear through the dry paper, but in all essentials it was undamaged. Moreover, the nude figures, which David drew before he clothed his models, the lines of architectural perspective, and other characteristics of the artist's careful method of approach were all shown. Only the drawings of properly posed bone skeletons of some of the models were missing. The composition was fairly complete, and it differed in many interesting details from the complete finished study in the Louvre and from the huge oil fragment at Versailles where the life-size portraits, nude or clothed, were finally painted.

Señor Madrazo, the owner of this fascinating item, was the ideal type of Spanish hidalgo, and he was also an artist of considerable academic accomplishment. Just then he needed funds to pay the medical expenses for his incurable illness and he agreed to part with the priceless David souvenir and other drawings, when he learned that they would not be hawked about in the picture marts but remain in the collection of Mr. Winthrop, one of his father's American patrons, and would ultimately serve to inspire a new generation of serious art students.

After this prize was secured, I found a complete watercolor version of the entire picture and, what was an equally unbelievable piece of luck, one of David's own sketchbooks of preliminary studies for the great unfinished oil paintings. This precious book, in its original mottled-cardboard binding, was one of a series of similar albums, most of which were purchased many years ago by the Louvre at the sale of David's effects, and each of its pages, like the ones in the Louvre, is signed with the initials of the artist's heirs-at-law. I hope that this precious volume will eventually be shown where it logically belongs, and where Mr. Winthrop in-

tended it to be shown, in a glass case in the room devoted to
David's works, and not in the Houghton library, where it and
similar volumes of original drawings by other artists that belonged
to the Winthrop Collection are being preserved.

Some of the sketches were on loose pages, and both sides of
these leaves were drawn upon. The loose drawings were carefully
mounted and framed for Mr. Winthrop, while the rest of the
original pamphlet was preserved. The work of mounting and
framing was entrusted to Leonard Clayton, who used only the
finest boards for the mats to avoid the danger of foxing. Wherever
possible, the full blank margin of the paper on which the artist
drew, was shown. After many experiments to insure uniformity,
a simple gold frame of a special design was decided upon for all
drawings in the Winthrop Collection. For this reason, many fine
frames and lovely old French mats were unfortunately sacrificed,
but, all in all, the result is dignified and scholarly.

The David group was further fortified by a classical painting
of the blind Homer and Calliope his Muse (formerly belonging
to the composer Thomas), dating from the time when the master
was painting classical subjects like some now hanging in the
Louvre. However, the real masterpiece among the David paintings was the celebrated portrait of Sieyès, the famous Republican
to whom the French Revolution can, in part, be traced. He was a
friend of the painter when David settled in Brussels to avoid the
ire of Napoleon. The purchase of this superb portrait, one of the
great works of the early nineteenth century, was a narrow stroke
of good fortune. I had just arrived in Paris, and while strolling
on a boulevard I was greeted with surprise by Monsieur André
Weil, to whom we already owed the acquisition of the magnificent
portrait of Madame Rousset by Ingres. This was one of the few
items borrowed from private sources for the great French Exhibition arranged by the Royal Academy in London.

"Why did you not answer my cable?" Monsieur Weil exclaimed,
on seeing me.

"What cable?"

It seems that to keep an early promise, he had wired me when
I was no longer in New York, to the effect that the portrait in

question, which had never been in the market, could be bought from a descendant of Sieyès. Receiving no answer, he had offered it to the National Gallery of London, and both Clark and Sassoon who crossed the Channel to see it, practically assured him that it would be purchased, but, according to custom, it must first be submitted to the purchasing committee, and the picture was already packed for shipping to London.

"But why not unpack it?" I suggested.

Monsieur Weil consented to do this, and on seeing the masterly work I secured it without hesitation for Mr. Winthrop, without asking the collector's advice, and shortly afterward it hung near the masterpieces of Perroneau on East 81st Street. In place of the David, the National Gallery acquired the smaller of the two portraits of Madame Montessier by Ingres, which we had finally rejected because we did not like the pose of the lady's hand, pressing a plump finger against her head. Months afterward, when Mr. Clark, Keeper of the Royal collection at Windsor, visited Mr. Winthrop, he was amazed to find the Sieyès portrait, which had been so mysteriously spirited away from Paris, hanging in the small reception room leading from the hallway where the Chinese jades, gold ornaments, ritual bronzes, stelae, and other sculptures were shown.

In the meanwhile, the Louvre had arranged a memorable exhibition of the works of David and his circle, and among the exhibits were two volumes of portrait studies for the colossal painting of the crowning of Josephine. These belonged to the daughters of the Duc de Bassano, Napoleon's friend, who also owned David's spirited unfinished portrait of the young Napoleon, and the even more celebrated portrait of his child, the King of Rome, painted by Sir Thomas Lawrence in Austria for Prince Metternich. The two albums contained sketch portraits of practically all the individuals in the crowd of distinguished persons appearing on the huge canvas, besides studies of the nude Napoleon and of the heads of the Pope and his Cardinal. After many trials and tribulations, I had secured the famous preliminary double oil portrait of these princes of the Church from the Marquise de Gannay for Henry McIlhenny, the curator of the Philadelphia Museum. For some reason known only to himself, Mr. McIlhenny missed the opportunity of securing these two priceless albums. Mr. Winthrop, however, did not fail me, and he also acquired the enchanting Lawrence, the portrait of the King of Rome, although the English school of portrait painting was not one in which he was particularly interested, perhaps because it was already admirably represented in many other American collections. He had authorized me to secure the portrait of the youthful Napoleon by David, as well, but in my anxiety to obtain it for a sum less than the elder daughter of the Duc de Bassano demanded, I failed, and the picture remained in France.

Years passed before it became known that Lawrence's enchanting canvas had reached America, for it was clearly understood that this transaction was not to be followed by a journalistic "Duveen" sensation. All this took place after I had tried to persuade George Blumenthal to secure these unique items for the Metropolitan. He refused to consider the purchase on the ground that it was unethical for him as a friend of France to help remove such important historical treasures, and he was amazed that the owners, the daughters of the Duc de Bassano, whom he knew personally, would sell them to a foreign collector. I warned Blumenthal that America would be the sufferer, if it once became known that such treasures were in the market, reminding him that we had lost the priceless primitive seated Greek goddess, which is now in Berlin, by not seizing the opportunity when it presented itself. Blumenthal, however, was not to be moved, and only then did I make my successful appeal to Mr. Winthrop, who generously permitted me to offer the albums to Henry McIlhenny first, before they became a part of the collection housed on East 81st Street.

Perhaps I may be pardoned at this point for parenthetically recounting the story of the acquisition of the great double portrait by David now in Henry D. McIlhenny's collection, to show how easily that masterpiece might have slipped through our fingers.

When I first saw this magnificent painting, in the course of a visit to the Marquise de Gannay with Herbert Haseltine, she said she would not sell it, but finally she put a price on it. I asked her to hold the painting until I could show it to an American collector, and she consented to do this. When Henry McIlhenny saw the picture, he was as enthusiastic as I was, but he said he would have to go to the Berkeley Hotel in London to persuade his mother to advance the funds for its acquisition, and he urged me to make the journey across the Channel with him. I had already met Mrs. McIlhenny on a memorable trip in the Canadian Rockies where I traced John Sargent's footsteps to Lake O'Hara in the company of Durr Friedley, a talented curator of decorative art at the Metropolitan Museum. Mrs. McIlhenny said she would take the David but could only pay for the picture after her return to America. Since that seemed entirely satisfactory to the Marquise, I agreed to buy the picture on my return to Paris. In the meanwhile I bound myself legally to pay at that time.

What was my consternation on arriving in New York, to find that Mrs. McIlhenny was not well, and could not be reached! She advised her son that she had reconsidered the entire matter and would not take the painting, although she had verbally consented to do so. Not relishing the idea of returning to France to face a lawsuit, I appealed to Professor Paul Sachs, who finally succeeded in persuading Mrs. McIlhenny to realize the position she had put me in and she finally agreed to cable the necessary funds. However, after my arrival in Paris, when I tried to reach the Marquise, I was told she could not see me, and in any case the picture was really her husband's property and he would not part with it! Immediately after this, a French dealer offered me the picture, but for a much higher price! I knew at once that the Marquis, following the grasping procedure approved by other French aristocrats who worshipped the franc, had been hawking the picture about, telling dealers that "M.B., an American millionaire" had made such and such an offer for the David. I was furious, of course, and refused to see the painting, which the dealers wanted to show me, and after a few more weeks of suspense, when the Marquis saw that the offers of the French dealers were not bona fide, he finally let me have it at the original price, and it is now one of the gems of the fine Henry McIlhenny Collection.

Even before the acquisition of the series of works by David for the Winthrop Collection, rare opportunities to secure examples by another enchanting French master presented themselves.

Anatole France was an ardent admirer of Prud'hon, the "Correggio of France." After the writer's death, his treasures were put up for sale in the ugly rooms of the Ventes Drouot. After seeing them, I cabled Winthrop, urging him to authorize me to buy the Prud'hons. He agreed that we should make every effort to add them to his collection, since they formed a link between the masters of the eighteenth and nineteenth centuries. Good fortune attended us at the public auction and at the subsequent sale of the collection of the Duc de Trevise where we secured the sober oil portrait of Doctor Dagoumer, the artist's physician. It had been bequeathed by the doctor to a poor devoted servant who was finally obliged to sell it to secure an annuity.

Hardly had we hung these acquisitions in East 81st Street when other equally rare examples were added, and Winthrop's group became worthy of the little room in the Louvre that is hung with masterpieces by Prud'hon and by his talented friend and pupil, Mademoiselle Meyer, whose works are often offered as genuine Prud'hons.

Among the most important additions to Winthrop's collection of the French master was a lost jewel that belonged to Lilly Lawlor, a spirited collector and *marchande amateur*. I must not succumb to the temptation of writing an outline of the career of this remarkable woman, whose indefatigable activities as a singer, art collector and real estate speculator in America extended from the Pacific to the Atlantic, and later to France. I met her originally at the sympathetic apartment of the Misses Gerson even before she had acquired a *pied-a-terre* in Paris on the Rue du Docteur Blanche, opposite the studio of the distinguished American *animalier*, Herbert Haseltine. Lilly Lawlor's greatest find was a masterpiece by Prud'hon, the praises of which she sang to me years after she had bought it at the Hoe sale in New York. It was indeed a masterpiece of the French artist, and was none other than *Le Cruel rit des Pleurs qu'il faisait verser*, one of three drawings ordered by Prud'hon's patron Comte Harlai. After many weeks of bargaining, Miss Lawlor was persuaded to accept a smaller amount than the sum she originally demanded.

The unfinished *Love Leading a Maiden* was a drawing by the master which was particularly important because it showed Prud'hon's patience and careful methods, and Winthrop always contrasted it with the carelessness and haste of the impetuous moderns. Still another gem of draughtsmanship which eventually became one of Winthrop's favorites was added at this time. It was a superb *academie* of a nude male figure formerly owned by Reginald Davis, a brother of Sir Edmund Davis who gave the fine collection of contemporary English art to France, where it was at one time shown in the Jeu de Paume. Whenever a modernist spoke slightingly of this magnificent drawing as "merely academic," I pointed out that its technique was unique and it was so personal in its feeling that in a group of ten thousand drawings this unsigned masterpiece would at once be recognized even by a superficial student as a drawing that only the inspired Prud'hon could create.

Beautiful as this drawing was, I wondered whether even such a chaste nude would find its place in the Collection. At the time Winthrop's project began to take shape it might well have been rejected, and I am almost ashamed to admit that the remarkably vigorous painting of a nude model by Gericault, now in the Metropolitan, was passed by when it was offered to me, because I thought it might offend Winthrop's taste, and be out of place in the irreproachable environment at 15 East 81st Street. Later, the series of beautiful drawings and sculptures of nudes made by his daughter Emily made my task easier. Even the great erotic drawings for Wilde's *Salome* by Beardsley, the Fra Angelico of Satanism, as Roger Fry called him, were accepted. Rops in his milder moods also found a place in the collection. However, when the masterpieces that Beardsley had drawn to illustrate Aristophanes' *Lysistrata* were offered to him by a careless specialist in London, Mr. Winthrop regarded the offer as a personal insult.

Delacroix was a more prolific artist than Gericault—and examples of his work were to be met with frequently in the French market—but the artist had been neglected in America, and he was therefore a salient figure whose works had to be well represented in the Winthrop Collection. Mrs. Potter Palmer of Chicago already had a magnificent example, the *Pasha and Giaour*—Byron's theme which inspired the great romantic painter. Delacroix made three paintings devoted to the subject, the one now in Chicago, Mr. Winthrop's superb picture which showed the two heroes when their struggle began, and the final and perhaps most exciting version, which was owned by the Comtesse de la Tour, a descendant of Baron Gros. Over and over again I tried in vain to persuade the countess to put a price on her fine Delacroix, even after I secured some masterpieces in watercolor by the great French romantic, and such rare items as an oil study for one of his decorations in the Hotel de Ville which had been destroyed by fire. Winthrop's fine group of Gericault's paintings and watercolors came chiefly from the collections of the Duc de Trevise, the Baroness Rothschild, and the gifted artist Dubaut, who was a familiar figure at French race tracks.

Chasseriau, the talented link between the followers of the classical Ingres and the romantic Delacroix, presented a far more difficult problem. He had had an almost meteoric career. The scorched fragments of his decorations destroyed in the earlier mentioned Hotel de Ville fire, were evidences of his great talents. His master, Ingres, resented his romantic tendencies; although portraits by Chasseriau clearly reveal the strong influence of his acknowledged master, the ingrained romantic spirit kept showing through.

A vast number of his works belonged to his nephew, the Baron Chasseriau, who was president of the Musée Rodin. I must have tried the patience of the genial old baron with my importunities, but it was generally known in art circles that his collection would be left to the Louvre, and he would not part with a single example, although I pointed out to him that it was not wise to leave the entire life work of a painter to one institution, whether that artist was Moreau or Watts or Rodin. He was interested in my efforts, but he explained how embarrassing it would be to change his will and all he would do was to help me find stray works by Chasseriau that were privately owned. While I was admiring the many examples in his apartment on the Rue de Neva and studied their resemblance to works by Ingres, Puvis de Chavannes, Delacroix, and Gericault, he put me in touch with Monsieur Pereire who owned the large Arabian battle scene now in the Winthrop collection, and a number of fine portrait drawings. A delightful small painting of a mother and child was owned by the baron's cousin, and since a replica was already in his possession, the baron allowed me to acquire this desirable item. It is now in the collection of the Rhode Island School of Design, a gift from its former president, Mrs. Gustave Radeke.

Mrs. Radeke was a self-effacing, public-spirited benefactor, but her quiet manner masked a remarkably happy flair for beauty and originality. She rarely waited for her fellow trustees to approve her suggestions. If there was any danger of losing a treasure, she would acquire it with her private funds and await their subsequent approval. When the Chicago Art Institute needed a Chasseriau for an ambitious loan exhibition, Mrs. Radeke's example was the only one available, since Mr. Winthrop made it a rule not to allow any works to leave his residence at 15 East 81st Street.

While still a member of the firm of Scott and Fowles, many old masters passed through my hands, and occasionally I had amusing experiences that did not always redound to the credit of our clients. Lord Duveen, who always enjoyed impressing me with his prowess, once took me to see the home of the late Jules Bache on Fifth Avenue, where the group of works sold to the collector by his lordship were shown from time to time before Mr. Bache finally bequeathed them to the City. By passing title to the public during his lifetime, Mr. Bache was permitted to live in the building and was spared the pain of paying huge income and estate taxes, even before the collection actually became a part of the Metropolitan Museum treasure.

When I paid my visit to the house, Lord Duveen introduced me casually as "the expert, Birnbaum," and Mr. Bache, whose dealings with Scott and Fowles had always been through my senior partner did not even recognize me, and confused me with some European visitor to America. He began to show me his collection. "This," he began, pointing to a canvas with which I was long familiar, having seen it in Potsdam, "is a Watteau which belonged to the German Emperor." My silence should have served as a warning, but he continued, to point out canvases, each time naming the illustrious individual whose collection it had once graced.

Did he believe that the social or political importance of a former owner added in some mysterious way to his own greatness?

Finally, we stood before a Gainsborough portrait. Blissfully ignorant of the fact that he had bought it in my presence from Stevenson Scott, he repeated his formula, "This great picture formerly belonged to Pierpont Morgan." It had been consigned to Scott and Fowles by Mrs. Hamilton who had inherited it from her distinguished father.

At about this time my integrity cost me an opportunity to help build up what might have become another great collection of drawings and watercolors. The first Mrs. John D. Rockefeller, who had done so much to establish the Modern Museum, paid a visit with me to the Winthrop collection on East 81st Street. She had already heard of me through her sister Miss Aldrich of Providence, and was so impressed by what she now saw that she asked me to assist her, if possible, in the same way that I was helping Mr. Winthrop. As so many of the units in the Winthrop collection were already fairly complete, I thought I could safely promise my assistance without letting the Winthrop collection suffer, when an outstanding item that he no longer needed became available. It was understood that he would always be allowed the first refusal. It was also agreed that I alone would be primarily responsible for the authenticity and importance of all items and for the general pattern of the collection, although Mrs. Rockefeller would be the principal and would remain entirely free to make her own decisions and purchases, especially when I was abroad and could not be consulted. This verbal agreement seemed simple enough, and when I saw Mrs. Rockefeller in Paris shortly afterward, I had a small but truly notable group of works by van Gogh, Constantin Guys, Seurat, Ingres, and other artists to submit to her. The source, provenance and net price of each, as given to me, were confided to her. She wanted them all, and this first transaction was entirely satisfactory to everybody concerned. I even went beyond the field of graphic arts and secured for her the priceless regal Meissen service already referred to of over three hundred pieces, each decorated with a unique landscape.

When I returned to America, one of my first visits was to the former Rockefeller residence on West Fifty-fourth Street, in answer to a telephone call from Mrs. Rockefeller. She wanted to submit to me two items that had been offered to her by some dealer. They were small drawings, one by Delacroix and the other by Corot, traced by the artists on translucent *papier calque* and each bore the government seal that guaranteed its authenticity. It is no exaggeration to say that many such drawings can still be found without any difficulty in the Paris art shops. I warned Mrs. Rockefeller that if she wished to acquire works of such minor or insignificant importance, she would find her house too small to contain the quantities of such works that were in the market. When visitors came to see art works in the Rockefeller Collection, I told her, they expected to see the "impossible," superlative masterpieces that had to be sought for with patience and discrimination. She may have decided that I was too dictatorial, or, worse still, that I did not praise the drawings because someone else had found them and offered them to her, forgetting our agreement that I was to be held responsible for the quality of the collection. In any case, I never submitted anything to her again.

To return to the collection of Mr. Winthrop, there was one group of English painters that he never neglected. He was repeatedly tempted by an attractive item created by one of the Pre-Raphaelites, or by related artists like the unfortunate mystic, Simeon Solomon, whom Swinburne called the "hellenist of the Hebrews." A respectable group of works by the English Brotherhood already adorned the walls of the old Winthrop residence on Thirty-seventh Street when I came upon the scene, and after securing many additional items we agreed that no more works by them should be added unless an outstanding masterpiece like Rosetti's *Blessed Damozel,* would come into the market.

It was rather embarrassing, therefore, to find on my arrival in London some years later that the collection of Lord Farringdon, famous for its paintings by the Pre-Raphaelites, was about to be sold at Sotheby's rooms on Bond Street. I cabled Winthrop and sent him a catalogue, pointing out that one of the most desirable items from a popular point of view was the celebrated *Sir Launcelot and the White Horse* by Watts. It was to be sold near the end of the sale, and since works by Burne-Jones, Millais, Albert Moore and others would be sold before that picture, I asked for further instructions.

When this immensely popular picture by Watts was first shown at the Royal Academy, it was greeted with wild acclaim. A great many visitors collected before it, and in this crowd Watts stood listening to their plaudits. The canvas had already been marked "Sold" when the Academy doors opened. Standing near the painter of the picture was William Cory, the headmaster of Eton. Cory who had changed his name from Johnston, was also known as "Ionicus." He was a great Greek scholar and a charming poet, and became one of my literary heroes. Knowing that the picture was already sold, he said to a companion, "I would have given anything I possess if I could have bought that picture to hang in the Great Chapel at Eton." Watts overheard the headmaster's remark, and he at once offered to paint a smaller version of this symbol of English idealism as a gift to Eton. That painting may still be seen today hanging in the lovely Chapel of the celebrated school.

I was anxious to acquire the large Farringdon picture, but Mr. Winthrop never bought on credit, and he had advised me to bid on the earlier items in the Farringdon catalogue rather than risk failure with everything. Accordingly, on the day of the sale, I spent all of his available funds on other items, among them being the magnificent *Days of Creation* by Burne-Jones, in a superb frame designed by the painter. This frame which I hope is preserved at the Fogg Art Museum should again be used to protect the set of pictures. The *Days of Creation* were reframed singly by Winthrop because there was no wall-space available in the Winthrop house sufficiently large to hang them as a single item. At the Farringdon sale I soon had no cash left, and could not bid when the picture of *Sir Launcelot* was put up for sale. Sorely disappointed, I then did something I had previously decided never to do. When Winthrop and I made our original agreement, it was understood that I would not sell him anything; I would merely buy items for him on our agreed ten percent commission. Now I broke my rule and suddenly began to bid on the painting. If my bid were successful, I intended to buy the picture with my own money, and then offer it to Winthrop, without any profit whatever, as soon as more Winthrop funds should become available.

As the bidding on the Watts progressed, it was not long before the limit of my personal funds was reached. My erstwhile partner, Stevenson Scott, was present at the sale. Divining that I was bidding for Winthrop, he had generously stopped raising my bid. He mistakenly thought that I was the successful purchaser, when actually a stranger was my rival, and the *Sir Launcelot* was finally knocked down to the unknown bidder. I cabled my failure to New York, consoling myself with the thought that, after all, we had secured some bargains.

A few days later, however, I received at my apartment off King Street, a note from a dealer, asking me to see him about an urgent matter. He told me that a rich client of his had accidentally entered the salesroom just when the Watts picture was put up for sale and he had impulsively decided that it was exactly what he needed to grace the overmantel of his large living room. Accordingly, he outbid me. When he took the large canvas to his residence, he found it was too high for the space. He would be obliged to lower the mantel or mutilate the picture by cutting down the canvas. Finding out that I was the under-bidder, he now offered it to me at considerably less than the price he had paid for it at the sale. I cabled all this to Winthrop, and the reply ordered me to buy it, for further funds had in the meanwhile arrived to the credit of his account at Robert Winthrop & Company, the bank founded by his father.

Winthrop already owned a portrait of Lady Lindsey by Watts,

and he was eager to acquire other examples of the popular Victorian master, so generously represented in the Tate Gallery, in the large rooms hung exclusively with his greatest works. Mrs. Watts, the charming octogenarian widow of the painter, who had written a two-volume life of her husband, treasured every scrap of his work. She was his second wife, his first experiment with the lovely youthful actress Ellen Terry having been a failure. Mrs. Watts had built a large gallery not far from her home, Limners Lease near Guildford, dominated by a colossal bronze group of a horse and rider, now a monument at the tomb of Cecil Rhodes in Africa. The sketch for this in bronze was already in Winthrop's collection. It was generally known that Mrs. Watts would bequeath all her husband's unsold works to the nation, and that they would be added to the gifts already hanging in the Watts Gallery.

Charles Ricketts had told me that she would sell to no one, although he had at one time persuaded her with great difficulty, to let a picture go to Australia. Nevertheless, he gave me a letter to the dear old lady, and I agreed to pay her a visit. After I sent my letter of introduction to Mrs. Watts, she invited me to lunch. I took my violin along, hoping I would win my way into her good graces. The day was a perfect one, and Limners Lease, with its lovely gardens in full bloom, was worth going a long distance to see. I soon confessed that the purpose of my visit was not purely social, and told her my story of Mr. Winthrop's remarkable collection. Mrs. Watts discouraged me immediately. She stated flatly that she would on no account sell a single item. But I was not easily put off, and began to argue with her. I claimed that she was not serving the reputation of her distinguished husband by holding the majority of his works in a secluded English village. His artistic message, such as it was, would be far better served if good original examples of his work were seen by students in foreign countries. If she persisted in her determination not to sell, the reputation of Watts would depend in a measure on a local museum rarely visited by foreigners, like the Gustav Moreau Museum in Paris, famous chiefly because Rouault, one of Moreau's pupils, was its curator.

Finally, Mrs. Watts invited Mr. Alston, the director of the Watts Gallery, which was close to her house, to come in to discuss the matter. To her annoyance, he admitted that I was right. I was then sent off to the garden to play with Mrs. Watts's pet spaniel. When I returned, she told me they had decided to let me have one of three works, but I would have to pay a very high price, although Watts's works were no longer in fashion. I was pleased, until I saw the group of pictures from which I had to make my choice. Then my face fell.

"Mrs. Watts," I exclaimed, "I'm afraid you do not realize that if your husband were represented by one or all of these unimportant examples his reputation would suffer instead of being enhanced. It would be unfair to his memory to hang such works among the masterpieces by Burne-Jones, Rossetti, Albert Moore, Millais, and his other friends. Such pictures as you offer me would make Watts appear as an artist of only slight importance, if any."

"Well," she replied, "what would you suggest?" I pointed with a smile to a lovely overmantel of Orpheus and Euridice.

"Nonsense!" she exclaimed. "Nothing could induce me to part with that picture. It was the wedding gift I received from my husband."

"Good," I replied. "Just such a noble sacrifice on your part would be applauded by your husband, for this picture might inspire students and other visitors to the Fogg Art Museum at Harvard, where Mr. Winthrop's collection will ultimately go. If you part with anything, let me take the finest available canvas, something as fine as his wedding gift. Can you think of a more fitting permanent place to hang it?"

"You are a dangerous man to deal with," she exclaimed good-naturedly.

I was backed up by Alston, the director, and Mrs. Watts finally said she would agree to part with the picture, but only for a very high figure, to increase the endowment fund needed to maintain the gallery at Limners Lease. That, I replied, would depend on Mr. Winthrop, and I would cable him from London. We parted on this friendly note, and she gave me an inscribed copy of the two-volume biography of her husband she had written.

When Winthrop's favorable reply arrived, I paid my second visit, armed with the funds. She told me that because I was a genuine admirer of her husband's talent she would present me personally with a lovely canvas, *The Spirit of Greek Poetry*, the final version of which already hung in the Watts Gallery. Soon afterward I left for London with the two pictures securely attached to the top of an automobile, from the window of which I caught a glimpse of Mrs. Watts standing in her doorway, weeping like a child.

The following year, when I paid her my last visit, I confessed that I had presented *The Spirit of Greek Poetry* to Mr. Winthrop, who had paid such a high price for the *Orpheus and Euridice*, for I felt that he, not I, was entitled to her generous gift. Mrs. Watts, however, wanted me to own something by her distinguished husband. She allowed me to pick out a collection of drawings and water-color studies for various works and some of these I still own. The others I have presented to the admirable and useful collection of drawings owned by Cooper Union.

While the works by Watts were being acquired, one of those strange coincidences occurred that became almost commonplace while I was building up the Winthrop Collection. We had agreed that only works of the greatest importance by the Brotherhood would henceforth be added, items that would give added significance to the group as a whole. Glancing one day through the pages of a monograph on the Pre-Raphaelites, I came to a full-page reproduction of Rossetti's *The Blessed Damozel*. The book had been published in the eighteen-eighties, and the picture then belonged to a gentleman living at Malvern, the town in the north of England where Shaw's plays were first produced at annual festivals. It was the only Pre-Raphaelite picture that Mr. Winthrop and I had mentioned as of sufficient importance to be added to the collection, but I had told Mr. Winthrop that we could dismiss it from our minds, as it was in the Leverhulme Museum. But I was mistaken. The museum owned a second bowdlerized version; the one reproduced in the book was the famous original. Although half a century had elapsed since the publication of the book, I wrote to the owner at Malvern, thinking he might be living, and asked whether he still owned the picture. By return mail I received a letter saying that the original owner had died, but had bequeathed this picture and his entire collection to his son, the writer. He added that if I ever found myself in Malvern, he would be pleased to show me his father's collection.

I never passed up such opportunities, and a few days later I was admiring the Dyson Perrins Collection in a fine house overlooking the town. Mr. Perrins was a well-known collector of English porcelain and encouraged the production of beautiful Worcestershire. His father's collection was a notable group of English pictures. After seeing excellent works by Turner, Cox, Holland, Rossetti, and many other masters, we came upon *The Blessed Damozel* in the original frame designed by the artist. It hung inappropriately on a landing among many family portraits. This famous picture had been condemned when first shown because the background and the predella were filled with lovers, and, as a concession to the early Victorian censors, Dante Gabriel Rossetti later painted a replica, leaving out the amorous couples. This second version was in the Leverhulme Gallery.

I hesitatingly told Mr. Perrins that I was acquiring paintings for private American collectors and museums, and if he ever wanted to dispose of *The Blessed Damozel* I would make an effort to sell it for him, and would give him the name of the purchaser. He told me that while nothing in his father's collection had ever been offered for sale, the Rossetti was always a source of irritation to his wife, because they could find no proper place to show it. He felt that Mrs. Perrins would be only too happy to have it removed from among the ancestral portraits. While enjoying tea on the beautiful terrace, we found that Mrs. Perrins would bless me if I would take the picture away, and she urgently advised its sale. We looked up the government list of appraisals made for inheritance tax purposes when Mr. Perrins' father had died. The value suggested by the government was eminently fair, for Pre-Raphaelite pictures had become *demodés*. I cabled Winthrop, received an immediate reply favoring the acquisition, and soon afterward the picture was packed and shipped to America.

We now felt that it would be wise to include a few prominent connecting links with the eighteenth century, and three of the principal men decided upon were Blake and Flaxman in England, and Prud'hon in France. The works of the last mentioned artist have already been touched upon. The Blake collection, once started, grew by leaps and bounds, for Grenville Winthrop recognized something overwhelming in the designs of the English mystic who was not in tune with the eighteenth century in which he saw light. The sale of the effects of the painter Linnell, who befriended the great English genius, was our first opportunity. The Linnell Collection had been stored away for a century, protected from light, and when the watercolors were shown at Christie's rooms, excitement ran riot, for they were seen to be unfaded, and in their pristine condition. My partner Stevenson Scott and I agreed that we should try to become purchasers of the set of drawings to illustrate Dante. However, Sir Alec Martin pleaded with us by cable not to make the attempt, explaining that every effort would be made to keep the set in England, and accordingly we refrained from bidding.

Various national collections pooled their interests, and at the sale in 1918, the Dante lot was knocked down to them for 7665 guineas. It was then realized that sufficient money had not been raised and we persuaded Sir Joseph Duveen to donate an additional two thousand pounds to the fund. Even then, the full amount needed had not been reached, and when it became obvious that the Dante set would not remain intact, Scott and Fowles were allowed to secure a portion of the series through the efforts of Sir William Witt, whose pattern of a great library of photographs was copied by Miss Helen Frick in New York when she inherited a portion of her father's estate.

Sir William Witt's house on Portland Square was like a magnet, that drew me to its threshold whenever I went to London. His unmatched collection of photographs, fortified by many preliminary original studies for famous pictures, was stored in large boxes alphabetically arranged, and these covered shelves on all the walls of his residence. Very often a student could identify a picture with absolute certainty by consulting Sir William's priceless documents. He was one of the chief spirits of the movement that encouraged contemporary artists in England, but Sir Joseph Duveen's generous contributions to that cause should likewise be acknowledged. Sir William had an amazing fund of anecdotes and his modest public addresses were not only lively and entertaining but notable for their display of knowledge and wisdom.

When I last saw him, hopelessly crippled by painful arthritis, he was still a cheerful enthusiast, and I possess an autographed copy of the following limerick about picture restorers and experts, which he gave me while we were identifying some drawings by Ingres with the aid of his photographs.

> As the picture grew cleaner and cleaner,
> The painting grew leaner and leaner;
> Cried Rembrandt van Ryn—
> "I'll be damned if it's mine—
> It's by Bode! Or else Valentiner."

Mr. Winthrop's Blakes were hung in a large room on the top floor of 15 East 81st Street. The drawings for Dante in the Linnell Collection had been distributed among various British and Colonial institutions, which had contributed to the purchasing fund. My friend Charles Ricketts, who was admirably presented in the Winthrop Collection and who had helped the national project in every way, was the only private collector permitted to acquire three particularly fine sheets. When his life-long friend Shannon was the victim of apoplexy, and needed costly medical attention, Ricketts sold his masterpieces of Persian art, including the unfinished Bihzad, a sensational item in the great Persian show arranged in London by my friend Arthur Upham Pope. They were acquired through me by Philip Hofer, later connected with the Houghton Library, at Harvard. When the expenses of caring for Shannon kept growing, Rickett's three remarkable Blake watercolors from the Linnell Collection were added to Mr. Winthrop's group.

Another famous item in the sale of the Linnell Collection was the second version of the watercolor illustrations for the Book of Job. The original and finer set now in the Morgan Collection was coveted by Blake's patron Linnell and he had ordered this second set, knowing that the first version was no longer available. This more highly finished group was brilliant in color because it had not been exposed to sunlight for virtually a century. The lot was knocked down at the Linnell sale for 3990 guineas to my enterprising countryman, Gabriel Wells, who in due course sold it to Mr. Winthrop but only after disposing of the finest sheet to the bibliophile A. Edward Newton. This watercolor was mounted and protected in a fine morocco Solander case, suitably inscribed.

There was a special reason why Mr. Winthrop wanted this particular item. Many years before, the distinguished American artist, John La Farge, had had an order from his friend Judge Patterson, a resident of New Jersey to create a stained-glass window and use Blake's magnificent imaginative watercolor drawing of the singing angels for the main design. I had been told that such a window, inspired by this same wonderful design, was once offered to Westminster Abbey as a Blake memorial but was rejected by the dean. After Judge Patterson's death, we acquired La Farge's stained glass windows from the judge's surviving daughter, and they were remounted and fitted into the window spaces on the top floor of 15 East 81st Street. Some of La Farge's original watercolors were also acquired from Judge Patterson's daughter and distributed around the room. Newton prized his famous item so highly that he refused to part with it at any price. However, after his death, when his famous library was sold at a series of memorable sessions under the direction of the Parke-Bernet Galleries, we finally secured it for a bid of $4,400. Several other Blake watercolors were acquired by me at the Newton sale, and all catalogues in England and America were eagerly scanned for possible further additions to enrich the walls of the room which was dominated by a picture of the *Youthful Christ* from the Jarves collection, the greater part of which is owned by Yale University. On almost the only occasion that Mr. Winthrop was persuaded to break his rule of allowing no pictures to leave No. 15, the Morgan Library, Philip Hofer and Mr. Winthrop showed all three versions of Blake's watercolor illustrations for the Book of Job at the beautiful library on Thirty-sixth Street, and when the exhibit opened, an illuminating lecture was delivered by Laurence Binyon. To have reproductions made for the publication undertaken by Quaritch in London, Binyon's daughter made very careful copies in color of the Winthrop set, since the originals were not allowed to leave America.

John Flaxman, Blake's schoolmate and friend, was equally well represented, not only by many of his classical Greek designs, but by the entire set of Dante drawings bound in yellow levant for

Lord Hope of Deepdene Castle, from whose descendant it was acquired at auction. Since Flaxman, who was among the first to follow Winckelmann's lead in the classical revival, had encouraged the youthful Ingres and was admired by Mr. Winthrop for his exquisite musical line and composition, it was natural that he should be represented by a large number of drawings. Besides the Deepdene drawings, many were secured from an old English gentleman who was an authority on Wedgwood as well as on Flaxman. The fine collection in Chicago owed much to the same Englishman, and Hutcheson and Ryerson had created a beautiful room at the Chicago Art Institute with additional material acquired from Scott and Fowles. When these collectors came to New York they chose the best drawings quickly and with unerring expert taste, whereas when Bryson Burroughs arrived with Edward Robinson the director, I was amazed to find that they chose only the cheapest items in the collection and passed by Flaxman's masterpieces. We presented their choice to the Museum rather than sell them for the few dollars at which they were priced. When Bryson Burroughs objected to the prices demanded for the best drawings, I pointed out that had he bought the entire collection at Christie's as we had done, the Metropolitan might well have been grateful to him. Flaxman was greatly admired by the Frenchman Prud'hon, another artist on the borderline of the eighteenth and nineteenth centuries, who is so well represented in the Winthrop Collection.

In the meanwhile, our fascinating search for works by salient figures in other schools and untilled fields, was never interrupted, and we soon made many fruitful excursions into the arts of other European countries. We had Fuseli, Segantini and Hodler from Switzerland, Goya and Fortuny from Spain, Leibl and the great Menzel from Germany, Marius Bauer, Mauve, the gifted Maris brothers, van Gogh, Jongkind, and others among the talented nineteenth-century artists of Holland, Stevens and Rops from Belgium, Zorn from Sweden, and Boldini from Italy, Bakst and Jacovleff from Russia, and last but certainly not least, our great nineteenth-century American masters Audubon, Sargent, Whistler and Winslow Homer, followed by La Farge, Mary Cassatt, Maurice Sterne and Hassam, with large groups of works by Mr. Winthrop's personal friends Augustus Vincent Tack and Albert Sterner. Eventually Mr. Winthrop also acquired a number of drawings and sculptures by his talented daughter Emily.

Although he never had an eye to the main chance, occasionally an opportunity would arise to buy a large group of works by a single master for a very reasonable sum. This happened when Hunt Henderson, once king of the New Orleans Mardi Gras, died. He and his sister, Miss Nellie Henderson, were the outstanding collectors of New Orleans, and besides magnificent collections of prints by Whistler and Zorn, he owned important paintings and pastels by Renoir, Manet, Degas and other masters. His dining room walls were hung with a group of works exclusively by Whistler, with the exception of the dominating portrait of Mrs. Henderson by John Alexander. Henderson's acquisition of the lovely portrait of Madame Renoir nursing her first child in a sunlit garden with a contented pet cat at her feet was an amusing incident. In the course of a visit to Scott and Fowles he assured me he did not want to purchase any new items. He merely wanted to rest and see if I had anything new to interest him. When I showed him the Renoir, he looked surprised and exclaimed, "How did you know that I *must* acquire this picture?" I tried to convince him that I did not understand or follow him. He continued, "Don't you know that after many years of married life my wife has just given birth to our first child, and I simply must present her with this painting?"

When he died, all his Whistlers were bequeathed to his son's alma mater, Tulane University. That institution, having no art museum, finally decided to sell the entire group, and I acquired them for the Winthrop Collection, of which they now form a part.

As his interests and ambitions widened, Mr. Winthrop began to collect groups of works that were the glories of China, Egypt, pre-Columbian America, Greece, Persia, and other remote countries, because he felt that comparatively few students would ever be able to travel to such remote regions to see the originals. It is always best to study arts and cultures on their native soil, and only when Mr. Winthrop felt that any of them were not sufficient-

ly well represented in American collections was he tempted to try
to fill the gaps, although both he and I deplored the fact that so
many important items had already been removed from their
original environment. To comment adequately on these small but
important groups, a series of essays would be required, which, in
all probability, the faculty and graduates of the Fogg Art Museum will eventually provide. For example, because American
museums and private collectors already owned fine examples of
oriental paintings, Mr. Winthrop specialized in Chinese stone
sculpture, bronzes, and early tomb jades, and passed by the works
of incomparable Chinese painters. The closely related Khmer
arts were favored by me as the result of my travels in Indo-China,
and we secured a few choice items like the large bronze statuette
of Vishnu and a Cham stone figure, one of the last items bought
through me by Mr. Winthrop. It was agreed that the group of
Cambodian sculptures, which the French Colonial Government
permitted me to acquire, could not go to a private collector, and
they were therefore offered to and acquired by the Metropolitan
Museum. Mr. Brummer was responsible for the inclusion of important reliefs from the Near East and many great Egyptian items,
as well as a fine collection of pre-Columbian masks and Mexican
stone halters. To this group I added, among other items, many
gold and silver Mayan and Inca treasures.

After I returned from an overland trip across the Sahara and
through the Belgian Congo, I wanted Mr. Winthrop to start a
nucleus of African aboriginal carvings, but he did not seem attracted to any of the savage phases of art flourishing on the Dark
Continent, and turned instead to the early American painters, intending to leave a fine group of these in memory of his brother,
Beekman. Whether the trustees of the Fogg Museum will eventually respect his often expressed intention to honor his brother
in a separate room for these pictures, remains to be seen.

When the curve of his life was descending he rarely accepted
invitations to dine or to go to a concert or play; he preferred to
devote hours of meditative idleness to his dream of assembling
this unique collection which he hoped might inspire future gener-

ations of American youth. After a lonely dinner, chiefly of fruit and vegetables, he would read some favorite book, or work on a card catalogue of his treasures, before the more relaxing pastime of the long evening would commence. Proust could have done the scene justice. The quiet of the cork-lined rooms at No. 15 was disturbed only by the chimes of the fine collection of grandfather clocks that stood in the rooms, hallways and on most of the landings. They were carefully adjusted so that their mellow bells reverberated successively without interfering with one another, and while their delicate peals vibrated through the house the master would move about the shadows hanging his drawings or cataloguing them, or rearranging the Chinese jades and gilt bronzes.

Strangely enough, he shared the social rebel Gauguin's feeling for music as applied to line, form and color. In each cabinet he patiently sought for a distribution of the contents that would result in perfect harmony and balance. His indefatigable arrangement and rearrangement of the gold, glass and stone objects resulted in subtle harmonious chords of strange greens and pale ivories, accentuated by a note of velvety black, brilliant cinnabar, or the gleam of burnished gold. His sensitive eye studied every shade or nuance of tint and tone, as though the cabinet were a musical composition for the eye and not for the ear, and the cabinets were poems of balanced composition.

Far into the night he might be discovered cleaning the verdigris from some strange Chinese ritual instrument, and his face would light up when his industry was rewarded by the discovery of gleaming precious metal under the layer of green metallic mold. Such self-imposed labors were for him like baths in a fountain of youth, and sustained him through his last years, but there is something poignantly pathetic in the life of one who, after always caring for others, becomes a solitary lonely figure in spite of great wealth. Had Henry James known of these activities, he might have left us an incomparable novelette of this enthusiast who had love affairs with especially favored bibelots, and who, by the force of his passion for beauty, actually brought the glory of his oriental items to life.

The longer he worked, the more deeply he became immersed in his task. On one crystal shelf his celebrated horses' heads of jadeite faced one another symmetrically but dramatically, separated by a magnificent carved "Pi" carefully selected for its size and color. It had once graced the collection of my dear friend Ned Bruce. Precious sets of gold implements discovered in a tomb by some unknown Schliemann of the Celestial kingdom had shelves all their own. The wonderful designs and mystic symbols on the backs of a notable group of silver mirrors were shown distributed against backgrounds of soft-toned velvet, chosen to show off their beauty to the greatest advantage. In the soft light of the spacious hallways, flying apsaras from the caves of Long-Mien and holy Buddhas with their bodhisattvas smiled down enigmatically from their pedestals as though they approved the efforts of the gentle recluse so deeply immersed in his tasks.

Finally, when Grenville Winthrop felt that his inspiration was wandering, he would retire to his bedroom, with its old Chippendale fourposter covered with crimson damask, and lie down to what may be hoped were pleasant dreams. Exquisite wooden jackals of Anubis, an unbelievably grand Chinese gilt dragon, and a noble Horus in the shape of a regal bronze hawk, once the property of his classmate William Randolph Hearst, guarded his slumbers, and when he awoke at dawn he was greeted by these beautiful objects and a scintillating oil painting, one of Sargent's engaging works, hanging over the mantel. It had belonged to Besnard and was only one of many of the great American painter's pictures that covered the walls of the bedroom, two of them being Sargent's portrait drawings of Emily and Kate, Mr. Winthrop's daughters.

Among other paintings in the room were the panels by Watts, formerly the property of Sir Edmund Davis at Chilham, and the celebrated self-portrait of Bracquemond, from the Watts-Dunton collection, which I first saw at the Biennale in Venice. At that exhibition a delightful small full-length portrait of Ruskin by Millais hung near it, and I tried, for many years, to acquire this for the Winthrop Collection, but always failed.

Some of the chief treasures in the bedroom, hidden behind the locked doors of an old wooden secretary, were shown only to a favored few. They included a group of Chinese shrines and some superlative small gilt bronzes of monks and dancers, which sur-

pass in quality and beauty all known works of the kind. When
Zamaguchi, the emissary of the Japanese Emperor, an ardent
royal collector, visited America, he was overwhelmed when he
saw these incomparable items, and no one present on that
occasion will forget his reverent oriental obeisances before the
mantel supporting the above mentioned striding dragon with
its lashing tail. To him, this was not a piece of sculpture
but a powerful spirit to be worshipped, like a Renaissance madonna or a holy Russian icon. Zamaguchi told us that the collection of the Japanese Emperor contained few masterpieces comparable to these works then hidden away in that little room on
East 81st Street. The Japanese gentleman's powers of appreciation
were so exhausted by what he had seen that he refused to go to
the upper story of No. 15 to see the room devoted to Whistler,
who owed so much to the orientals, or to learn something about
William Blake and our great American, Winslow Homer.

Zamaguchi's countryman, the indefatigable Baron Matsukata,
would not have missed seeing these treasures. Well do I remember
how he exhausted me and all other vendors of art works when he
visited America or Europe on one of his treasure hunts. His appearances at Scott and Fowles were always timed for an hour
when I was about to leave my desk to swallow a hasty light
luncheon. I would perhaps start showing him our examples of
French Impressionists, and he would ask the price of each one.
Then he would ask to see more items and inquire whether any
reduction would be granted if he bought a group of them. This,
of course, was almost always possible, and he would want to
know what concessions would be made. Then other items in our
collection had to be submitted, and again new combinations of
groups and special prices would be asked for. After the price of
a particular group under consideration was fixed, he might suddenly ask what they would cost if the costliest picture were
omitted. The collection might have had to be submitted again
and again, in new combinations and a special price would be demanded for each group. This technique of his was invariably
followed until I was thoroughly exhausted and confused. At
about three o'clock, when I was fainting from hunger, he would
suddenly arise and say, "I am hungry. I will return after I have

eaten." And he would leave me to return at another time, never specifying when exactly his next visit would take place. Finally, if he did return, the farce would be enacted all over again, and I considered myself favored if he made a purchase. I have often wondered what happened to Matsukata's collection during the Second World War.

I must digress here and touch upon Mr. Winthrop's philanthropies. A notable activity was a long association with the Woman's Hospital in New York City, the presidency of which he gave up only after his last lingering illness. Dr. Grethe Stohr, who may still be a member of the staff of physicians there, told us that Grenville Winthrop assumed his obligations with exemplary seriousness, and that for many years he paid regular visits to the hospital, inquiring into the minutest needs of the institution, which counted on his undeviating support. Illness alone prevented his attendance at a board meeting.

A comparable devotion to the maintenance of a public library at Lenox, Massachusetts, also absorbed him. The books are housed in the interesting old Court House built in 1816 which he helped to restore, and while he was at Groton Place hardly a day passed without his visiting the librarian, to discuss the progress of all branches of her work. He encouraged the collection of association and presentation copies of books and musical manuscripts, useful to summer visitors who were attracted to Koussevitsky's concerts at Tanglewood. He also had restored the Congregational Meeting House and the Lenox Academy Building, and, as mentioned before, he purchased and saved Bald Head Mountain and left it to the community, which already had a famous bird sanctuary not far away. He had a fascinating little museum of natural history on his grounds, and he also took pleasure in a fine series of aquaria, filled with beautiful tropical fish.

These interests helped to compensate for long periods of loneliness, and made his bucolic months at Lenox enjoyable. The magnificent avenues of trees on his Lenox estate were almost all planted under his direction, and the finely proportioned fountains on the spacious lawns were often made after his own designs. He made excellent use of natural granite rocks on the grounds in his land-scaping and the award of the Hunnewell Gold Medal for his out-standing achievements as a landscape gardener already referred to, was a distinction that filled him with a mild transport of pride, although he was never guilty of angling for honors, and he even refused a trusteeship of the Metropolitan Museum.

The culminating point of his activities, the manifestation and revelation of the real man behind that placid exterior, was his col-lection of art treasures. This was to be his way of trying to stem what he thought was the current invasion of ugliness, and of bet-tering the lot of men in the chaotic world that he was leaving. He wanted these wonderful objects to sow seeds, primarily at Harvard among the youth of America, and thus help to shape the course of our artistic progress.

With this end in view, another Harvard man, Ronald Pearce, an architect who had done important work under Whitney on the restored Louvain Library, designed a fine building, already re-ferred to. The façade is intended to harmonize with the existing building of the Fogg Museum of Art, and the two buildings were to be connected by a corridor. It is hoped that this new wing will some day not only house the collection, but provide students with perfect working laboratories. Such a museum will be a fitting mon-ument to the donor's enlightened munificence.

V

Travels and
Art Adventures

Many of the more romantic, artistic incidents of my travels relate to the discovery of certain works of art, the spell of which seems to be temporarily losing its hold on a generation influenced by dealers in the works of contemporary anarchists. Sadness overwhelms me when I think of the changes in taste of many of our collectors.

My travels were not carefully planned far ahead. I decided first of all to soothe my restless spirit by visiting the scenes of Flaherty's *Moana of the South Seas*, a picture I had privately seen over and over again in the original uncut version. After voyages to Tahiti, Fiji, Samoa and Hawaii, I could roam at will across Asia, Africa or Europe. I might find a divine sculptured fragment in Greece, a lovely basket woven by a queen in Ruanda, a bronze Siva in Angkor, an apsara from a rifled cave in China, a study for a fresco by Chasseriau in Paris, or attend a sale at Christie's to acquire a rare Gericault. Some of my friends who had faith in my knowledge, taste and integrity would surely want such items, and I would be helping them while enjoying myself in a hitherto undreamed-of way. The search for such treasures became an absorbing passion, and a few of my adventures in this form of activity will now be described.

I cannot assert that my travels resulted in the discovery of "self." Always I found something lacking. Who knows whether a wife and children would have altered the meaning of it all? Perhaps they would only have made life more perplexing. The wanderings were pleasant enough, and perhaps they will continue after I pass into the Unknown.

When I learned that a vessel in the port of Papeete was about to sail for Fiji, I hastily made preparations to go on board as a passenger. In Tahiti, my inspiring companion was the botanist Gerritt Wilder, of Hawaii, and I longed to go to Easter Island and even more to Rennel Island, described by Dr. S. M. Lambert in his fascinating book, *A Yankee Doctor in Paradise*. Unfortunately, I had no rich friend with an ocean-going yacht who would venture to such spots on the map merely to please me. After a long sojourn in Fiji, and a shipwreck in Samoa, where I visited the natives who appear in Flaherty's great picture, I found a vessel bound for Hawaii, where I hoped to see the famous Bishop Museum and visit the home of my beloved friends, Gerritt and Lillian Wilder, before sailing on a Japanese vessel for Yokohama. I had been provided with letters by Miya and Tanaka of the Yamanaka firm, so that I could see the No plays and visit shrines and attend ceremonies closed to the average tourist.

With friends, I crossed the Sea of Japan and entered Seoul, where we admired the huge Siberian tigers in the zoo and studied the magnificent collection of Chinese ritual bronzes in the museum. We worked our way slowly down through Manchuria into China, and there we found special treats in store for us. Naturally, we took long walks on the Great Wall, lounged in the already partly ruined temples, and wandered through the great avenues, lined with stone monsters, leading to the royal tombs. We had interesting social experiences there as well, for we arrived in Pekin with a letter of introduction from Galen Stone to Chen Chi Fou, the president of the Chinese American Bank. A unique experience which disclosed the high regard the Chinese hold for culture and courtesy, resulted from the presentation of this letter.

Galen Stone was the real head of the institution and was known as the American president. His letter of introduction created quite a sensation among the bank employees, for they mistook me for a fabulous American millionaire who must be ceremoniously ushered without delay into the private sanctum of Chen Chi Fou. He, too, was visibly excited, and asked his English-speaking secretary to invite me to dinner at his residence. This in itself was a signal

honor, for foreigners were usually entertained in luxurious restaurants built especially for that purpose. My host was known as
the Rosewood King, because he had purchased many pieces of
elaborately carved furniture that had belonged to the late Em-
press before she was deposed.

When I arrived in the evening, the courtyards were already lit
by subdued lights, fixed in niches and covered by glass on which
charming pictures were painted. The walls of the rooms through
which I was guided were decorated with an occasional picture or
with a poem in the beautiful handwriting of the great aesthetic
emperor, Chien Lung. The dinner was a delightful stag party.
Our host was kept busy flitting around the table filling the glasses
of his guests with warm wine which we sipped very noisily, imitating our host, to show our appreciation of his hospitality and of
the quality of the beverage. Several of the guests were German,
and one of them was married to a Japanese lady who, I was told,
was the social leader of Pekin. I not only played a few short selections on my violin, but succeeded in entertaining the company still
further by telling them incidents of Li Hung Chang's visit to
America.

My attempt to entertain Chen Chi Fou's guests with my violin
was deeply appreciated and richly rewarded. My host asked
whether there was anything in China I particularly wanted to see,
and I told him that I had hoped to have an opportunity to hear
Mei Lan-fang, the great actor and female impersonator, whom I
had never seen. "Unfortunately the actor is at present touring
China," the secretary explained, "but perhaps we can persuade
him to return for a few days and give a special performance for
you. You may know that Chen Chi Fou is the illustrious actor's
great friend, and often supplies him with priceless original furniture and antique costumes for his productions. When Mr. Stone
was here, private performances were arranged for him."

"And what," I asked, "did Mr. Stone do in return to show his
appreciation of such a rare honor?"

"Oh," said the secretary, "he merely made out a handsome
check payable to the great artist."

Having no bank balance that could even remotely compete with
Stone's, I felt obliged to forego that chance to see China's foremost

actor, but when I left Pekin I was overwhelmed to find my gracious, thoughtful host and his secretary waiting at the railroad station to see me off, and I was presented with a box of Mei Lanfang's best records, as a souvenir of my visit.

From China I eventually worked my way down through Indochina, feasting on the wonders of Khmer and Cham art and I determined to return at some future time to study them more carefully. Siam, Burma and India were visited in turn. Letters from Dulac and Laszlo to the beautiful Maharani of Kooch Behar, whose children had posed for Dulac, gave me rare opportunities for enjoying social life in the Far East, and I travelled slowly overland from Calcutta to Bombay, visiting the Jain temples to the north, and the sculptured shrines on the island of Elephanta to the south. I had to wait thirty-two years more before I saw the incomparable treasures in the caves of Ajanta and Ellora.

The winter of 1927 was spent in Egypt chiefly on the Nile, before going back to Europe to revisit my old playgrounds. There were always new romantic art experiences in store for me. Whenever I returned to Europe or to America, I plunged back into interests with which my previous life had been associated, although I had not long before been thankful enough to abandon those activities.

In Paris, for instance, a morning would be spent watching Sudbinin, nude to the waist, at work in the open air on his Mellon portraits, and this would be followed in the afternoon by calling at the modest studio of the highly gifted sculptor Despiau, who was putting the finishing touches on the superb bust of Mrs. Eugene Meyer, one of the first clients I had in 1910 when I took charge of the fortunes of the Berlin Photographic Company. Despiau was just then having his troubles. The artist worked slowly and patiently and only rarely without having his living models before him. He was completing a seated figure, calling to mind the *Penseur* of Rodin whom Despiau at one time assisted. The Russian model had disappeared with an infatuated opera singer and sittings could not be resumed until the lady had tired of her love affair and sent back the discarded model to Despiau. I acquired the entire edition of the original version of that figure for American collectors. There were six replicas, and as a reward for my interest, the artist gave me a number of drawings, studies for that bronze, and some small bas-reliefs which were dedicated to me.

As soon as my presence in Europe was discovered, my old friends and some of the dealers in Paris and London began to swamp me with letters, asking whether I had made any "finds" or they offered some of their own outstanding treasures. This partial reimmersion in the business side of the art world seems a logical place in my narrative to tell of a few experiences out of the ordinary that excited me after I attempted to retire completely from business and devote my entire time to writing and travel.

After my retirement from active commercial life, it was primarily to Gari Melchers that I owed my first appointment to act as America's *Commisario* at the Biennale of Venice. My second appointment to help organize the international retrospective portrait show of nineteenth-century artists came from the Italian Government, and I settled down as the owner of the lovely Casa del Leone on the Giudecca.

I had fallen in love with Venice many years before, and I have remained ever since its faithful *amoureux fou*, to borrow Henry James's French phrase. Many were the enchanting hours I spent there intoxicated by the odor from my giant magnolia, the Persian lilacs, the golden mimosa trees, the delicate jasmine blossoms, the roses, and great clusters of white and violet wisteria, which hung from vines that completely covered the old walls, and even the roof. The Casa del Leone had been originally a convent, adjoining the monastery and grounds of the great Church of the Redentore; I engaged the talented architect Del Giudice to restore the crumbling romantically situated ruin after I bought it from the estate of Miss Holland of London. In this delightful spot, with its pergola overlooking the lagoon, I enjoyed some of the happiest days of my life. It lent itself admirably to entertainment on a large scale, but I did not attempt to rival Countess Annina Morosini's banquets, Princess Polignac's informal musicales at which great artists like Artur Rubinstein performed, or such fabulous parties as the dinner given by the Mdvanis on the pier of the Excelsior Hotel at the Lido, with a display of fireworks visible for miles around and two orchestras providing a stream of music while choristers on a decorated Chioggia boat, anchored just beyond the pier added vocal color. At my modest gatherings, I too had celebrities from all over Europe and America as my guests, but I had ample time as well, to devote to my duties in connection with the Biennale.

A canal separated my premises from the Giardino Eden, still the residence of the beautiful and gracious Princess Aspasie, widow of a former King of Greece and mother of the young Princess who later became Queen of Jugoslavia, as the wife of King Peter. From time to time, the children of Dorothy Caruso and Lord Melchett (who were Princess Aspasie's summer house guests) were the playmates of the future Queen and I often went swimming with the children at the Lido. Dorothy Caruso was shocked when I reported that a caretaker of the cemetery at Naples permitted visitors who paid a small fee to see the embalmed body of the great tenor, dressed in his evening clothes. The mausoleum was unlocked and through the glass cover on the sarcophagus the guardian pointed out that the pearl studs in Caruso's shirt were real and that quite regularly his fingernails were again carefully manicured. Adjoining was a beautiful tomb, an exact replica of Caruso's, made on the grateful tenor's orders to hold the body of his singing teacher. An end was put to these ghastly, morbid exhibitions by Dorothy Caruso.

I could fill a separate volume with an assortment of romantic recollections dating around this period spent in Venice. Many fine parties were given by the beautiful social leader, Countess Annina Morosini, whose palazzo on the Grand Canal I had shared with my friend Potterton while the Casa del Leone was being rebuilt. Other fleeting memories were teas at the Palazzo Barbaro where the Curtis family had entertained John Sargent and his beloved friend Henry James who wrote *The Wings of a Dove* in one of the rooms. Delightful afternoons in the adjoining Giardino Eden and moonlight gondola parties given by the spirited Constance Gower to honor George Blumenthal, are also pleasant memories, and naturally there were many receptions in honor of the King and Queen of Italy at the Biennale.

Sinclair Lewis and his brilliant wife, Dorothy Thompson, paid me an interesting visit. It was their first trip together in Venice, and Dorothy wanted me to introduce her to a living princess, not at all a difficult task at the time. "Lulo" de Blaas, a handsome fellow but an indifferent portrait painter, was giving his annual prize for the most attractively decorated fishing boat at Chioggia, and he had asked my friend Countess Luling, then the Princess Marina Ruspoli, the lovely elder daughter of Count Volpi, to act as one of the judges, along with me and "Lulo" himself. Dorothy and Sinclair Lewis were guests on "Lulo's" yacht, and when we arrived at the fishing village the meeting between Dorothy and the Princess was arranged, but, alas, Sinclair wandered off and became so hopelessly drunk that his wife was obliged to take him back to Venice in a swift motorboat before the prizes were actually distributed. Countess Luling is now the mistress of the famous house at Maser, decorated by Paolo Veronese. Several books have been written about it.

My first effort in Venice, in the American Building designed by Delano and Aldrich, was notable. A room was given over to the work of Arthur B. Davies, who had just lost his life while travelling in Europe. Another room was almost filled with a group of paintings by George Bellows, including his Dempsey-Firpo Prizefight, lent by the Whitney Museum. A third room contained works by Melchers, Sterne, Hawthorne, the gifted Miss Bishop, and other artists. The fourth room became one of the outstanding features of the Biennale; a remarkable group of paintings, rugs, beadwork, silver, and ceramics by American Indians was shown there. Two years later I gathered a collection of portraits by Sargent, Whistler, Mary Cassatt, Eakins and Chase, as the American unit in the retrospective international exhibition of nineteenth-century portraits.

That year the American Building was presided over by Mrs. Harry Payne Whitney, and in it her director, the late Julianna Force, arranged an exhibit of American art, that was hung by the late Gerald Kelly. On the opening day, it was found that William Randolph Hearst had succeeded in having a portrait of Miss

Marion Davies, by the Polish painter Tadé Styka, hung in the entrance lobby. Styka was a facile artist with a youthful talent not unlike our own Albert Herter's. Earlier in his career, the young Pole who never developed into a more vigorous artist had executed a portrait of my friend, Mrs. Annie Bertram Webb, and as a result, her beautiful Villa Certosella, in Capri, became the property of the Styka family.

When the portrait of Marion Davies was discovered in the entrance hall, Julianna Force was greatly upset, and demanded its removal, for Styka was not an American, and in any case the picture had not been invited by Mrs. Whitney. I knew that Count Volpi, the head of the Biennale, was commercially involved with Hearst, and would not remove the picture. Furthermore, I pointed out to Mrs. Force and Kelly that if they took no action the portrait would hardly be noticed, whereas if a suit were brought the portrait would become a center of attraction, and the influential Count Volpi could easily arrange to have the case postponed to a remote date on the court calendar, so that it would not be tried until after the close of the Biennale. The portrait was not removed, and my reasoning proved correct.

A year or so later Kelly died in Paris, and among the wreaths of flowers that went with him to his grave was one from the Duchess of Windsor. Not long afterward, my own humble efforts at the Biennale exhibitions were rewarded by an Italian decoration conferred on me in the palace of Count Volpi on the Grand Canal. On the day appointed for the ceremony, the palace was crowded with royalty, ambassadors and lesser dignitaries. Escaping from the crowded rooms I found myself with Elsa Maxwell on a quiet balcony overlooking the Grand Canal. She told me that she was bored by the huge gathering, and a few minutes after our conversation I observed her sitting in the middle of one of the crowded reception rooms at a bridge table absorbed in a game of solitaire!

During that season Mussolini, accompanied by his brilliant friend and biographer, Donna Margherita Sarfatti, made one of his rare visits to Venice. After an operatic performance at a banquet in the great hall of the Fenice, Count Volpi found me in a passageway as I was about to leave the august assemblage.

"Commendatore," he exclaimed, "you must not go away! You are to be presented to the Duce!"

This embarrassed me for a moment, for I intensely disliked the dictator, whom I had seen several times pompously haranguing the crowd from a balcony in Rome. I remarked that I felt ill and completely exhausted by the festivities and simply could not remain, adding that I was certain my absence would not be noticed.

Volpi's eyes twinkled, as he said, "Don't confide to anyone else the fact that you left and did not take advantage of this signal honor."

I am convinced that Volpi was not an admirer of the odious Duce, but had he been openly anti-fascist, he not only would have lost his position, but his great fortune would almost certainly have been confiscated and even his life might have been endangered. The brilliant Count, whose addresses were models of diplomatic eulogy and flattery, died in exile—and later it was a satisfaction to learn that his courageous, attractive daughter, the Countess Luling, was one of the people who helped Bernard Berenson while he was hiding from the Nazis and writing his magnificent diary, *Rumor and Reflection.* As for Donna Margherita, because of her Jewish ancestry, she was eventually obliged to flee penniless from Italy, to escape the jealous wrath of Edda Ciano. Her daughter and grandchildren were held as virtual hostages to prevent her from publishing a second biography of Mussolini who was no longer her friend. Later she took refuge in Uruguay, but I believe she has since returned to Italy. Count Volpi's place as the leading citizen of Venice has been taken by Count Giorgio Cini, a former Senator, who has restored the Palladian Church of San Giorgio Maggiori, founded a remarkable reference art library, created the lovely Teatro Verde, established a model technical school and orphanage for the sons of Italian war veterans, and otherwise helped to revive the cultural importance of Venice.

When the Second World War threatened us, I sold the Casa, a transaction that I have never ceased to regret. The purchaser was the Infante of Spain, Eulalie's notorious younger son Louis Ferdinand, whose aged wife already owned the Chateau of Chaumont in France. She had foolishly married the young prince to become a royal highness. When the great war menaced our security, I returned to America and offered my services in vain, for the officials in Washington decided that I was too old, so I travelled instead in Central America and the West Indies, and continued to find treasures for Mr. Winthrop and my other collector friends.

Greek art had always appealed to me more strongly than any other, and I shall always regret not having devoted more of my life to its study. Fortunately, I had several opportunities to visit Greece and to steep myself in its glorious culture. I never dreamed that I would be instrumental in bringing some of its treasures to America, and the circumstances surrounding the acquisition of a unique work of great interest remain among the thrilling incidents of my career.

After visiting the museum on the Athenian Acropolis, one realizes how hopeless it is to try to acquire primitive works of major importance, since Greece wisely prohibits their export and any attempt to smuggle them out of the country is severely punished. What was my surprise, therefore, when, in the course of an annual visit to London I came upon a well-preserved and fairly complete stone sphinx or harpy; only the tail and one wing were missing, and otherwise it was only slightly damaged. Its feathers were still fairly brilliant with paint, which the Greeks were in the habit of using to enhance the beauty of their sculptures. Its enigmatic smile fascinated me. I was familiar with the type from an old silver coin presented to me by a young diplomat, whose art collection—he carries it about with him—consists of a group of gold and silver Greek coins, many in almost mint state, locked in small morocco cases. I recognized my sphinx as a decoration for a funeral monument like those preserved in the museum on the Athenian Acropolis.

When I brought the broken fragments to New York, Miss Gisella Richter, now living in Rome, was the active curator of the classical division of the Metropolitan Museum. Knowing that she was one of our ablest authorities, I at once submitted my find to her. She agreed that it had probably surmounted a stele and she was as enthusiastic as I was, because the marble had retained its color so well. There was a tall stele on exhibit in the Museum at that time, acquired many years before by Cesnola, a former director. It showed two figures in relief, a man and his small daughter. The original head of the little girl, which was in the Kaiser Friedrich Museum in Berlin, had been taken to Russia during the war, and a plaster copy of it was used by the Metropolitan Museum to complete as far as possible our own stele. Miss Richter at first thought as I did, that my sphinx was too large a figure to surmount a tall slender funeral monument. She was, however, wondering how ungainly it would look if raised to the requisite height and placed on top of a plaster cast of the Cesnola stele. To our amazement and delight, the stone paws, only slightly mutilated, exactly fitted the cast of the four damaged paws still preserved on the top of the Museum's stele. There was no question whatever that by a strange coincidence I had found not only the portions of a sphinx as fine as any in the Museum on the Acropolis but these fragments were some of the missing parts of the Cesnola stele, an item that had been on view at the Museum for half a century. George Blumenthal, then president of the Metropolitan, hemmed and hawed when told the price asked for these fragments, but eventually they were acquired, and my first triumphant adventure in Greek art seemed to be concluded.

But that was not the case. I returned several times to the premises in London where I had found the missing pieces, and about five years later I was shown the contents of another valise containing a number of small broken marbles of Greek origin. Some of them still retained the ancient paint and seemed similar to the colored feathers on the New York sphinx. It was an exciting moment, for one of the largest pieces was, I felt certain, the greater part of one of the wings of our sphinx. Naturally, I took the entire parcel to New York, and again we found that we had discovered more of the missing pieces which fitted exactly. All day we worked with the other fragments, hoping they too would turn out to be parts of our stele. To our utter joy, we soon found ourselves on the right track, but a strange puzzle presented itself when we tried to put the creature's tail together. For hours, we toiled to complete the creature's tail. As so often happens in jigsaw puzzles, we had no trouble with some of the fragments, but others completely baffled us. I was finally exhausted and left the Museum believing that some of the pieces of the creature's tail which was twisted into a strange knot, were still missing.

Next day, however, Miss Richter called me on the telephone to tell me that all the fragments fitted one another perfectly and were in place. I rushed to the Museum at once, and there, smiling mysteriously at me, was the curious, partly-human figure, its tail complete, as it may now be seen in the Museum.

A carefully prepared plaster cast copy of my find was made, and this surmounts the original stele. The stone original is beside it in a glass case to allow students to study it at eye-level. Several parts of the monument, notably a section of the all-important inscription on the base, are still missing, but even these may still exist, and may turn up some time as a piece of repair work in a ruined wall in Greece, for precious marble fragments were sometimes put to such ignoble uses by ignorant Greek plasterers. The copy of the head of the little girl on our stele ought to be secured from Russia. It would be a splendid gesture on the part of the institution which now possesses it, to give it to the Metropolitan in exchange for some of the fine Egyptian treasures we have in duplicate.

Not all my adventures with Greek sculpture ended so happily. In the meantime my relations with Miss Richter and her talented sister developed into a pleasant friendship, and on one of my visits to the Museum I saw a small terra cotta relief that reminded me of a huge head of a gorgon discovered in Corfu by a German archaeologist. Miss Richter was surprised when I told her I had seen the Corfu Gorgon *in situ* before it was removed to the local museum.

Once a remarkable helmeted head of a Greek *hoplite* or warrior, was offered to me. The unknown owner, who was in England, sent me a photograph of the piece through an agent. It was a unique and extremely important fragment. Again, however, George Blumenthal balked at the price, though I pointed out that no marble head of this type and quality had hitherto been discovered. I urged the owner to send it on from England, thinking that I might persuade Blumenthal to change his mind when he saw the original. But, alas, a German bomb fell on the warehouse where the marble head was stored, and it was blown to atoms.

At about this time we in America were prevented from obtaining another unique piece of sculpture, although fortunately not by its destruction. I had become friends with the charming Milani family in Florence, who possessed many treasures inherited from their father, a distinguished archaeologist. They asked me to come to see a superb dinner service of the finest Meissen porcelain, each of the three hundred-odd pieces of which was decorated with a unique landscape. I felt that the first Mrs. John D. Rockefeller, who already possessed several magnificent Meissen sets, would surely want this service, and I was not mistaken. In the course of my negotiations with Dr. Milani, a son of the former owner, I observed a life-sized stone figure standing in a shadowy corner of the room where we were conversing. At first I thought it must be a plaster cast, for it was a primitive votive offering to Apollo similar to those in the National Museum at Athens. A superficial glance convinced me that it was certainly equal in quality, perhaps even finer, than any I had seen in Greece or Germany. On closer examination, I was excited to find that it was actually a stone original dating from the early part of the fifth century B.C. The owner told me that his father had found it many years ago in Etruria, with a mutilated torso of the same period. This, too, was in the house. Such heavy marble figures might have been used as ballast by ships trading between Greece and Italy. Their importance and great value have only recently been recognized. The price asked for this item was very high but not fantastic. The first Mrs. Rockefeller, to whose husband I wished to submit it, told me that he would not consider such a costly purchase unless I could bring the original item to him for his inspection. So I left her and went to see Edward Robinson, then director of the Metropolitan Museum. After discussing the matter with Gisela Richter, they agreed, without seriously questioning my judgment, that if the figure was really as fine as I claimed, they would recommend its acquisition by the museum.

Dr. Robinson insisted that it must first be examined by Mr. Marshall, at that time the museum's official foreign expert on Greek art in Europe, and if he agreed with me, negotiations for the purchase would be started. I felt that I could not fairly object to such a condition. Mr. Marshall's cable came soon afterward and was satisfactory; my judgment was flatteringly vindicated. In the company of a famous German expert (Dr. Arndt, I believe) he went to see the Apollo, and both men agreed that only one of the chorae in Athens could compare with the sculpture in question. However, although the item was Greek and not Italian, the Department of Antiquities in Italy refused to allow it to be exported, although we engaged one of the finest attorneys to obtain permission to ship it to America and the museum offered a large pecuniary gift to the Archaeological Department of the Italian Government to allow its exportation. It was finally taken away from the family to grace the Museo Mussolini in Rome.

An adventure in an entirely different field came my way in the summer of 1935, in Paris, when I received a cable from my friend Robert MacIntyre, then head of the old New York firm of Mac-Beth & Company, the first dealers to specialize exclusively in American art. McIntyre asked if I would undertake to find a painting he thought was in France. He wanted the picture for an important client whose name he refused to divulge, although I had retired from active business in 1926 and there was no longer any question of rivalry involved in such an exchange of confidences.

I wrote in reply that I might make the effort, but I could not give a definite answer until I knew more about the picture and what clues there were to its possible whereabouts. It was a comparatively simple matter to find a celebrated picture that would be listed in some *catalogue raisonné* with the former owner's name, but to find a work by a master almost unknown to American collectors was quite a different problem. Some weeks later, when Bob MacIntyre knew that I was in London, he cabled to me again. This time he informed me that his client was Bartlett Arkell, head of the Beech-Nut Packing Company, and he advised me to get in touch with the gentleman who was staying at the Savoy with his wife.

This I did without delay, and I was thereupon invited to a typically sumptuous Arkell repast over which we discussed my host's problem. He told me that a portrait of Seigneur Van Diemen d'Arkel, a forerunner of his family, by the painter Luytichus, a contemporary of Hals and Rembrandt, had been sold at auction at the Parke-Bernet Galleries. Firmly believing the picture to be a portrait of one of his ancestors, Mr. Arkell had authorized Mac-Beth & Company to bid as high as fifteen thousand dollars for it, a very high price for such an item. To his great surprise Bob MacIntyre failed to secure it. Mr. Arkell also attended the sale in person, and was amazed to find that some stranger was willing to pay even more than fifteen thousand dollars. He then unwisely took the matter out of Bob MacIntyre's hands and began to do his own bidding, going higher and higher, raising his bids by a thousand dollars each time. Soon the sum of twenty thousand dollars was offered, and still the stranger persisted until twenty-eight thousand dollars was bid by Mr. Arkell. His unknown rival, with exasperating insistence, raised the offer another thousand, whereupon Mr. Arkell, irritated and discouraged, stopped bidding. The picture was knocked down to the anonymous bidder for twenty-nine thousand dollars.

Hardly had the hammer fallen than Mr. Arkell regretted his decision. He wanted that picture at all costs, and shortly afterward he authorized MacBeth & Company to find the new owner and purchase the picture, even if the price went above thirty thousand dollars. The auctioneer, however, refused to reveal the name of the successful bidder, and it was then that Bob McIntyre sent his cable to me.

At the Savoy, Mr. Arkell told me he would not only pay practically anything to acquire his ancestor's portrait, but a generous commission as well if the picture could be found and bought for him. He protected me by giving me authority and instructions in writing. We soon got to know each other more intimately and it did not take long to find out what a genial, generous, and lovable man he was, and what a remarkable friend. We went on a short motor trip through England to Chilham Castle, owned by Sir Edmond Davis and to other estates of well-known English collectors. Finally, he and Mrs. Louise Arkell sailed for America and I returned to Paris.

After my conversation with Bart, as he was known to his intimate friends, I divined that he had made a fatal blunder by appearing at that auction sale. It was easy for anyone to guess why he, known to be a very rich man, was bidding on the portrait of an Arkell. The greedy vendors probably had learned of his wealth and had assumed that he would bid to a far higher figure. He disconcerted them when he stopped bidding, and they suddenly found themselves again the owners of the picture, which I assumed they had probably taken back to France, unsold.

The catalogue of the American sale was mailed to me and I engaged several agents who knew the various branches of the French family to find the portrait, I offered a tempting sum to anyone who would help me to acquire it. First I put the problem into the hands of an ingenious hunchbacked girl who made dresses for members of many aristocratic families, but she failed to locate the painting. Then I appealed to a familiar figure in the Parisian art world, a clever French official expert in art matters. He soon reported that the picture was owned by the divorced wife of one of his clients. The Luytichus had been in the collection of her former husband and was one of many pictures given to her as part of a divorce settlement. At that moment, however, the picture was on exhibition in Rotterdam, for the Dutch Government had invited it to a loan exhibition that was being held there. As soon as I learned of its whereabouts, I took a train to Rotterdam and lost no time visiting that exhibition.

I found the portrait without difficulty, and it proved to be a very attractive picture, in excellent condition. I introduced myself to the organizer of the exhibition speaking only in German, for I feared that if he knew I was an American the price of any items that might be for sale would be substantially higher than his quotations to German or other continental dealers. To secure his good will and set at rest any suspicion he might harbor, I bought a fine Fortuny watercolor of an Arab which he personally owned and which is now in the Winthrop collection. We discussed many of the privately owned items that were being shown, and when I casually looked at the Luytichus he smiled and said, "Can you imagine that the picture you are now examining was almost sold to some wealthy American at a sale in New York, where it was foolishly bid in by the former husband of the present owner for twenty-nine thousand dollars?"

I agreed that it was a fantastic price, and wondered what the divorcée, who, I was then told, needed money, would accept for it.

"Why don't you make her an offer if you are really interested?" said the organizer of the exhibit. "Luytichus is an artist who is not in demand in the present market, and I think she would accept any good offer."

He thought that sixty thousand francs (at that time about two thousand dollars) would be a fair offer, and I authorized him to telegraph it, which he did. The next morning he showed me her reply. She was infuriated by his wire, for, she said, the picture had been insured for twenty-nine thousand American dollars, and she demanded that the portrait, with all other items she had sent to the exhibit, be immediately returned to her.

When I was assured that the picture had actually been shipped, I took the train back to Paris and at once advised my friendly expert, who was recognized as one of France's shrewdest dealers, to start negotiations. He offered the lady only thirty thousand francs. Angered by this, she told him that a journalist and dabbler in art had offered her ten thousand American dollars for it. This, I knew, was not the case, but past experience enabled me to understand the reason for her statements. The man had obviously heard of Mr. Arkell's vain effort to acquire the portrait and had told the lady that if she would entrust the picture to him he would take it back to America, where he might secure as much as ten thousand dollars for it. I explained all this to my friend the French expert, who agreed with me, and he hastened back to the lady to tell her what he thought the real facts were. Fearing however that she might weaken and let the picture out of her possession, we did not bargain too long, and I finally made a cash offer which she accepted.

Not long afterward the picture was in Bart's hands, having cost him, with all commissions, less than one-third of the amount he would have gladly paid for it. It now hangs in the Canajoharie Museum, a unique institution built and maintained by Mr. Arkell, as one of a collection of fine paintings—notably an exceptional group of oils and watercolors by Winslow Homer—acquired with

the intelligent help of Bob MacIntyre. The museum was created
for the cultural benefit of the town, and since many descendants
of the early Dutch settlers live there, Bart ordered some excellent
copies of famous Dutch masterpieces by Rembrandt and other
masters, which are also hung in the gallery.

Bart was so delighted with the way I had handled the Luytichus
transaction that my success was crowned with his devoted friendship. With many others I was invited to the huge house party
in London celebrating the accession to the throne of King George
VI in 1937. Later I secured some other fine treasures for him.
Among the most interesting of these was an association picture
by Corot, which the artist had presented to a dear friend. It had
been shown in an exhibition of the Cent Chef-d'oeuvres de France.
The gracious letter that accompanied the Corot gift was attached
to the back of the frame. An even more important acquisition was
a pair of well-known paintings by Gilbert Stuart. These are the
portraits of Governor and Mrs. Winthrop Sargent, painted about
1805. The decoration Governor Sargent is wearing shows that he
belonged to the Society of the Cincinnati. These portraits once
hung on loan in the Metropolitan Museum, and I had tried in
vain at one time to secure them from the owner for Grenville
Lindall Winthrop because they were portraits of his collateral
relatives. However Mr. Winthrop had died in the meanwhile, and
when I showed them to Bart he bought them instantly and
graciously presented them to Mrs. Arkell on her next birthday.
Another important Stuart, a Washington portrait, was given to the
Canajoharie Museum. It may have been sent to France with the
full-length Peale portrait now in the Fogg Art Museum referred
to earlier in this book, because, like that painting, it once belonged
to a descendant of the Vicomte de Noailles, the Princess Poix.

I have many pleasant memories of vacation days spent with the
hospitable Arkells at Phoenix, Arizona and in their delightful home
at Manchester, Vermont, a town that boasts of its art center, one
of the liveliest and most progressive of its kind in the country.
During his lifetime, Bart was recognized as the outstanding
patron of the annual Manchester Exhibition and on the opening
day it was his custom to buy many canvases to encourage the

painters who had settled in that beautiful region. Happily, his talented son-in-law, Orland Campbell, and his friend Leonebel Jacobs, a born portrait painter, have left us sympathetic likenesses of the genial philanthropist. Now that he is universally mourned, Mrs. Louise Arkell, an enthusiast in the field of music as well as painting, continues to be a leader in Manchester's cultural activities.

A center of the arts, especially of music, even more ambitious than the one at Manchester has recently been established at Katonah, by the late Walter Tower Rosen, with whom my friendly relations dated back almost half a century. His residence on West Fifty-fourth Street was always a place where artists, literary men and musicians were warmly welcomed. The names of Ambrose McEvoy, Arnold Genthe, Clare Sheridan, Prince Troubetskoy, Augustus John, Michael Arlen, Anna, one of the loveliest of the Duncan dancers, Malvina Hoffman, Muriel Draper, Caro Delvaille, Rosita Forbes, and hosts of others come back to mind.

Walter himself was an excellent pianist, one of his brothers was a painter of attractive figures that recalled the work of Dewing; his sister married the French poet Maurice Magre, and Walter's widow, Lucie Bigelow Rosen, whose willowy grace reminded me of Botticelli's *Simonetta* was among the first to give public concerts on that strange electrical musical instrument the Theramin, named after its inventor. Painters enjoyed making portraits of Mrs. Rosen and one of the gifted McEvoy's best American works is a happy tribute to her beauty.

No one who had the good fortune to be invited as a guest on their midnight excursion to the great cathedral on the island of Torcello will ever forget that experience. The silver moonlight, the singing of the gondoliers, the delicious dinner on a yacht, the procession of the guests into the vast dim mysteries of the noble ruin—each of us holding a long candle—are treasured memories. Although artists, literary men and musicians often lack social graces, most people enjoy entertaining them, and they were always a feature of the gatherings at the Rosen residence.

I cannot resist the temptation to repeat what we overheard on one of those occasions. While at the dinner table, a woman with a serpent's tongue startled us by saying to Michael Arlen, "Mr. Arlen, I have been observing you closely. Do you know that you might almost be mistaken for a lady!"

"Indeed?" he replied. "Well, madame, I feel certain that no one would ever mistake you for one!"

Walter Rosen, while in Venice, bought an amazing collection of interiors, rescued from ruined European palaces. When he built Caramoor in Katonah, they became an integral part of that fine house. A notable performance there of a Mozart opera, comparable to the best English performances at Glyndebourne, began a series of annual productions that augurs well for the future of this magnificent memorial to the donor and his heroic son, a young volunteer aviator killed during World War II.

Another home in which I was proud to be welcomed for many years was that of the Misses Stettheimer, and no account of contemporary artistic activities in New York could be complete without mentioning them. Florine, the youngest, was an artist in her own right. Fame knocked at her door when her unique cellophane stage decorations were revealed to delighted New Yorkers in the production of Gertrude's Stein's *Four Saints in Three Acts*.

After her untimely death, the Museum of Modern Art arranged a memorial exhibition in her honor, which gave Henry McBride occasion to write a sympathetic account of all three sisters. Miss Cora, a born social leader, was the *grand dame* of the family, and her doll's house, in which the rooms are hung with miniature drawings and paintings by frequenters of the Stettheimer salon, is an appropriate souvenir of her reign. It can be admired at the Museum of the City of New York, where it is now exhibited. Miss Ettie, the last survivor, who died in 1955, received her Doctor of Philosophy degree from the University of Leipzig, and was highly but too briefly praised by Van Wyck Brooks. Her contributions to literature under the pseudonym of Henri Waste were in advance of her time. Shortly before her death, she published a remarkable volume reprinting some of her best work and containing appreciative articles written by her critics. The book bearing the title *Memorial Volume of and by Ettie Stettheimer*, deserves to be better known.

The apartment of the three sisters was the scene of many delightful dinners where one was stimulated by scintillating conversation as well as choice food. Madame Maeterlinck (known on the stage as Georgette Leblanc), Carl Van Vechten and his gifted wife Fania Marinoff, Henry McBride, Marcel Duchamp, Carl Sprinchorn, the beautiful Marie Doro, Marie Sterner and her second husband Barney Lintott, Kirk Askew, Lloyd Goodrich, Virgil Thomson, and many other figures in the artistic field, were to be met with there.

Here may I parenthetically add a word about the late Miss Maude Wetmore and her surviving sister, Miss Edith Wetmore, who is a collector of rare discrimination? The latter's enthusiasms include not only a fine group of drawings and watercolors, but she owns many fine pieces of Meissen, and her unique collection of illustrated children's books was recently given to a library in Newport. The great Wetmore house on Bellevue Avenue in Newport is filled with many treasures—exceptional Copley portraits, interesting lacquer furniture brought from the Orient by Wetmore ancestors, and fascinating silhouettes of colonial worthies. One can only regret that the sisters did not care to create a traditional salon in the grand French manner, for they were devoted to all civilized delights and Miss Maude, the founder of the Women's Republican Club, was an able student of politics.

A less ambitious collector, one of an altogether other type, was the late Dr. Herman Lorber.

At the tragic funeral of my gifted nephew, Dr. Jerome Martin Ziegler, Herman Lorber was one of the many mourners. He had heard of me as a dealer in works of art, and it did not take us long to become friends after he introduced himself. Dr. Lorber had few of the characteristics of an art collector, but I soon found that, although far more modest, he was as catholic and independent in his tastes as John Quinn. When he was an immigrant living on the teeming East Side of New York, Jacob Epstein, then on the threshhold of his notable career, used him as a model for illustrations to a book by Hutchins Hapgood. Later he became a well-known surgeon and gynecologist; before he retired from active practice he had brought more than eight thousand children into the world. His circle of friends included many artists and celebrities. Mabel Dodge Luhan mentions him in one of her books, and the walls of his office on Park Avenue were covered with admirable examples of the work of Sargent, Renoir, Corot, Rafaelli, Mauve, Delacroix, Israels, Max Weber, Georgia O'Keefe, Walkowitz, Picasso, Emily Winthrop Miles, Abram Poole, Leon Kroll, Jacovleff, and Alfred Stieglitz.

Many of these works were bequeathed to the Art Museum in Haifa, Israel. Dr. Lorber was the first American to buy the works of the talented Isenburger, when that artist made his debut, and he encouraged many other young artists, then unknown. His example in this direction ought to be followed by more collectors.

Since I have mentioned Sir Jacob Epstein, a brief account of our first meeting may be worth recalling. I was then in London, and the mild sensation caused by Epstein's new sculptures on the façade of a building on the Strand had not yet died down. They did not unduly excite me, although I recognized a certain architectural fitness in the stark figures looking down on the passing crowds. Epstein was known to be at work on a funeral monument for Oscar Wilde's grave in the Père Lachaise Cemetery near Paris, and as I was then on the lookout for new exhibitions, I arranged to visit the sculptor in his studio on Chelsea Embankment.

When I arrived at the appointed hour, the large studio door which opened on the street was slightly ajar. Nevertheless, I knocked loudly before venturing to enter. After a minute of waiting, there being no response from the interior, I shoved the door open and found Epstein theatrically posed, with his back to me, in front of the famous male sphinx. Apparently he was anxiously following every movement of a workman who was merely polishing the flat base for the figure. The sculptor seemed to be trembling and one arm was extended backward toward me, his unseen visitor, in a cautionary gesture against disturbing him at such an exciting moment. The disagreeably sensational features of the figure startled me for a moment, and then I greeted him.

"Good morning, Mr. Epstein. Surely you have no reason to be worried by your remarkable achievement, since it is now finished."

"Oh," he replied, turning, "it will never be finished until it is unveiled. The minutest detail is highly important."

We mentioned the possibility of an exhibition of his smaller bronzes, but although I felt his power and occasionally his charm, which is revealed in his portrait of Augustus John's baby, we came to no agreement, and his first American exhibition was shown elsewhere. Many of his bronze heads were shown from time to time at Scott and Fowles, and I recommended him rather guardedly to the notice of his namesake, the wealthy Baltimore merchant Jacob Epstein, one of the important clients of Lord Duveen. A brutally powerful but certainly not flattering portrait was the result. When I first met Epstein the collector, he walked into Scott and Fowles, a humble, almost shrinking figure, asking to see me. Without knowing who he was, I greeted him very cordially, and he was soon at his ease telling me he had heard of me through Lord Duveen. Without much encouragement he began to tell me what a wonderful friend he had found in His Lordship, just then absent in Europe.

"I have just returned from a cruise around the world," he added, "and at every stopping port, whether in Naples or Singapore, Lord Duveen sent me gifts and cables, expressing concern over my health and general welfare, and otherwise showing his affection for me. His cablegrams gave me so much pleasure that I still carry them about with me."

Without further ado he proceeded to read some to me, giving me additional evidence of the remarkable manner in which Joe kept his hold on an important customer whom other dealers had ignored.

I have since learned that neither Mr. Epstein of Baltimore nor his family liked the bust that Sir Jacob made.

Every time I met the sculptor, some unfortunate note was struck that interfered with our friendly relations. The last occasion was a chance meeting at Tooth's Gallery, on Bond Street. My friend Jacovleff had just died suddenly, on a Paris surgeon's

operating table, and I came at the request of Jacovleff's aged
mother to collect some pictures that had been left in London on
consignment. Epstein was in the gallery at the same time, and
when I commented on the tragic unforeseen passing of the brilliant Russian artist, Epstein almost sneered.

"Are you referring to that traveller?"

"A genius," I retorted, "who enjoyed travelling. Had he lived,
he would have developed color as an emotional factor, and would
have been spectacular. He might have become one of the greatest
artists of all time."

After settling Mrs. Webb's legal affairs, I spent many exciting
evenings in Paris attending the theatres, the opera, and the concert halls. Among the most sensational of these experiences were
the first performances of *Cleopatra* and *Scheherezade* presented
by Diaghilev's unique company of artists, which included Pavlova,
Karsavina, Ida Rubinstein, Nijinsky, Fokine, and a host of other
stars.

Like the rest of the great Parisian audience, I was carried away
by the series of Russian ballets that have never been surpassed.
I had no way of knowing then that a few years later I would have
the signal honor of introducing the genius of Leon Bakst, whose
sets and costumes played no small part in the huge success of the
ballets, among American art lovers.

My meeting with another dance divinity was much happier and
more exciting than meeting Pavlova. Harrington Mann, the English portrait painter, came to see me one afternoon in New York
and, to my surprise, told me that Isadora Duncan wanted to meet
me. Would I call her on the telephone and make an appointment?
I did so at once, reached Isadora immediately, and agreed to stop
at her apartment that very evening after I left the gallery. Long
since I had been one of her silent, unknown worshippers, when
she and the "Isadorables" revived the spirit of ancient Hellas on
the vast stage of the Chatelet in Paris. Would I ever forget those
gestures, those toes turned up at just the right instant to remind
me that the antique vase painters were realists?

I could hardly wait for the gallery to close, and within minutes after I left it, I was driving hastily to West Sixty-seventh Street and Central Park West. I was ushered into a large room entirely hung with grey-blue curtains in the style originated by Gordon Craig, the father of her two children. There I found Isadora reclining on a mattress that rested flat on the floor covered with attractive textiles.

"Miss Duncan," I exclaimed, as I bent down to kiss her outstretched hand, "I never thought when you were dancing with those angelic children on the stage of the Chatelet, that I should have the honor of meeting you in person."

Cocktails were brought in by one of her graceful pupils whom I recognized as the charming original who had posed for our friend Arnold Genthe. Isadora Duncan had not only revolutionized the dance, but the setting and lighting as well, and now I was privileged to hear her speak. She talked almost rhapsodically of Rodin and Bourdelle and Carriére, and of many lesser men who had been inspired by her dancing, and my nerves tingled.

Shortly after that memorable evening, alas, she left New York, because of a quarrel with her friend and patron, Paris Singer, and I never met her again. Nevertheless I went to see her dance on every possible occasion, even when she had gained in weight and it would have been wiser to win the public through such gifted disciples as the lovely Anna, Vera (Mrs. Maurice Sterne) and Therese (Mrs. Stephen Bourgeois), all of them living in New York. One of Isadora's last performances in New York was at the Metropolitan Opera House. Lying on the stage in full center, an image of the divine Demeter, she writhed like a woman in labor, while her brother Raymond intoned the lines of the Book of Job in mournful, lugubrious fashion, and the orchestra accompanied their efforts with music by Beethoven. As her squirming and rather meaningless contortions continued, the impatient audience became obviously bored, and I was guilty of exclaiming, "On with the dance, let Duncan be confined!"

The celebrated American dancer Loie Fuller, who had won Paris with her famous Fire Dance and kindred inventions, was on friendly terms with Rodin, and her cast of *Le Penseur*, a gift

from the great sculptor, became a part of the Winthrop Collection.
La Loie was a stimulating personality, a woman of rare intelligence resembling in certain ways the unapproachable Isadora.

A Japanese mime whom I met in London during the First World
War was Michio Ito. There was something macabre about this
thin Oriental. Dulac's full-length portrait caught all his qualities
and he was ideally suited, physically and technically, for the role
of the sinister bird that guarded the waters of immortality in
Yeats's poetical play, which I helped John Murray Anderson to
produce in America. The play was an interesting mélange of occidental and oriental elements, and Ito's birdlike movements were
admirable. He remained in America for many years, teaching the
dance and giving recitals, first in New York and later in Hollywood. He was interned when we entered World War II, and subsequently he was sent back to Japan.

Through Ito I first met Koscak Yamada, one of the best-known
Japanese conductors of occidental music, and he wrote the incidental music for Yeats's play. I spent many pleasant evenings discussing European composers and their styles with this highly
intelligent musician.

Other Japanese friends were Gensaku Sano, who studied at
Columbia and became the first man to print a Japanese newspaper
in the Latin alphabet, and Mr. Miya of the Yamanaka firm, who
founded and owned a Shinto temple in Japan. They all helped to
prepare me for my sojourn in Japan, as did the remarkable translations of Arthur Waley, which opened the doors of my understanding to the fascinating No plays. I am told that this distinguished English scholar had until recently never travelled in the
Orient. Nevertheless he became an outstanding Orientalist and
his voluminous translations of Chinese and Japanese classics are
models of their kind.

During one extended stay in New York I received an invitation
to his home, from William Delano, the eminent architect, whose
firm of Delano and Aldrich was responsible for the American
Embassy in Paris and other fine buildings. Dr. Walter Damrosch,

Charles Dana Gibson, Paul Manship and other prominent officials of the Academy were present, and I soon learned the reason for this pleasant gathering. The general public had hitherto taken only a slight interest in the activities of the National Academy of Arts and Sciences, and it was thought that I might have some suggestions to make that, if carried out, would result in arousing the city—and possibly the country—to a realization of their importance. It had been founded on the lines of the great French Academy, and owned a fine group of buildings generously given by Archer Huntington.

I thought at once of a large exhibition in which every member would be presented by works not hitherto exhibited, and I wanted to include not only paintings, sculptures and the graphic arts, but also plans of architects, designs for stage decorations, manuscripts and first editions of authors, and the original scores of musicians. The members of the committee were not enthusiastic; they pointed out to me that previous attempts of this kind had failed because many of the members ignored the invitation to exhibit or took no notice whatever of such exhibitions. I calmly replied that if I were entrusted with such a task, every member, without a single exception, would be represented. I assured them that there would be no absentees. I would accept no compensation, but I would brook no interference from anyone.

After these conditions were agreed to, and William Delano, following my suggestions, divided the huge single exhibition gallery into several rooms, I wrote to every member asking that he send me one or more of his best new works from which I would make my choice. Authors were asked to send first editions and manuscripts as well as photographs of themselves taken when young and after they had become famous in the literary world. Musicians were requested to send original scores; architects, plans for their finest buildings; and stage designers like Robert Edmond Jones, small maquettes of the settings used in plays. These miniature scenes were to be skillfully lighted to resemble their actual, full-size effect. I even arranged with the Steuben Glass Works to send a beautiful group of its vases decorated with designs engraved after the drawings of several Academicians.

Finding that some of the members had ignored my first letter, I sent another more urgent demand, and when time began to grow short I sent a final warning. If the dilatory members persisted in ignoring my request, I made it plain that I would personally search for and collect their works wherever available, and if they found themselves represented in this important exhibition by early works, no longer worthy of their mature effort, they had only themselves to blame. This elicited a reply from practically everybody except two or three members who were seriously ill.

No reply came from Archer Huntington who had tried in vain to resign when one of his personal friends had been refused a seat in the Academy, although the constitution clearly provided that vacant Academy seats could only be filled by election from among the Associates. I was thus obliged to represent Mr. Huntington by a photograph of him and a trifling song that he had at one time composed. These were shown in a glass case beside Walter Damrosch's beautiful manuscript score of the opera *The Scarlet Letter*, finely bound, with photographs of the genial president of the Academy as a little boy, and as a well-known conductor. Needless to say, Huntington's items did not create a favorable sensation.

Among the exhibits were two fine works of my friend Cecilia Beaux. These were hung in the main hall, and Miss Beaux was awarded the gold medal of the Academy. She was already blind, and did not long survive the honor bestowed on her. Many letters from her are among the touching souvenirs I have of that exhibition, and I treasure them as much as the beautiful Steuben table glassware presented to me by the Academy.

I spent many delightful hours with Miss Beaux, not only in her Nineteenth Street studio but also in her enchanting country home, Green Alleys, at East Gloucester. It was there that I played violin solos for Mrs. Jack Gardner. Later I was enraged by reading a fantastic libelous novel dealing with an imaginary love affair between her and John Sargent. After Sargent's death, Miss Beaux sent me a poetical tribute to the great portraitist who had strongly influenced her. The dirge has never been published, and although it is not a flawless poem, it merits quotation for its emotional judgment, and it reflects my own feelings.

SARGENT

Fallen is the tree;
Its great branches crashing;
Empty its wide space upon the sky.
Low upon the ground
Are the leaflets of its crest,
Proud, that knew the upper air.

Fallen is the Chief:
Princes, lay the purple robe upon him.
Purple as the wine,
Ruddy as the fruit,
Yellow as the corn,
He gave to all, generously bestowing.

Death has conquered now,
In the night softly lurking;
Sapped the bold eye's magic,
And the swift hand's daring;
Quenched the Beacon flame,
Quenched the Fount majestic,
Darkened sky and thirsty land.

Come, ye pallid starvlings
Nature's unendowed,
Here the banquet waits,
Envy shrinks away,
Take, and satisfy,
Parched soul, and withered eye.

Death is captive here,
Where the heaped-up treasure gleams.
Labor's dower to the ages,
Fruit of travail,
Strong creation's urge.
Here's abundance,
Come, ye People—feast and mourn.

Since that successful Academy exhibition in May 1942, when, to open it, a delightful al fresco party was given on the terrace, gay with large colored umbrellas, the Academy each spring has followed more or less the plan that I initiated. At the same time,

I rehung the permanent exhibition gallery, I brought out the collection of Childe Hassam's own works that he had bequeathed to
the Academy, and I hung Blashfield's *Academia* over the stage.
It now dominates the hall where the annual ceremonies are held
and the Academy prizes are awarded. Some members should be
persuaded to add two other works to complete the decoration of
the assembly hall.

After this interlude I again left America on further wanderings
in Europe, Asia and Africa, to continue my search for outstanding
items that would add importance to certain collections, particularly Mr. Winthrop's.

VI

Epilogue

The building up of Grenville Lindall Winthrop's collection, which kept me busy for so many years, was in a sense the culmination of my career. I have already referred to the encouragement my activities received from my lamented friend, Richard Henry Dana, at whose father's summer residence at Manchester, Massachusetts, I spent many happy holidays, while I was a guest of the Longfellows, not far away. It was there that I first met John Singer Sargent, and an account of my relations with the great painter resulted in my writing a little book that won considerable acclaim. Fortunately, in the course of my reading I came upon a book that is not sufficiently well known in America. This was *The Story of My Heart* by Richard Jefferies.

In the chapters of this remarkable prose poem, which still thrill me when I read them, I found a perfect *apologia pro vita mea*. The author not only came to my rescue with passionate words; he provided, whenever I felt depressed, a mild justification for my activities and those of others who are engaged in the collection and preservation of noble works.

Jefferies bewailed pessimistically that "out of all the toil of many millions through vistas of time, down to the millions who at this hour are rushing to and fro," so little has been accumulated in past ages for our benefit. The good result of the ceaseless labor and movement vanishes the moment it is done. Disease and weaknesses, crossed and cultivated and rendered part and parcel of our very bones, seem to be the only things stored up. Why do we not long to do something that would render future generations happier? The very thought would make this hour sweeter! Then, in the same poetic frenzied breath, realizing that his statements were obviously too sweeping, Jefferies admitted that when his soul was weary and thirsted for beauty, "with all the thirst of the salt sea, and the sunheated sands dry for the tide," he would sit down in the National Gallery near some divine fragment of Greek sculpture or before a glowing Titian to which his heart was drawn.

"I lived in beauty; without beauty there is no life for me. . . ." Amen!

MARTIN BIRNBAUM

May, 1960

Index

Index

255